This introduction to African religious history focuses primarily upon traditional African religions. It also includes substantial treatment of religion and nationalism, African Islam, and independent Christianity. It is thematically organized to show the structural unity of African religions in terms of symbols, ritual, and community.

BENJAMIN C. RAY, Ph.D., University of Chicago, is Assistant Professor of Religion, Princeton University. He is a member of American Academy of Religion and African Studies Association. In 1972 the American Council of Learned Societies awarded him a Study Fellowship for research in Uganda, where he was also Visiting Professor, Department of Religious Studies and Philosophy and Department of Sociology, Makerere University, Kampala.

African
Religions

PRENTICE-HALL STUDIES IN RELIGION SERIES

SERIES EDITORS

John P. Reeder, Jr.
Brown University

John F. Wilson
Princeton University

BENJAMIN C. RAY

Princeton University

African
Religions

Symbol, Ritual, and Community

BCLTT BIP88
PRENTICE-HALL, INC., *Englewood Cliffs, New Jersey*

Library of Congress Cataloging in Publication Data

RAY, BENJAMIN C. (date)
African religions.

(Prentice-Hall studies in religion series)
Bibliography: p.
1. Africa—Religion. I. Title.
BL2400.R34   299′.6   75-17519
ISBN 0-13-018630-9
ISBN 0-13-018622-8 pbk.

© 1976 by PRENTICE-HALL, INC., Englewood Cliffs, New Jersey

Printed in the United States of America

10 9 8 7 6 5 4 3 2 1

PRENTICE-HALL INTERNATIONAL, INC., *London*
PRENTICE-HALL OF AUSTRALIA, PTY. LTD., *Sydney*
PRENTICE-HALL OF CANADA, LTD, *Toronto*
PRENTICE-HALL OF INDIA PRIVATE LIMITED, *New Delhi*
PRENTICE-HALL OF JAPAN, INC., *Tokyo*
PRENTICE-HALL OF SOUTHEAST ASIA (PTY.) LTD., *Singapore*

Contents

v

Series Foreword

The volumes in this series are intended to contribute to the development of the study of religion. It seems to us that it is especially important that appropriately conceived and well-written materials be available for use in undergraduate and graduate instruction. Moreover, it is our hope that this series will not only be a useful teaching instrument within the formal curriculum, but will also play an important role in shaping the study of religion.

Individual volumes fall into one of three subsections in the series. One set of studies, small in number, will be concerned with theories of religion or methodological approaches to the study of religion. Our attempt will be to offer books where none are available or where the existing materials are inadequate. A second group of books, also small, will deal with general aspects of religion in various traditions. Mysticism, symbol and myth, religious ethics, and other comparable topics deserve theoretical and systematic treatments not available at present. The third section of the series consists of particular studies of various religious traditions, periods, or movements. The editors will try to identify areas of study to which sufficient attention has not been given, as well as classical subjects which deserve or even require fresh approaches.

We hope that each of the volumes in the series will be sufficiently lucid to serve as an introductory study, while also providing insights that will contribute to the work of specialists. Scholarly apparatus and bibliographies will be included to provide directions for further study. Throughout the project the editors will seek out studies which manifest unquestioned quality in scholarship and writing.

JOHN P. REEDER, JR.
Brown University

JOHN F. WILSON
Princeton University

Preface

In writing this book I have had two primary concerns: to present African religions in as much depth and variety as possible and to provide a framework for understanding them. Previous introductions to African religions have suffered from an excessive generality. To overcome this problem, I have utilized a series of case studies and juxtaposed particular ethnographic materials. The superb quality of these materials makes it possible to present something of the general nature of African religions through analysis of a few well-portrayed examples. The aim of this book is thus to put the reader in a position to grasp the general in terms of the particular.

In presenting the fruits of research of so many different scholars, I have also introduced the reader to a great variety of approaches to the study of African religions. My intention has been to allow these approaches to open up different levels of interpretation of the phenomena. At the same time I have attempted to provide an obvious structure and some sense of the historical whole. Unfortunately, I have had to emphasize structural themes at the expense of historical process. This is largely due to the characteristics of the ethnographic sources which generally lack significant historical depth. Current research is beginning to tackle this problem, but we are still a long way from being able to write the history of an African religion, even over the last century. The prospects for serious historical work in relation to Islam and Christianity in Africa are somewhat better, and here I have been able to be more historical.

The main purpose of this book is to facilitate the understanding of African religions. At a recent conference on the historical study of East African religions, the Ugandan author Okot p'Bitek warned against "intellectual smuggling"—importing into African religious history Christian theological terminology and assumptions. I have tried to avoid this difficulty by using terminology drawn from the history of religions and from anthropology and by pointing up problems of interpretation. I have also attempted to provide enough descriptive depth so that the reader may perceive the materials within their own living contexts. The process of interpretation actually begins within the religious materials themselves. It arises from the semantic richness of religious language, and it is expressed in the different interpretations offered by the participants. The best fieldworker, African or non-African, tries to record not only religious texts and ritual performances but also informants' exegesis of them. This kind of activity represents an extremely important stage in the interpretive process, and I have made extensive use of such materials in the present work. Upon this foundation the fieldworker then presents his own explicitly Western interpretation. When done in a perceptive manner, this is not "intellectual smuggling," but rather the continuation of an interpretive process which began with the participants' own attempt to understand their religious situation. The aim of the present book is to carry on this process at a more comparative level. For this reason I have preferred to write about the thought and behavior of actual individuals and about specific religious events rather than to present abstract summaries of religious "beliefs" and "systems."

This effort would have been impossible without first-rate ethnographic sources. They have provided me both with the materials and with the concepts for understanding them. In this respect, my first and deepest expression of indebtedness goes to those scholars whose work I have used. If despite my efforts, distortions have occurred, I am of course responsible. I also wish to express my indebtedness to those who have helped me while this work was in progress. Professor Terence O. Ranger of Manchester University and Professor Peter J. A. Rigby of the University of Dar es Salaam have read the manuscript and have made many important suggestions. The editors of the Prentice-Hall Studies in Religion series have also given me much welcomed advice and encouragement. Mr. Rogers Miles has helped with numerous stylistic matters. Obviously, I take full responsibility for any of the weaknesses that remain.

Benjamin C. Ray
Princeton University

Perspectives on African Religions

The study of African religions has recently emerged from the shadow of African politics, history, and sociology and has become something of a special field with a sizable body of literature. Since this literature contains a wide variety of perspectives on African religions, e.g., anthropological, theological, and historical (and varieties thereof), it will be useful to begin with a brief review, so that at the outset, the student will be aware of the important questions of perspective he will encounter in this and other works. At the same time, I shall indicate the significant contribution which the study of African religions has made to Western anthropology, especially anthropology of religion.

The study of African religions has passed through several phases, each involving different purposes and points of view. The first extended accounts were written in the eighteenth and nineteenth centuries by travelers, missionaries, and colonial agents. For the most part these were not scholarly or systematic studies but collections of random observations and superficial opinions designed to appeal to the popular European mind. The next phase, beginning in the late nineteenth century, was marked by more objective and systematic field studies by trained anthropologists. The best work of this nature began in the 1930s and includes some outstanding monographs written by both European and African authors. A third and more recent phase consists of a small but growing number of philosophically and theologically oriented studies written primarily by African authors. More recently still is the attempt to combine anthropological and historical methods. This development combines the search for evidence of specific forms of change with the construction of adequate "models" of change in religious structures over time.

ACCOUNTS BY TRAVELERS
AND MISSIONARIES

The general unreliability of most early accounts by European travelers and missionaries renders them of little use to the serious student. But they are significant in revealing the cultural bias of the authors

2

who wrote them and of the public for which they were written. For this reason they are worth mentioning, if only briefly, for such biases have a way of lingering on in the popular mind, even when abolished from scholarly work.

Usually based on inaccurate information and cultural prejudice, early travelers' accounts made African religions appear to be a morass of bizarre beliefs and practices. As the late Sir Edward Evans-Pritchard once noted in connection with travel reports from the southern Sudan, such accounts seemed to have been concocted according to a standard "recipe":

> a reference to cannibalism, a description of Pygmies (by preference with a passing reference to Herodotus), a denunciation of the inequities of the slave trade, the need for the civilizing influence of commerce, something about rain-makers and other superstitions, some sex (suggestive though discrete), add snakes and elephants to taste; bring slowly to the boil and serve.[1]

What underlies this early perspective is the view of Africa as a savage "other" world, the reverse of European civilization. As such, Africa readily became the symbol of the European world expressed in upside-down fashion, a primitive version of Europe onto which a variety of European fantasies and fears were projected.

Religion was given special prominence in the travel genre because it was regarded as one of the chief measures of the African mind. In most instances observations about religion were used to justify especially strong judgments about African mental and moral character. In 1867 the explorer Sir Samuel Baker presented the following report to the Ethnological Society of London on the Nilotes of the southern Sudan: "Without any exception, they are without a belief in a Supreme Being, neither have they any form of worship or idolatry; nor is the darkness of their minds enlightened by even a ray of superstition. The mind is as stagnant as the morass which forms its puny world." [2] Baker himself knew nothing of the language of the people he was so confidently describing, and he spent only a short time among them. Considering what later anthropological studies have shown about the complex notions of supreme divinity, ritual sacrifice, and religious morality among the Nilotes, it is evident that Baker was far more interested in reinforcing popular prejudices than in reporting ethnographic fact.

If Baker was somewhat extreme in denying Africans even a modicum of religion, other Victorian travelers held only slightly higher views. Referring to West Africa, the famous explorer-adventurer Sir Richard Burton wrote:

> The negro is still at that rude dawn of faith—fetishism—and he has barely

advanced to idolatry. . . . He has never grasped the ideas of a personal
Deity, a duty in life, a moral code, or a shame of lying. He rarely believes
in a future state of rewards and punishments, which, whether true or
not, are infallible indices of human progress.[3]

This statement appeared in an essay eulogizing the racial views of
James Hunt (the founder of the Ethnological Society). It was aimed at
showing that the mental inferiority of Africans required their being
"held in labour," if not in slavery, for their own improvement. Yet, of
all the explorers, Burton had the most brilliant (if erratic) mind. He
was capable of knowledgeable and perceptive observations which frequently ran counter to accepted opinion. In describing the religion of the
Fon of Dahomey, he credited them with a *"sensus numinis"* and with
a philosophic concept of Supreme Being comparable to that "of many
thinkers in modern or in ancient Europe." [4] Burton was also the first to
recognize the fundamentally religious basis of human sacrifice practiced
by the kings of Dahomey, whereas others attributed this custom to
innate cruelty. This misapprehension provided the French with a pretext
for military invasion and conquest of Dahomey.

In contrast to the travel writers, Christian missionaries stayed
longer among Africans and often became more knowledgeable and sympathetic observers. One was the American missionary Thomas Jefferson
Bowen, who compiled a dictionary of the Yoruba language. Writing in
1857, Bowen pointed to certain "higher" aspects of Yoruba religion:

In Yoruba many of the notions which the people entertain of God are
remarkably correct. They make him the efficient, though not always the
instrumental, Creator. They have some notion of his justice and holiness,
and they talk much of his goodness, knowledge, power and providence. . . .
They may extol the power and defend the worship of their idols, whom
they regard as mighty beings, but they will not compare the greatest idol
to God.[5]

Bowen also insisted that "fetishes," usually depicted as the sum and
substance of African religion, were nothing more than symbols, analogous
to the many images and charms used by Catholic Christians. Yet even
this enlightened missionary ultimately sided with the racial theorists,
for he attributed the higher elements of Yoruba religion to the presence
of Caucasian blood. Only this, in Bowen's eyes, raised the otherwise
"uncivilized" tribes of the interior above the "degraded and supersti-
tious" Negroes of the western Coast, whom he thought it was impossible
to Christianize.

Perhaps the most sympathetic and informed missionary of the time
was the famous David Livingstone. His portrayal of an "argument with

a rain-doctor" shows an unusual degree of fairness and objectivity about African beliefs. At one point he has the "rain-doctor" say:

> I use my medicines, and you employ yours; we are both doctors, and doctors are not deceivers. You give a patient medicine. Sometimes God is pleased to heal him by means of your medicine: sometimes not—he dies. When he is cured, you take the credit of what God does. I do the same. Sometimes God grants us rain, sometimes not. When he does, we take the credit of the charm. When a patient dies, you don't give up trust in your medicine, neither do I when rain fails. If you wish me to leave off my medicines, why continue your own? [6]

But Livingstone, too, was a child of his age and ultimately regarded Africans as culturally "degraded."

Unfortunately, such prejudices still haunt some learned minds today. Lord Kenneth Clark begins his widely acclaimed survey of Western art by conjuring up a comparison between a Hellenistic statue of Apollo and an African ritual mask. The African mask, he suggests, embodies a lower state of "civilization" because it reflects a religious attitude of "fear and darkness," while the Hellenistic statue reflects a loftier attitude of "light and confidence." [7] The same inverted perspective also pervades some of our basic terminology, such as "primitive," "nonliterate," and "premodern." No matter how "value-free" these concepts may be, they still characterize Africa as the opposite of the West and thus reinforce a negative perspective.

AFRICAN RELIGIONS
AND EVOLUTIONARY ANTHROPOLOGY

Fetishism

Stimulated by the growing publication of missionary and travelers' accounts of "primitive" societies in the 18th and 19th centuries, a new interest developed in the origin and evolution of human culture. In quest of the origins of culture, scholars culled through missionary and travel literature for appropriate examples to illustrate their speculations. In 1760 Charles de Brosses proposed the theory that religion originated in the "fetish" phenomenon, long observed on the west African coast by Portuguese sailors. *Fetish* comes from the Portuguese word *fetico* which was used to refer to west African images and charms. For de Brosses, "fetishism" referred more generally to the "primitive" phenomenon of endowing natural things (trees, mountains, waters, pieces of wood) with sacred and divine power. This, he supposed, represented the origin of religion and the first stage of man's religious history. The second and last stage he believed was represented by the monotheistic religions of the western world. De Brosses' theory was later taken up and modified by the French philosopher, August Comte, who made fetishism the first stage of a three-fold scheme of religious evolution: fetishism, polytheism, monotheism. This theory held sway until well after the middle of the nineteenth century when fetishism was replaced as the initial stage by Sir Edward Burnett Tylor's more specific concept of "animism" (belief in souls) which was also based in part on African examples.[8]

Divine Kingship

African religions also played a prominent role in the evolutionary theory of the great Victorian anthropologist Sir James G. Frazer. The central theme of Frazer's monumental work, *The Golden Bough,* was the institution of divine kingship. In Frazer's scheme, the origin of the divine king, or god-man, stood somewhere between the godless Age of Magic and the later Age of Religion, characterized by the worship of spiritual beings. For Frazer, the central feature of divine kingship was regicide: the technique of killing an ailing or enfeebled king to protect the divinity within. In Africa Frazer found what he considered to be the oldest and best examples of this practice. Taking regicide as his central fact and the Shilluk of the southern Sudan as his primary ethnographic example, Frazer argued that all the ritual and symbolism associated with sacred kingship in other civilizations (mock-kings, scapegoat kings, ritual combat, dying-rising gods) were later modifications of the earlier principle of regicide. Into this general framework, Frazer fitted virtually all that was then known of myth and ritual in non-literate and ancient civilizations and in European folk practice. As a result of Frazer's theory, later anthropologists have concentrated upon African kingship and have recently made it something of a methodological proving ground for their own theories of ritual and symbolism.

"Primitive Monotheism"

It was not until the beginning of the twentieth century that evolutionism, together with its premise about the inferiority of the "primitive" mind, was successfully challenged and finally overturned. This resulted in part from the discovery among certain non-literate peoples, especially hunter-gatherers in Australia and North America, of a genuine notion of a supreme being ("Creator," "Allfather"). This proved, if nothing else, that even the most technologically primitive peoples could conceive of "higher" religious ideas. Seizing upon this discovery, the Catholic ethnologist Father Wilhelm Schmidt declared it showed that monotheism, not fetishism or animism, was the earliest form of religion and that these other forms were later "degenerations." Schmidt argued that the earliest survival of this primitive monotheistic belief was to be found among the hunting-gathering, forest Pygmies of Central Africa, who in his opinion represented the oldest surviving culture on earth. Schmidt also claimed that the supreme beings of the pastoral Nilotes of East Africa represented the fullest survival of this original monotheistic concept. But most anthropologists, except for a few Catholic scholars, rejected the monotheistic bias of Schmidt's monumental work (published in twelve volumes titled *Der Ursprung der Gottesidee*).[9] Yet Schmidt's work signaled for later scholars the widespread significance of supreme beings in African religions. Today African supreme gods have again become the focus of considerable scholarly attention and debate.

ANTHROPOLOGICAL APPROACHES TO AFRICAN CULTURE

With the decline of evolutionary theory and the advent of social anthropology, systematic fieldwork studies began to be made of African societies. Anthropological approaches, however, developed in different directions and became divided along national lines or "schools," primarily British and French. Unfortunately, this slanted fieldwork studies according to the nationality of the author, and thus imposed a "colonialist" structure upon the interpretation of African social and religious systems.

The British School

Following the fieldwork approach of Malinowski and the social-functionalist theory of Radcliffe-Brown, British anthropologists concentrated, until recently, upon the sociological aspects of African culture, that is, upon kinship systems and political organization. Consequently, less attention was given to the cosmological and symbolic dimensions of African life. When British ethnologists did turn to religion, they were primarily interested in its function within the social system: how mythology served as a "charter" which legitimated sociopolitical institutions, how ritual "maintained" the social order, how religious ideas "reflected" the social structure. Myth, ritual, and symbolism were investigated more as functional components in the social machinery than on

their own terms as intellectual phenomena. For this reason, British anthropologists tended to portray religion in Africa as merely a "reflex"
of the social order. Typical of this approach is Max Gluckman's treatment of rituals of symbolic reversal as rituals of "rebellion": "I start
from the empirical fact that African rituals are frequently organized to
exhibit rebellion and protest, and to emphasize the [social] conflicts
which exist between those who participate in the rituals." [10] Until recently, few British anthropologists have produced separate monographs
on African religion, preferring to write short chapters on the subject
within works devoted primarily to social and political organization.

A new approach developed at the hands of Evans-Pritchard,
which has been characterized as a shift from function to meaning. His
accounts of Zande witchcraft and Nuer religion concentrate less on
sociological "functions" and more on Zande and Nuer linguistic categories. In this way Evans-Pritchard sought to explain Zande and Nuer
behavior according to a system of ideas within their own universe of
thought. Much of his analysis can thus be called phenomenological in
the sense that it is an attempt to understand concepts, beliefs, and
cosmologies through an analysis of their own logical patterns. Yet, for
Evans-Pritchard the social context of religious beliefs also remained
essential, for he saw that the two were fundamentally related: "We have
to account for religious facts in terms of the totality of the culture and
society in which they are found. . . . They must be seen as a relation
of parts to one another within a coherent system. . . ." [11] In reference
to his study of the Nuer, Evans-Pritchard called attention to his dual
phenomenological/sociological perspective: "I have tried to show how
some features of their [Nuer] religion can be presented more intelligently
in relation to the social order described in earlier volumes but I have
tried also to describe and interpret it as a system of ideas and practices
in its own right." [12]

Outstanding applications of this perspective have appeared in the
works of Evans-Pritchard's associates and pupils, such as John Middleton,
Godfrey Lienhardt, and Thomas Beidelman, whose analysis of Lugbara,
Dinka, and Swazi cosmology and ritual I have utilized in the present
study.

It was, in part, the increased emphasis on fieldwork that led to this
move from function to meaning among British anthropologists in Africa.
Ideally the anthropologist was to steep himself so deeply in the language
and behavior of the people he was studying that he learned not only
to speak the language but also to think of the world in the way his informants did. In this way the anthropologist's explanations conformed
more closely to his informants' explanations and followed their own

mode of thought. John Middleton tells how this shift to the semantic, mythological level occurred in the course of his fieldwork among the Lugbara:

> They realized . . . that to understand their culture I would have to learn to think in mythopoeic terms: literal or historiographical concepts were not sufficient. . . . I had concentrated first, as I think I had to do, on what seemed then to be the basic matters of technology, farming and homestead organization; but the Lugbara soon took charge of my learning and taught me the things [myths] that they considered essential if I were to understand the life around me. These myths are at the basis of all Lugbara culture, its basic symbolic statements, and once I had a rudimentary knowledge of the technical, the Lugbara saw to it that I turned to the more symbolic, the essence of what was meant by "Lugbara." . . . They would speak of what I would think of as "politics" by telling me of myths; they would tell me of topography by telling me cosmologies, and so on. When I saw this I had learnt something that opened the doors to their culture to me in a way that I had not imagined possible.[13]

A similar experience among the Ndembu led Victor Turner to concentrate his attention upon ritual symbols and to emphasize their "exegetical," "operational," and "positional" levels of meaning. Turner was stimulated towards this line of inquiry by a wise old Ndembu diviner nicknamed Muchona, "the Hornet," whose interest in Ndembu ritual matched Turner's own. Turner tells of his excitement upon first meeting Muchona and of his sense that a new level of meaning had been reached:

> I had heard many other Ndembu interpret plant symbols, but never so clearly and cogently as this. I was to become familiar with this mode of exposition, the swift-running commentary on unsolicited details, the parenthetical explanations, the vivid mimicry of ritual speech, and above all, the depth of psychological insight: "What hurts you, when discovered and propitiated, helps you." . . . I felt that a new dimension of study was opening up to me. Sympathy was quickly growing between us and when we parted we arranged to meet again in a few days.[14]

First of all, Turner recognized it was necessary to take seriously what he was told about the meaning of a ritual symbol, distinguishing between popular and esoteric interpretations. He also saw the importance of observing precisely how a symbol is used in a ritual context and by whom, in addition to its emotional import. Finally, he realized it was necessary to see how the meaning of a symbol is derived from its relationship to the totality of symbols which comprise the society's world view.[15]

The French School

In contrast to the early British functionalists, French anthropologists adopted roughly the opposite approach. Where the British focused upon the social order, the French focused upon the symbolic-philosophical order, regarding this as the determinant of the social structure. In adopting this perspective, the French made great advances in elucidating African cosmological systems and implicit philosophies, as shown, for example, by the brilliant work of the Griaule mission among the Dogon of Mali. This approach demonstrated that African religious systems are not simply reflections of socioeconomic relations but that they form coherent and autonomous spheres of thought and action.

Commenting upon this approach, Mme. Dieterln, a member of the Griaule research mission, tells how it was suited to understanding Dogon culture:

> It became clear in the course of this work that African peoples had, like others, reflected on their own customs, that these customs stemmed from norms which were proper to themselves but which were nevertheless fundamental standards which it was indispensable for the ethnographer to understand. Enquiry, enriched by such an approach, was at the same time complicated by it, for it was by no means easy for minds attached to occidental logic to penetrate systems of thought such as these in which analogies and the power of symbols have the value of facts. . . .
> Religious gestures, whether spectacular or secret, and generally uncomprehended by outsiders, show themselves under analysis to be of an extreme subtlety in their implications. The smallest everyday object may reveal in its form or decoration a conscious reflection of a complex cosmogony.[16]

In the course of Griaule's research, it became clear to him that the Dogon "live by a cosmogony, a metaphysic, and a religion which put them on a par with the peoples of antiquity, and which Christian theology might indeed study with profit." Like Turner, Griaule was greatly assisted in his work by a wise elderly informant named Ogotemmeli:

> In October 1946 he [Ogotemmeli] summoned the author to his house, and on thirty-three successive days, in a series of unforgettable conversations, he laid bare the framework of a world system, the knowledge of which will revolutionize all accepted ideas about the mentality of Africans and of primitive peoples in general.[17]

Unfortunately, Griaule was less interested in the social processes in which Dogon thought was shaped; hence he presented a somewhat static and idealized account of Dogon religion.

Most French and British anthropologists now agree that their perspectives are not contradictory but complementary. Hence, at a recent joint French and British symposium on African systems of thought, Turner suggested that "what was required was a theoretical frame which would take full account of both the structural-functional and 'logical-meaningful' (to use Sorokin's term) modalities of religion and would reveal their hidden interconnexions." [18]

The same need has also been recognized by some historians of religions whose perspective has been largely phenomenological. Referring to the study of African and other traditional religions, Charles Long has stressed the necessity of achieving "a unified approach to religion encompassing not only the phenomenology and morphology of religion but equally the existential, social and practical dimensions of religion." [19] The present study draws upon both social-functional and phenomenological approaches and attempts to integrate them within a unified perspective.

HISTORICAL PERSPECTIVES

None of the above approaches has, however, paid much attention to the historical dimensions of African religion. This stems partly from an anthropological bias against history and partly from a lack of information. It also stems from the enormous errors and prejudices of earlier culture-historians of Africa. As a result, most anthropological accounts have been limited to a more or less timeless "ethnographic present."

Fundamental to the culture-historical view was the popular "Hamitic" theory according to which the "higher" elements of civilization were conferred upon the indigenous Negro races of Africa by the so-called "Hamitic" race. The Hamites were alleged to be a branch of the Caucasian race which had entered Africa and become indigenized there. "The incoming Hamites," wrote Seligman, "were pastoral 'Europeans'—arriving wave after wave—better armed as well as quicker witted than the dark agricultural Negroes." [20] According to this theory, wherever iron-working, large-scale political organization, sacred kingship, the concept of supreme being, "Caucazoid" racial features, or certain linguistic elements were found, separately or together, the presence of Hamitic civilization or influence was indicated. In this way a crude "historical" dimension was imposed upon sub-Sahara Africa as scholars tried to sort the "earlier" more "primitive" Negro layers of culture from the "later" more "advanced" Hamitic layers. This theory, which fitted comfortably with European notions of racial superiority and with the colonial enterprise, has now been completely abandoned. In Africa, as elsewhere, it is recognized that race, language, and culture are independent elements. The presence of one or two items (or aspects of them) does not indicate the presence of a whole race or culture, Hamitic or otherwise.[21]

The problem of early religious and cultural history is extremely difficult because of a serious lack of archaeological and culture-historical information and because of the highly mixed cultural situation which now exists. For example, there are no purely hunting-gathering societies left, apart from a few relatively isolated Bushman bands in the Kalahari Desert, and it is difficult to generalize from these few cases about the hunting-gathering "stage" which once existed throughout Africa. In some instances linguistic information provides useful evidence, but this alone is not enough. For these reasons, it is almost impossible to reconstruct with any certainty the more ancient and radical forms of religious change, e.g., developments in the notions of supreme deity, ancestors, or culture heroes.

More fruitful results are now being obtained by shifting attention to more recent limited forms of cultural and religious change. Because suitable historical information rarely exists in the published literature, much of it has to be provided by specially designed fieldwork projects, utilizing oral tradition, political history, and contemporary socioreligious analysis. A number of recent studies have been carried out along these lines in East and Central Africa and published in an important volume, *The Historical Study of African Religion*.[22] This book advances new and significant views concerning royal cults and recent socioreligious change, some of which are discussed in the present study.

COMPARATIVE STUDIES

In addition to the anthropological and historical approaches just described, there have also been a small number of philosophically and theologically oriented comparative studies by both European and African authors. The general reluctance of anthropologists to attempt broad comparative studies of African religions has meant that this task has fallen to theologically and philosophically trained scholars. Understandably, they have neglected the cultural and social context of African religious ideas and behavior. Inevitably such efforts have resulted in both superficial and distorted representations.

Using the Bergsonian notion of "vital force," Father Placide Tempels' well-known *Bantu Philosophy* was the first European attempt to interpret African religious concepts according to Western philosophical categories. Tempels saw the idea of "vital force" as the unifying notion underlying all Bantu cosmology, ethics, and ritual. His interpretation greatly influenced European—especially French—understanding of African religions, but its limitations become apparent the more deeply one penetrates into African ritual and symbolism. On this level, such general notions as "force" and "vitality" are not precise enough to deal with the complex logic of the ideas and symbols involved. More recently, the Rwanda scholar, Father Alexis Kagame, has interpreted the Bantu world view according to Aristotelian methods and concepts. But, unlike Tempels' work, Kagame's *La philosophie bantu rwandaise de l'etre* is too systematic and abstract, and forces Bantu terminology into a rigid Western philosophical scheme.

In partial defense of these efforts, Robin Horton has emphasized the need for Western philosophical dialogue with African traditional thought. Contrary to much current British anthropology, Horton argues that philosophical concepts can deepen our understanding of African cosmologies if we look at them as systems of "explanation, prediction, and control" based on "theoretical models." In proposing this approach, Horton nevertheless clearly dissociates himself from the Frazerian view of traditional thought as a form of pseudoscience. Still, Horton believes there is an underlying similarity between African cosmology and Western science such that "African religious systems . . . can be seen as the outcome of a model-making process which is found alike in the thought of science and in that of pre-science." [23] Thus Horton argues,

> Once we have seen that many traditional religious statements are simply theoretical statements couched in an unfamiliar (because personal) idiom, all their more puzzling features at once become intelligible.
> . . . The gods appear as unobservable entities equivalent in many ways to the atoms, molecules and waves that feature so prominently in the explanatory statements of the sciences.[24]

Unfortunately, Horton rejects the use of Western theological and ontological categories (specifically those of Thomistic philosophy) because, in his view, they do not always correspond to African concepts and religious experience. There are differences, to be sure, and extreme caution must be used, but it does seem that if Western concepts are to be used at all, those taken from theological and metaphysical discourse are as useful for elucidating African religious thought as concepts from the philosophy of science.

More descriptive surveys of African religions by Parrinder (*African Traditional Religions*) and Mbiti (*African Religions and Philosophy*) suffer from another set of problems. They try to be exhaustive and to cover too many societies and too many types of religious phenomena.

Consequently, these surveys present little more than superficial catalogues of examples extracted in Frazerian fashion from concrete socioreligious contexts. For the most part, they concentrate upon "beliefs" without giving due recognition to the sociocultural and ritual fabric within which they are imbedded. Thus they reduce African religions to a set of "doctrines" analogous in structure to Western faiths: God, at the top, followed by a graded order of divinities, then the ancestor spirits, and lastly, the forest spirits and magical objects.

I have tried to avoid this problem by organizing my discussion around a small number of case studies, each drawn from the work of a recognized authority. I have also striven for geographical representativeness; however, ethnographic quality has been the selective principle. Thus some of the societies described here are remote and numerically small, while others which are more numerically prominent have been ignored.

AFRICAN RESPONSES
TO WESTERN SCHOLARSHIP

As previously mentioned, African authors have made significant contributions of their own to the study of African religions. Thus far, I have referred to works by Kagame and Mbiti. In concluding this historical survey, it is appropriate to mention the work of African scholars, for the future of the study of African religions obviously lies in their hands.

The earliest group of African writers produced basically descriptive and ethnographic accounts. Another generation of scholars emerged with more critical and constructive perspectives. Joseph B. Danquah was the first to mount a major attack on European anthropological interpretations. Danquah was trained in philosophy, and in his *The Akan Doctrine of God* he tried to expound the African idea of supreme being in Western philosophical terms. In the face of the European tendency to reduce African religions to mere polytheism, Danquah also argued that the Akan religion knew only one God. He also contended that African supreme beings were not as "remote" and "abstract" as Europeans had maintained. Unfortunately, Danquah greatly exaggerated the case for Akan monotheism and was later forced to modify his views. He did, however, draw attention to the active moral role of the Akan supreme god in personal life. In this respect he confirmed and added significantly to Rattray's earlier ethnographic evidence on this question.

More recently, the Yoruba scholar E. Bolaji Idowu has argued for a monotheistic interpretation of Yoruba religion. Like Danquah, Idowu attacks European views of the supreme god as a *deus incertus* or *deus remotus*. Among the Yoruba, he argues, the concept of supreme deity is the "one essential Factor by which the life and belief of the Yoruba cohere and have sustenance . . . since He is so urgently real." [25] In his view, the lesser gods, which form the bulk of Yoruba religion, should be regarded as attributes and functionaries of the one supreme god, thus making Yoruba religion a kind of "diffused monotheism." In addition, Idowu upholds the theological doctrine of universal revelation and the assumption that Yoruba religion was originally a "primitive monotheism." Idowu is rightly indignant at much of what has passed for the study of African religions. But his own purpose is avowedly theological, not merely anthropological, and he thus goes beyond the descriptive level to the level of metaphysics, which in his view "makes religion *religion*." [26] Despite his urgent appeal to study the African mind, the metaphysics which Idowu chooses is that developed by Western theological thought.

Following in this tradition, John Mbiti has presented a synoptic survey of African supreme beings in nearly three hundred different societies. Mbiti's premise in *Concepts of God in Africa* is the conviction that African concepts of supreme deity spring from an "independent reflection" upon the "One Supreme God" recognized in the Judeo-Christian tradition. On this basis, Mbiti extracts supreme gods from the various socioreligious systems to which they belong and constructs a composite, larger-than-life picture which goes far beyond the scope of any single African divinity. As in his previous work, *African Religions and Philosophy*, Mbiti's primary purpose is theological. Like Idowu and other contemporary African theologians, Mbiti is attempting to lay the basis for a distinctively African theology by blending the African past with the Judeo-Christian tradition.

To all of this, the Ugandan writer Okot p'Bitek has taken strong and vigorous exception. His recent *African Religions in Western Scholarship* is written from the standpoint of a cultural nationalist. He is especially critical of African philosophers and theologians whom he attacks for Hellenizing and Christianizing African religions. Much of p'Bitek's criticism is penetrating and well taken. His two major conclusions are worth noting, even if they overstate the present situation:

First, that whereas different schools of social anthropology may quarrel bitterly over *methods*, they may all share the same view that the population of the world is divisible into two: one, their own, *civilized*, and the rest, *primitive*. The second conclusion is that Western scholars have never been genuinely interested in African religions *per se*. Their works have all been part and parcel of some controversy or debate in the Western world.[27]

Unfortunately much of p'Bitek's criticism tends toward literary bombast. As Professor Ali Mazrui has aptly put it, "in a fit of fury Okot p'Bitek enters the temple thus erected by the first wave of African religious scholars, and indignantly pulls off those resplendent [Christian] robes, in an attempt to reveal the real essence of African deities." [28] In the final analysis, p'Bitek's interpretation of African religions turns out to be nothing more than what has already been shown by conventional field-work methods.

ARCHETYPAL SYMBOLS, RITUAL, AND COMMUNITY

From the preceding survey, it will be apparent that questions of perspective have been and continue to be central to the study of African religions. It remains for me to say a word about the perspective I have used in the present study and the themes I have chosen to explore.

For the purposes of this book, I have adopted a flexible and synthetic approach, using a combination of perspectives depending upon the nature of the materials involved. In most instances I have been strongly guided by the perspectives of the anthropologists and historians whose ethnography I have used. In addition, my purpose is to introduce students to as rich a variety of perspectives as possible, so that they will become acquainted with different methods. In this sense the present study is as much an introduction to the study of African religions as it is an introduction to African religions themselves.

Quite apart from the particular aims of this book, I also believe that a polymethodic approach of the sort I have adopted is demanded by the very nature of African religions. As numerous scholars have recognized, African religions are part and parcel of the whole fabric of African cultural life. Religious phenomena are thus closely interwoven with social, psychological, and moral dimensions. As such, they contain a variety of semantic features which Western thought can interpret only by artificially dividing them up according to sociological, psychological, philosophical, and historical methods of analysis. For this reason, the study of African religions must be polymethodic and multidimensional. In this study I try to combine these several perspectives as much as possible in order to reveal the full semantic, existential, and social meanings of African religious systems.[29]

I have organized the book around three major themes which are fundamental, though not unique, to African religions: archetypal symbols, ritual, and community. These are the keys to understanding any religion, and they open up both phenomenological and sociological levels of analysis.[30]

By "archetypal symbols" I mean sacred images, whether they be gods, ancestors, sacred actions or things, which make up the traditional universe. Such images, enshrined and communicated in myth and ritual, provide a network of symbolic forms, uniting social, ecological, and conceptual elements into locally bounded cultural systems. They give order to experience by framing the world in terms of sacred figures and patterns. Thus encapsulated within local universes of archetypal forms, traditional African thought tends to abolish both time and chance by shaping experience to interrelated moral and ritual patterns.

In this sense, archetypal symbols are models for behavior as well as modes of thought. To reenact the deeds of the gods, to become possessed by divinities, to manipulate sacred objects, to speak sacred words, is to conform experience to normative patterns of meaning and thereby to control and renew the shape and destiny of the world. The ritual sphere is the sphere *par excellence* where the world as lived and the world as imaged become fused together, transformed into one reality. Through ritual man transcends himself and communicates directly with the divine. The coming of divinity to man and of man to divinity happens repeatedly with equal validity on almost every ritual occasion. The experience of salvation is thus a present reality, not a future event. The passage from the profane to the sacred, from man to divinity, from moral conflict to moral unity occurs Here and Now. In short, almost every African ritual is a salvation event in which human experience is re-created and renewed in the all important ritual Present.

Mythical symbols and ritual acts are thus decidedly instrumental. They not only "say" what reality is, but they also shape the world to conform with this reality. In this respect religion plays an enormous role in African societies. Archetypal symbols express a community's past and they structure collective rites for corporate benefit. In the traditional context religion cannot be a purely personal affair; the relation to the sacred is, first of all, a communal one. Ritual specialists, priests, prophets, diviners, and kings are the servants of the community and their role is to mediate the sacred to the people. The life of priests and kings is bound up with the life of the societies they serve; rites which "strengthen" them "strengthen" the people as a whole. African ritual has a specifically social-functional character, and this is clearly recognized by the participants themselves. Every sacrifice is a re-creation of the group's solidarity, every rite of passage a reforging of the corporate life. In times of colonial oppression and rapid social change, ritual symbols have also served to create and reinforce new religious and political movements.

Suna's Shrine

It may be useful to illustrate more concretely what I mean by these themes with an example drawn from my own fieldwork among the Ganda of southern Uganda.

In 1972 the members of the Lungfish clan consecrated a new shrine to Kabaka Suna II, one of the kings of Buganda, who ruled from 1824 to 1854. The kingship itself dates back to the fifteenth century, and all the dynastic ancestors have shrines dedicated to them. In this case the construction of Suna's shrine was the culmination of years of work by the Lungfish clan to which Suna belonged. Several days prior to the ceremonies, people gathered at the shrine to clear the small country road leading to the hill top where the shrine was located. The dedication would be a three-day affair, attracting members of royalty and ritual attendants associated with the shrines of other kings. When I arrived early on the second day, trucks and taxis were still bringing numbers of people. Singing and dancing had already begun as the gathering awaited the arrival of the Head of the Princes and the assistant Curator of Antiquities who would officially open the ceremonies. The songs expressed the deep Ganda reverence for their kings. Women, many of whom were princesses and mediums of the spirits of the kings, danced to the songs. On the sidelines sat a group of elder princes talking among themselves and receiving the salutations of friends and kinsmen.

When the Head of the Princes arrived, he took his place among them. He was an old and respected man and immediately became the center of attention, and people came forward on their knees to greet him with a gentle touch of the hands. In his opening remarks, the Head of the Princes recalled that Suna II was the twenty-ninth Kabaka of Buganda. In this way he drew attention to the antiquity of the kingship which until recently had been the central institution of Ganda society. He also pointed out that Suna was the first in Buganda to adopt Islam, which indicated the forward-looking and cosmopolitan character of Suna's reign long before the colonial period. As he spoke, his words expressed what everybody felt—the dedication of the shrine was a rededication of Ganda historical identity. By contrast, the assistant Curator, who represented the national government, emphasized the view that the shrine had significance for "the whole" of Uganda, which now embraced many other ethnic groups.

The shrine itself was constructed in the traditional conical thatched roof style. It was a large round structure about eighty feet in diameter with a high domed roof. After a ceremonial trimming of the thatch over the entrance, the shrine's drums boomed out a royal welcome, and there was a great rush of people to get inside. The first to enter carried large decorated vases on their shoulders. These sacred objects are called "Twins," and they represent the royal ancestors who had come to pay their respects to Suna in his new home. Upon entering, everyone left sandals and shoes outside before crossing the threshold into the sacred domain within. In the dimly lit interior a barrier of spears and shields could be seen standing at the center in front of a large barkcloth curtain. The curtain stretched from side to side and concealed the rear portion from view. The area behind the curtain, called the "forest," is where Suna's spirit dwelled. According to Ganda mythology, Kintu, the sky-born founder of the kingship, "disappeared" into a forest near his palace after establishing the kingdom of Buganda. The symbolism of this primordial event has become part of the royal ideology, and it serves as an archetype for the architecture of the shrines. Like Kintu, deceased kings do not die but go into the "forest" sanctuaries of their shrines. The "forest" is the "other" world of the royal spirits, and it enables them to remain in contact with this world, and this world with them. Within the shrine the two worlds meet precisely at the center, at their point of juncture directly under the roof dome. Today, the shrines are clustered together in the small county of Busiro, which is the ancient center of the kingdom. The kingdom is thus oriented around a sacred center, which is the realm of the royal ancestors.

At Suna's shrine the mediums of the royal spirits came forward to introduce themselves to Suna in front of the curtain. On this occasion the curtain was slightly parted at the center to give access to the "forest," thus enabling the two worlds to meet. The mediums soon became mildly possessed with the spirits of their kings and they sang and danced before the people, Suna himself among them. The people responded with the royal salutation, "You have conquered! You have conquered! You have conquered us (your subjects)!" and they came forward to place offerings of money in the baskets before the opened "forest." Later the mediums, called "bearers," ran out of the shrine brandishing their royal spears in a triumphant display. This recalled enthronement ceremonies, when a new king is paraded before his people on the shoulders of his running bearer.

As this ceremony suggests, the shrine stands as an archetypal symbol. It is a sacred center representing the mythic, spiritual, and historical foundations of the kingdom. The shrine also acts as a sociological center, pulling together the segmented royal class and the different clans which have participated in the kingship. The periodic ceremonies held at this and other shrines reinforce the social identity of the royal class and the historic continuity of the kingdom with its sacred past. In the course of the ceremonies the past is made present through the ecstasy of the mediums. Time is transcended, and once again the Ganda bask in the radiance of their kings.

Much more could be said about the details of the shrine ceremonies which make them uniquely Ganda events. What I have emphasized here are their enduring symbolic, ritual, and social aspects, which, as I have indicated, are common themes in this and other forms of Africa religious behavior.[31]

In chapters 1 and 2 I deal with the archetypal realms of myth, history, and divinity. In chapter 3 I examine techniques of ritual expression and control. In chapters 4 and 5 I discuss the social sphere of religious leadership and moral categories. At the same time, I consider these themes simultaneously, for they are mutually related. Hence I examine the ritual aspects of myth, the symbolic aspects of social experience, and so on. Chapters 6, 7, and 8 carry forward these themes into the historical context of colonial resistance movements, African Islam, and African Independent Christianity, showing how traditional religious forms have shaped (and have been shaped by) recent religious and political developments. The book thus has an historical as well as a thematic organization, though much of what is described as traditional in the early chapters is of course based upon contemporary studies.

NOTES

1. E. E. Evans-Pritchard, "Sources, with Particular Reference to the Southern Sudan," *Cahiers d'Etudes Africaines* 11, no. 41 (1971), 144-45.

2. Samuel Baker, "The Races of the Nile Basin," *Transactions of the Ethnological Society of London*, n.s., 5 (1867), p. 231, as quoted in E. E. Evans-Pritchard, *Theories of Primitive Religion* (Oxford: The Clarendon Press, 1965), p. 7.

3. Richard F. Burton, *A Mission to Gelele, King of Dahome*, 2nd ed., 2 vols. (London: Tinsley Brothers, 1864), 2: 199.

4. Richard F. Burton, *A Mission to Gelele, King of Dahome*, 3rd ed. (New York: Frederick A. Praeger, Inc., 1966), pp. 291-92.

5. T. J. Bowen, *Adventures and Missionary Labours* (1857; reprint ed., London: Frank Cass & Co. Ltd., 1968), p. 310.

6. David Livingstone, *Missionary Travels and Researches in South Africa* (New York: Harper & Brothers, Publishers, 1858), pp. 26-27, as quoted in Margery Perham and J. Simons, *African Discovery* (London: Faber and Faber, Ltd., 1963), pp. 131-32.

7. Kenneth Clark, *Civilisation* (New York: Harper & Row, Publishers, 1969), p. 2.

8. For an assessment of the theories of de Brosses, Comte, and Tylor, see EVANS-PRITCHARD, *Theories of Primitive Religion,* chap. 2.

9. A partial summary of this work appears in WILHELM SCHMIDT, *The Origin and Growth of Religion: Facts and Theories,* trans. H. J. Rose (London: Methuen & Co. Ltd., 1931).

10. MAX GLUCKMAN, *Custom and Conflict in Africa* (Oxford: Basil Blackwell & Mott Ltd., 1966), p. 110.

11. *Theories of Primitive Religion,* p. 112.

12. E. E. EVANS-PRITCHARD, *Nuer Religion* (Oxford: The Clarendon Press, 1956), p. 320.

13. JOHN MIDDLETON, *The Study of the Lugbara* (New York: Holt, Rinehart and Winston, 1970), pp. 37, 39.

14. VICTOR TURNER, *The Forest of Symbols* (Ithaca: Cornell University Press, 1967), p. 133.

15. *Ibid.,* pp. 50-58.

16. G. DIETERLEN, Introduction to MARCEL GRIAULE, *Conversations with Ogotemmeli* (London: Oxford University Press for the International African Institute, 1965), pp. xii-xiv. Used with permission.

17. GRIAULE, *Conversations,* p. 2.

18. VICTOR TURNER, "Ritual and Symbolism," in *African Systems of Thought,* ed., M. Fortes and G. Dieterlen (London: Oxford University Press for the International African Institute, 1965), p. 15.

19. CHARLES H. LONG, "Prolegomenon to a Religious Hermeneutic," *History of Religions* 6, no. 3 (1971), 254.

20. C. G. SELIGMAN, *Races of Africa* (London: Oxford University Press, 1930), p. 96.

21. On the sources and history of the Hamitic theory, see EDITH R. SANDERS, "The Hamitic Hypothesis; Its Origins and Functions in Time Perspective," *Journal of African History* 10, no. 4 (1969).

22. T. O. RANGER and I. N. KIMAMBO, *The Historical Study of African Religion* (Berkeley: University of California Press, 1972).

23. ROBIN HORTON, "Ritual Man in Africa," *Africa* 34, no. 2 (1964), 99.

24. ROBIN HORTON, "Philosophy and African Studies," in *Africa in the Wider World,* ed. David Brokensha and Michael Crowder (Oxford: Pergamon Press, 1967), p. 266. See also ROBIN HORTON, "African Traditional Thought and Western Science," *Africa* 37, Nos. 1 & 2 (1967).

25. E. BOLAJI IDOWU, *Olódùmarè: God in Yoruba Belief* (London: Longmans, Green and Co., Ltd., 1962), p. 202.

26. E. BOLAJI IDOWU, *African Traditional Religion: A Definition* (London: SCM Press Ltd., 1973), p. 10.

27. OKOT P'BITEK, *African Religions in Western Scholarship* (Nairobi: East African Publishing House, 1970), p. viii.

28. ALI A. MAZRUI, Epilogue to *African Religions in Western Scholarship,* p. 125.

29. See Professor Ninian Smart's definition of the study of religion as "an enterprise which is aspectual, polymethodic, pluralistic, and without clear boundaries" (NINIAN SMART, *The Science of Religion and the Sociology of Knowledge* [Princeton: Princeton University Press, 1973], p. 8.).

30. My exposition of these themes is drawn from the work of anthropologists to whom I have referred throughout the book and from several other scholars, especially JOACHIM WACH, *Sociology of Religion* (Chicago: University of Chicago Press, 1945); MIRCEA ELIADE, *Cosmos and History,* trans. Willard Trask (New York: Harper & Row, Publishers, 1959); CLIFFORD GEERTZ, "Religion as a Cultural System" in *Anthropological Approaches to the Study of Religion,* ed. Michael Banton, Association of Social Anthropologists Monographs, No. 3 (London: Tavistock Publications, 1965); I. M. LEWIS, *Ecstatic Religion* (Hamondsworth, England: Penguin Books Ltd., 1971).

31. For a fuller discussion, see B. RAY, "Royal Shrines and Ceremonies of Buganda," *Uganda Journal* 36 (1972).

1

Myth and History

In most African societies there is little speculation about the origin of the universe. African thought tends to be bound up with daily life, and hence there is little interest in questions that do not concern practical matters. Most African myths deal primarily with the origin of man and with the origin of certain social and ritual institutions that account for real-life situations. These myths explain the basic conditions of human life as the people now find it.

For this reason, African mythology contains a good deal of what we would call "history." Indeed, in African oral tradition "myth" and "history" generally overlap and shade into one another. Myth blends into history as cosmic and archetypal events bear upon local situations, and history blends into myth as local and human events become ritualized and infused with cosmic and archetypal meaning. It is important to see how African myth-history as a whole gives meaning to the world: how the sacred and true events of the past serve to represent and explain the world as it ultimately is, and how these same events may serve as ritual archetypes for the renewal of the natural and human order.[1]

CREATION MYTHS

Dogon Cosmogony

The Dogon of Mali are unusual in having developed an elaborate cosmogony and a highly complex cosmology. The creation myth which I shall summarize below was collected and pieced together over a number of years by Griaule and Dieterlen.[2] My interpretation adheres closely to their own analysis and point of view. In their view, the creation myth provides the symbolic categories by which the Dogon understand and organize their world and it provides the ritual patterns by which the Dogon seek to maintain the world in existence. I shall also indicate how the creation myth explains the world in terms of a binary structure.

In the beginning, Amma, the Supreme God, existed alone and depended upon nothing but himself. Amma had the shape of an oval egg made out of his four collar bones joined together. The bones divided the egg into four quarters containing the four elements—fire, air, earth, and water—and the joints between the bones represented the four cardinal directions of space. The morphology of the cosmic egg thus contained both the substance and structure of the universe.

Amma traced within himself the design of the cosmos and its future development by placing in the egg 266 cosmic Signs. These signs manifested the creative thought of Amma, and they contained the structure, essence, and life-principle of all things.

After making the 266 Signs, Amma embarked upon the creation of the world. He placed the four elements and the Signs together with the Seeds of plants and crops in a flat disk, and set the disk revolving between two cosmic axes. But as the disk began to spin, it threw out the water, drying up the Seeds. The creation was a failure. Amma destroyed it and began again. This time he would make mankind the instrument for preserving the order and life of the world.

Amma began his second creation by placing a tiny seed grain within himself in the center of the cosmic egg. Into this grain he spoke seven creative "Words" bearing the creative force (*nyama*) of sacred speech. This caused the seed to vibrate seven times and to turn in a spiral fashion extending itself in seven directions within the womb of the egg.

The seven protrusions prefigured an anthropomorphic shape, the image of man, around which the world would be organized. The seventh projection, however, broke through its enveloping sheath and produced a separate segment which was shorter than the others, and incomplete. It represented the principle of incompleteness (imperfection, singularity, disorder) which together with the principle of completeness (perfection, duality, order) constitute the structure and dynamics of the Dogon cos-

Figure 1. The first seven vibrations of the egg of the world.

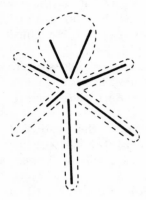

Figure 2. The prefiguring of man in the egg of the world.

mology. This was foreseen and determined by Amma from the beginning.

Amma then transformed the egg into a double placenta. In each he placed a set of twins, male and female. Before the process of gestation was complete, one of the males, named Ogo, became impatient. He feared that Amma would not give him his female counterpart after birth. Despite Amma's assurances, Ogo grew increasingly anxious. Feeling desperately alone and incomplete he could no longer wait for the completion of the gestation process, which took sixty years. Instead, he burst forth from his placenta with the intention of seizing his twin for himself before the time of birth. But Amma had foreseen Ogo's revolt and removed his twin to the other placenta.

Unable to recover his twin, Ogo revolted completely. He broke all the cosmic rules and tried to take over all the secrets of the universe for himself with the intention of creating another world. He traversed the

Figure 3. "The life of the world." The heavenly and earthly placentas.

area inside the cosmic egg in a spiral motion contrary to the original spiral direction and thereby imposed his own disorder upon the creative process. He declared himself to be as wise as Amma and capable of creating his own universe, for he knew that Amma had implanted within him the important Signs, Words, and Seeds of creation. He stole what he thought was the original Seed grain, intending to create a new world of his own. But this seed turned out to contain only the seeds of inedible plants and insects. When Ogo tried to utter the sacred Words, he discovered that he lacked the special quality of speech with which to say them properly and thus launch a new creation.

Undaunted, Ogo burst forth from the celestial egg-womb, tearing off a piece of it as he went and taking it with him as he descended through the void below. Amma, who stood ready to reorganize Ogo's destructive efforts, transformed the piece of placenta into the Earth. With the addition of this new element, the world again took on the shape of a human figure. The celestial egg was the head, the lower placenta was the hips and legs, and the space between represented the trunk and arms.

Still intent upon acquiring his own twin, Ogo copulated with the Earth. In this way he acquired a "wife" as a substitute for his lost female twin. But he unwittingly defiled the Earth, for being Ogo's placenta it was also his mother, and mating with it was therefore an act of incest. This made the Earth sterile and dry and bereft of its creative potential.

Instead of destroying the now disordered universe, Amma resolved to restore the disorder caused by Ogo's revolt. He would sacrifice the other male twin, called Nommo, who shared the placenta with Ogo and thus shared in the responsibility of his revolt. Amma strangled Nommo and scattered his dismembered parts in the four directions. In this way, Amma regained control over the creative Words and Signs located in the body of Nommo. By scattering Nommo's body over the expanse of the celestial world, Amma was able to reimpose his own order upon it.

After five days, Amma gathered together the pieces of the sacrificed Nommo and restored him to life, and made him the master and ruler of the universe. From the parts of Nommo, Amma also created four other Nommo spirits, whose offspring became the ancestors of the Dogon people.

Amma then sent Nommo and the ancestors down to Earth in a great ark provisioned with everything needed to restore and fructify the Earth and to sustain the human race: all species of animals and plants and all the elements of human society and culture. As the ark descended, Nommo shouted out Amma's creative words. In this way the creative Word was transmitted to Earth and made available to all mankind. Upon landing, Nommo stepped out of the ark and placed his foot on the soil. In this manner he demonstrated his dominion over the Earth, and he impregnated it with Amma's creative Signs.

Meanwhile, Amma transformed Ogo into an animal called the Pale Fox. Solitary and incomplete, always in revolt, the Fox now wanders over the surface of the Earth in a fruitless quest for his female soul. The Pale Fox is the forerunner whose steps reveal the dangers man must avoid. In the course of his wandering, the Pale Fox guides mankind through the mysteries of life by the tracks he leaves on the ground, which are interpreted by the Dogon diviners.

Amma's final act of restoration was the sending of the rains to Earth and the performance of another sacrifice to purify and revitalize the soil. This time Amma sacrified one of Nommo's offspring, named Lebe. Later, Amma restored Lebe to life in the form of a snake, while his bones remained buried in the ground where they continue to fructify the land. From this time onwards, men began to cultivate the land and to spread out over it in increasing numbers. Aided by Nommo, mankind continues to follow the way originally blazed by the Pale Fox, the miscreant forerunner of human civilization.

Before we examine the content of the myth, let us notice its binary structure. So closely is this structure correlated with its content that the structure itself expresses the central doctrine of the story: the world oscillates between order and disorder.

The narrative proceeds through three temporal or diachronic phases: Creation, Revolt, and Restoration. In the first phase Amma brings forth Thought, Signs, Seeds, Word, and Twins: the principles of order. Before this phase can be completed, it is interrupted by an oppositional phase, the revolt of Ogo, which introduces emotion, irrationality, sterility, and singularity: the principles of disorder. This is followed by a third and final phase which partially mediates the opposition between order/disorder and thus serves to restore the original order.

The narrative begins by reference to the abstract and moves forward by reference to the processes of realization and concretization: Thought becomes Sign, Sign becomes Word, Word enters Seed, Seed becomes Womb, Womb engenders Twins. This ordered and rational process proceeds with almost inexorable necessity. But just before it can be brought to completion, a disruptive counter-process arises stemming from the irrational personality of Ogo, the Pale Fox. Implicitly, the central question is posed: Why did Ogo revolt? On the narrative level, he revolts because he is impatient; the gestation process takes too long. But there is also a deeper reason.

To see this, we have to turn to the synchronic or structural level of the myth. Here we encounter the controlling principle of twinness. This is the principle of binary opposition, which symbolizes the idea

of completeness and perfection. Each phase of the myth generates a set
of binary pairs—e.g., thought/sign, sign/word, small/expanding, male/
female, sacrifice/resurrection, order/disorder—and these serve to move
the myth forward. They are its basic building blocks. In the imagery
of the myth, the male twin becomes impatient and finally rebels. In
logical terms, there is a clash between the principle of the unity of
paired opposites, represented by the twins, and the process of creation
itself, represented by the period of gestation. The unity of the Pale
Fox and his female twin, required on the structural level, is held off
by time on the diachronic level. But the principle of twinness cannot
be ignored, and it finally asserts itself, fracturing the creative process.
The impatient Fox revolts and attempts to acquire his missing twin,
thus introducing chaos into the original order. The perfection of the
universe as originally conceived by the Creator is thus compromised by
the very process of bringing it into existence. In ontological terms, being
becomes qualified by becoming, essence by existence.

From this point onwards, it is a question of repair and restoration,
of creating order out of disorder, being out of becoming. The narrative
moves forward again, in terms no longer of creation and realization
but of ritual transformation and renewal. These ritual acts set the stage
for man's involvement in creation as the ritual agent who mediates the
opposition between order and disorder by repeating Amma's archetypal
acts.

The creation myth thus answers not only the speculative question
of how the world came into being; it also answers the more practical
question about the nature and purpose of human existence.

According to the myth, the human world is a fallen place which
has been partially restored. The world originated in disobedience, not
by man, but by a son of God. God restored the world by sacrificing
another of his sons who, together with mankind, now rules over the
world in God's stead. Because the world is a remade version of a fallen
realm, it is not perfect. It is in a perpetual state of becoming because
it still contains the elements of darkness, sterility, and death which
resulted from the revolt of Ogo, the Pale Fox. These elements of disorder, or becoming, have not been abolished but are merely offset by the
elements of light, rain, fertility, life, or being, introduced by Nommo.

Man, for his part, is a direct descendant of the son of God who
restored the world. His task is to continually push back the boundaries
of disorder, the tides of time and becoming, by spreading out the canopy
of civilization over the Earth and by performing periodic rituals to restore its life. This role was predestined for man from the beginning, and
the myth provides the archetypal symbols that man duplicates on Earth.
This can be seen in Dogon social organization.

The Dogon system of kinship and alliance represents a reorganization of the original set of disrupted relationships between Amma, Nommo, and the Pale Fox. According to the Dogon, the maternal grandfather symbolizes Amma. In the next generation, the mother and her brother are the twin Nommo. The offspring of the next generation represent the Pale Fox.

Just as the Pale Fox, in taking a piece of his mother's placenta, is still a part of his mother, so the child remains partly identified with his mother. For this reason the child is classified as belonging to his mother's generation. If the child is a male, he is symbolically regarded as the "brother" of his mother. Since his own parents represent the twin Nommo, they should ideally be brother and sister. But in real life this would be incestuous, so the child's parents are symbolically replaced by the wife's brother and his wife. A male child can therefore regard his real father as a stranger and his maternal uncle as his ideal genitor. Recalling the incest of the Pale Fox, the son may also call his aunt "my wife" and behave in a sexually intimate way with her. He may also take freely from his uncle's household, as the Fox stole from the Nommo. In addition, the child is permitted to express feelings of hostility towards his father, who has generated the incomplete being the son feels himself to be. In his early years, the son, like the Fox, lacks a wife. In the myth, this resulted in disaster, but it is brought to a satisfactory resolution among the Dogon by the uncle, who finds a wife for his nephew, a substitute for his "aunt-mother." In one sense, every marriage is a repetition of the mythical incest of the Fox, because the husband's wife is his "mother." But since she is a substitute "mother," this avoids the otherwise destructive consequences of sons marrying their real mothers! The existing kinship and alliance system thus represents a reorganization, under the direction of the Nommo-uncle, of the original mythical situation, which was a result of the rebellion of the Pale Fox.

The myth also presents a model for structuring the territorial, village, and homestead organization into a coherent system.

The Dogon inhabit the mountainous area of central Mali. They live in small villages scattered among the cliffs and plateaus, wherever flat spaces of land may be found for their millet and rice fields. In accordance with the principle of twinness, the villages are often built in pairs, referred to as the Upper and Lower villages. A pair of this sort is regarded as Heaven and Earth (Nommo and the Pale Fox) joined together. The basic structure of the village also represents a pair of Nommo twins. At the northern end of the village is the head, the men's meeting house where collective decisions are made. The family houses are the chest, and the women's huts are the hands. The village altar is the male sexual organ, and the stone on which women crush fruit is the female organ. The communal altars at the southern end of the village are the feet.

The ground plan of the individual household also reproduces a mythical archetype, in this case the male Nommo lying on his right side in the position of procreation. The kitchen represents the head and the two hearth stones are the eyes. The trunk is the central room of the household, while the storerooms on either side are the arms. The sex organ is the entry passage to the work room. This contains jars of water and grinding stones used in crushing new ears of corn whose liquid, associated with the male seminal fluid, is poured over the ancestor shrines located at the end of the passage.

Thus far we have seen how the myth provides a metaphysical and moral answer to the question of human existence and how it provides systematic knowledge about the world and a set of archetypes for social, territorial, village, and domestic organization. To this extent the myth resembles a form of philosophy. But it is more than this. The knowledge it conveys is not merely systematic and metaphysical but existential and ritualistic. It is this which enables the Dogon not only to know the origin and nature of the world but also to enter into dynamic relationship with it. It enables the Dogon to ritually control and shape their world and their experience of it according to the archetypal patterns displayed in the creation myth.

A few examples will illustrate this existential and ritual dimension. First, the Signs. As we have seen, these refer to the basic ontological properties of the world. But they are more than "ideas." They are ritual symbols that enable the Dogon to control the things they represent. The placement of these Signs on sacred objects is an efficacious act that "produces" the things to which the Signs refer. Diagrams representing the complete table of 266 Signs are painted under the main altar of Amma. This altar represents "Amma in the sky" and the "center of Amma's egg." The painting of these Signs upon the altar helps to maintain the world in existence. Another altar of Amma, located in the main section of each village, contains the Signs governing the development of things. It represents the "opening" of the cosmic egg and ensures the efficacy of Amma's Signs on earth. Signs are also painted upon the major totemic sanctuaries in order to perpetuate the totemic animals and natural species associated with them. In executing the Signs the priest also prays for the strengthening of his own powers through them: "Let the mind of Amma pass into me; let Amma place me before mankind, let him add life to me." During the spring agricultural rites, the head of the family inscribes at the center of his fields a pattern representing the 266 Signs and cosmic Seeds. This, together with Amma's blessing, will fructify the newly sown fields. In this way, the Signs revealed in the myth function as the archetypal forms enabling the Dogon to both comprehend and control their universe.

The same function may be seen in the ritual repetition of Amma's sacrifice, the act by which Amma took control of a disordered universe and renewed it. A series of altars located between the Upper and Lower villages represents the several aspects of Amma's cosmic sacrifice. Some altars are associated with the vital parts of Nommo's dismembered body and with the Words contained in it. Others are associated with the stages of the sacrifice: the strangulation, dismemberment, and resurrection. Still others are associated with the four cosmic directions, the mythical ancestors, totemic clans, and other elements of the social system. At these altars all aspects of Amma's primordial sacrifice are reenacted over a period of five years. This series of altars provides the Dogon with a mechanism for periodically re-creating and renewing the world. In this sense, the Dogon universe is truly anthropocentric. Like Amma in the beginning, the Dogon take control of the world, whose duration has been placed in their hands, and renew its life and substance through the repetition of ritual acts. These acts mediate the original opposition between order and disorder and thus help to restore the total cosmos.

This pattern is built into almost every African mythical system. Myth posits an original situation against which the world develops. An opposition or division arises between order and disorder, divinity and humanity, sky and earth. The "problem" of religion is to overcome this divine/human polarity through ritual action.

Myths of "Paradise Lost"

One prominent myth, found throughout Africa, tells of a primordial separation between the sky and the earth and between God and man. The primary theme of this myth is its statement about the nature of the human condition. It explains the origin of suffering, illness, death, and separation from God in terms of a sky/earth polarity. We have already seen one version of this theme in the Dogon creation myth, and we have seen how it is related to Dogon cosmology and ritual in general. In other societies there are different versions, and to understand them we have to see how they fit into the larger context of the socioreligious systems to which they belong.

According to the Nuer cattle-herders of the southern Sudan, the sky and the earth were originally connected by a rope sometimes said to be attached to the Tree of Creation from which man entered the world.

Every day people climbed down the rope from the sky to obtain their food. When people died on earth, they ascended to the sky via the rope for a short time and returned rejuvenated to earth.

The Nuer have different versions explaining how the rope was severed from the sky, making death a permanent feature of the human condition. In one version, a mischievous hyena and a sparrow climbed to the sky, but the Creator, named Kwoth, ordered them guarded so they would not cause trouble. At night they eluded their guards and escaped to earth down the rope. Then, as a prank, the hyena cut the rope at the bottom, whereupon the remaining segment withdrew to the sky, never to return. In another version, a girl descended from the sky with some companions to get food on earth. While on earth, she met and had sexual relations with a young man. He, too, had originally come from the sky, but he had spent his whole lifetime growing up on earth. When it came time for the girl and her companions to return, the girl refused. Declaring her love for the young man, she announced her intentions of staying permanently on earth. When the urging of her companions proved to be of no avail, they ascended to the sky and cut the rope, severing forever the means for immortality.[3]

Before turning to the meaning of this myth, we may look at a similar but contrasting myth among the Tutsi cattle-herders of Rwanda.

In the beginning, Imana, the supreme god, existed alone, prior to the creation of the heavens and the "world below." He created both worlds simultaneously, so that the two realms together formed a single totality. But the "world below" was the opposite of the world above. It lacked the beauty and prosperity of the divine realm of the sky. It contained nothing but misery, suffering, work, and rebellion. In the heavens, Imana created all species of plants, trees, and animals, and, last of all, mankind. Man lived in the sky close to Imana and enjoyed without labor the fruits of the trees and fields. Even hunting involved no risk or effort, for the animals did not fear man and run away. Sickness and death were unknown. When people died, they were brought to life again by Imana after three days.

There was one couple, however, who remained childless. In desperation the wife, Nyinakigwa, made an offering to Imana and asked for a child. Imana was moved by her plea and promised to give her a child, providing that she did not reveal its true origins. Nyinakigwa agreed, and Imana made her a son Kigwa in a pottery jar. When she asked for more children, Imana gave her another son Lututsi and a daughter Nyinabatutsi.

Nyinakigwa had a sister who was barren, and she became jealous of Nyinakigwa's newly acquired children. After much persuasion, the sister prevailed upon Nyinakigwa to reveal the origin of her children. Upon learning that it was Imana, she set off to ask the same favor of him.

Realizing the seriousness of her indiscretion, Nyinakigwa cried out, "I have killed my children! . . . I have offended Imana, I have killed my children!" Then the floor of the sky trembled and opened up and the three children fell to the "world below."

> Seeing this, Nyinakigwa lamented, what have I done to my children, unfortunate mother that I am? I have lost them. They have left me for the land of work and suffering. Imana has punished me for my sin. What should I do without my children? Can I not accompany them? Why have they been punished instead of me? My children, it is I who am guilty, you poor innocents who expiate my sin. . . . All the beautiful things which Imana has placed in the sky! Below, he tells me, it is misery, famine, thirst, and work. O, my children, it is I your mother who has killed you.[4]

The two sisters begged Imana for forgiveness, but he promised only to show pity upon the children and alleviate their condition in the world below. One day, he promised, their expiation would be complete and they would return to the sky.

Here, then, is another separation myth explaining the origin of the human condition—suffering, toil, and separation from God—as the result of a loss of paradise. Yet, it is obvious that these two myths present very different views of the cause and significance of this situation.

For the Nuer, the loss of paradise did not result from disobedience to the Creator. It was the consequence of accidental and unforeseen circumstances. In one version the separation was caused by a mischievous and destructive animal, apparently to spite the Creator. In the other version it was caused by an impetuous young girl and her vindictive companions. Here there is a suggestion of disobedience and rebellion, but the situation is fundamentally ambiguous, for no explicit rule was broken. Indeed, the girl's behavior reflects customary marital practice in which girls leave their childhood homes and companions for their husbands and their kinsmen. Thus one can imagine that the Nuer look upon the girl's act more or less indulgently as a prelude to the development of human society. Both versions represent the separation between the sky and the earth as an accidental event. The hyena version stresses the prank, and makes it a rather senseless, almost "absurd" event. The girl's abandonment version suggests that it was a necessary feature of human experience. But in neither version is it conceived as a rebellion against the creator god.

The Tutsi myth expresses the opposite point of view. The loss of paradise resulted from an explicit act of disobedience against the creator's will. There is no ambiguity. It was a breach of an agreement between a supplicant and her master.

How do we interpret these two mythologies of the "fall"? Why do the Nuer and Tutsi have such different points of view? As we have seen, myths of origins attempt to explain the present order of things; they are not mere speculations. We can therefore gain some insight by looking at the different religious and social situations which these myths reflect.

The Nuer cattle-herders live in small villages widely dispersed over the flat riverine country of the upper Nile basin. The Nuer are transhumant, moving about during the dry season and returning to their villages during the wet season for cultivation. Nuer political organization is non-centralized and segmentary. It is built up of kinship relations among dominant or "aristocratic" lineages on the village, clan, and sub-tribal level. At the basis of this system are the villages and family homesteads. The village is subject to the authority of the elders of the dominant lineage. The homestead is subject to the authority of the father, who controls and protects the interests of his children.

Nuer religion is organized in much the same segmentary fashion, except that it is ultimately unified around the supreme god, Kwoth. The spirits of the sky are Kwoth's "sons." They are the dominant or "aristocratic" powers, superior in rank to the clan-spirits, which are said to be the "children of Kwoth's daughters." Each of these powers operates at a different level of social experience: family, lineage, village, clan, sub-tribe.

Nuer also conceive their relation to Kwoth in the idiom of kinship. They are his "children" and he is their Father and Ancestor. As such, Kwoth also is the Spirit of the Homestead Shrine and the Spirit of the Village, for he is the ultimate ground of family and village unity beyond the clan-spirits. He is also the Spirit of all Nuer, and hence the basis of the widest ethnic unity, surpassing the limited scope of the sky-spirits.

As the above titles suggest, Nuer conceive of Kwoth in intimate, personal terms. In addition to being a Father and Ancestor, he is, more generally, a Friend. Nuer feel he is constantly near them and directly concerned with everyday life. He is involved in virtually all ritual occasions: agricultural and seasonal rites, healing, oath-swearing, peace-making, marriage, purification, and rites for protection against lightning. In times of sickness and drought or other personal or collective crises, Nuer make direct appeal to his creative and saving power. In response Kwoth frequently sends his "sons" to inspire prophets and assist his people.

At the same time, Nuer also refer to Kwoth in more transcendent terms as Creator of the Universe and as Spirit of the Sky. Nuer admit that Kwoth sometimes seems to be far away and that he does not always heed their prayers. They say they are mere "ants" in his eyes, too "ignorant" to comprehend his ways.

Thus, although the Nuer see themselves to be clearly separated from their Creator, who is ultimately beyond their grasp, they do not experience this separation in radical form. For the Nuer, the cause of the separation was both accidental and natural; it did not stem from a moral breach which keeps God and man fundamentally apart. Kwoth still remains their Father and Ancestor, transcendent in his authority and power, yet very close to them in moral and ritual terms.[5]

By contrast, the Tutsi experience of Imana is more abstract and distant. He is the First Creator and Eternal One who determines men's destinies but otherwise remains aloof from the world. People know him only indirectly through the medium of divination, which reveals the destinies he has set for them.

Tutsi religion is more immediately concerned with the family ancestors and cult-spirits and with the dynastic ancestors of the kingdom. As the ultimate ground of the world, Imana completely transcends the ordinary ritual sphere of mutual exchange and transaction between men and the ancestors and cult-spirits. Between man and Imana there is a fixed destiny, an unbridgeable gap.

This pattern of relationship resembles the traditional sociopolitical system of the now defunct Tutsi kingdom. The keystone of this system was what Jaques Maquet has called the "premise of inequality." Individuals entered into multiple forms of clientship relations with different feudal lords to whom they owed immediate loyalties and obligation in return for personal protection and favor. At the top of this system stood the cattle-owning Tutsi aristocracy, who constituted a caste unto themselves. They were the lords of the agricultural Hutu who constituted the majority of the population. At the bottom of the scale was a small number of Twa pygmies who were hunters. Imana established this order in the beginning, after the Tutsi "fell" from Heaven to the "world below." This world was already inhabited by Hutu and Twa, who had been previously expelled from the sky, and who, it is said, would never be allowed to return. At the very pinnacle of this system was the Tutsi king; he was the Lord of the lords. He was an autocratic ruler from whom all order and government flowed and to whom everyone owed ultimate allegiance.

Like the Tutsi king, Imana governed absolutely but from a distance. Only rarely did he intervene in human affairs—for example, in times of extreme personal crisis when all other powers failed. But his intervention was not guaranteed, and people had no other recourse than to wait upon his wishes. He kept constant watch over the moral lives of the people, as the king kept constant surveillance over his subjects, but the sense of separation was still complete.[6]

The Tutsi interpreted this situation in terms of the basic moral premise of their society: the agreement between a client and his lord. Nyinakigwa's violation of such an agreement nullified the original mutual relationship between Imana and the Tutsi and caused their expulsion from his realm. Thereafter Imana was no longer responsible for them, though he did watch over their general destiny while they served out their fate in the "world below."

By looking at these differences in social and religious experience, we can go some way towards understanding the differences in the mythologies of the lost paradise. For the Tutsi, the separation myth is cast in the form of a moral breach that explains the gap they experience between man and God. For the Nuer the myth is cast in a more ambiguous form that fits in with their experience of Kwoth's nearness. Seen against this broader experiential background, theological differences we might otherwise attribute to the arbitrariness of mythological "Just-So" stories become meaningful expressions of fundamental contrasts in religious and cultural form.

Mythic Archetypes in Lugbara Cosmology

As we have seen, African mythology explains the world by reference to symbolic oppositions and polarities that serve to categorize complex social and moral relationships.

According to the Lugbara of northwestern Uganda, human society evolved through three social phases.[7] The first was a primordial, mythic phase in which the world was the inverse of what it is now. The second was a transitional, mythic-historical phase consisting of both inverse and normal characteristics. The third is represented by the present (right-side-up) sociocultural system. This tripartite scheme is fundamental to the Lugbara world-view and it serves as a conceptual model by which the Lugbara define both their present social circumstances and those of the recent past.

In the beginning, the Creator (Androa) made the first man and woman. They produced another pair of male-female offspring, who did the same in turn. These first couples were essentially non-human beings. They acted through magical means and performed marvelous deeds. According to some versions, they did not have sexual intercourse in the human manner. Since the couples were siblings, incest prevailed; there were no marriages and no bridewealth was given.

The last pair of siblings produced the two Lugbara heroes, Jaki and Dribidu. These transitional beings exhibited both human and non-human characteristics. Before they came to Lugbaraland, Jaki and Dribidu lived as non-human beings "outside" the bounds of normal social relationships. Dribidu was a hairy cannibal who ate his own children. Both heroes begat offspring incestuously and did not exchange bridewealth, thus repudiating all bonds of kinship and alliance.

But when they entered Lugbaraland, they shed their anti-social characteristics and established the social rules which now obtain in Lugbara society, though they still remained partly magical beings. Their children were normal people who lived according to established social rules. This marked the beginning of human society as the Lugbara now know it.

This mythic scheme applies not only to the distant past but also to recent historical experience. Thus the Lugbara say that the first Europeans they met were cannibals, like the first ancestors who lived "outside" Lugbara territory. They were "inverted" people who could disappear under the ground and walk on their heads. Europeans who arrived later were associated with characteristics belonging to the second or mythic-historic phases. Like the Lugbara heroes, these later Europeans (the Belgians and the first District Commissioner) were regarded as essentially magical people who performed miraculous feats. Today, Europeans whom the Lugbara have come to know better are regarded as normal people.

This same scheme also applies to contemporary social experience. The local group to which an individual Lugbara belongs exists, as it were, at the center of a series of concentric circles, each representing spheres lying at greater social and spatial distance. The center is where normal upright people live, one's own kinship community. Outside this central area lies a larger social sphere containing other Lugbara and peoples of other societies who are not regarded as entirely normal. They possess magical powers and are often suspected of sorcery. Beyond this sphere lies the rest of the world. Here, people are completely inverted and, from the Lugbara point of view, entirely "outside" the bounds of humanity. They walk on their heads, eat rotten meat, practice cannibalism and sorcery, and live in forests on the border of the open country of Lugbaraland.

As in the preceding myths, the concept of inversion is important, for it explains the world in dialectical terms as the relation between two opposing spheres: order/disorder, cosmos/chaos. Whether the original state of affairs is conceived as cosmos or chaos, it is always the opposite of the human situation—hence it is sacred or divine. Thus the Lugbara see their world as a cosmos situated within a universe of chaos ultimately controlled by the Creator. Lugbara would like to keep the two spheres apart in order not to introduce chaos into the cosmos. It is the task of the diviners and prophets, who participate in both spheres, to control this relationship by ritual means.

Dinka Myth-Ritual

As we have seen, ritual often derives its forms from mythic patterns established in the sacred sphere. The Dinka cattle-herders of the southern Sudan tell of an original opposition between themselves and their culture hero, Aiwel Longar. They have converted this opposition into a ritual form which now serves to benefit themselves.

In the primordial time, before Dinka society was fully established, a serious drought occurred in the land. As the pastures dried up, Dinka cattle began to grow thin and to die. But the cattle belonging to Aiwel Longar remained miraculously fat and sleek, for Longar knew of a magical means of getting water by pulling up tufts of grass. Longar summoned the Dinka elders and told them that he would lead the Dinka to a new "promised land" of rich pastures "where there was endless grass and water and no death." But the elders refused, and Longar set off alone. When the Dinka tried to follow, they found that Nhialic, the supreme god, had placed mountains and rivers in their path to hinder their progress. Across one river, Nhialic had made a dike of reeds, the kind Dinka use when spearing fish. "As the people tried to pass this fence of reeds to cross to the other side, Longar stood above them on the opposite bank of the river, and as soon as he saw the reeds moved as men touched them, he darted his fishing-spear at them and struck them in the head, thus killing them as they crossed." Finally, a man named Agothyathik made a decoy from the sacrum of an ox. When Longar speared it, mistaking it for a human head, his spear stuck fast. Agothyathik then climbed out of the water and siezed Longar from behind. "There they remained for a long time locked together until Longar was tired with wrestling." "Aiwel Longar now told Agothyathik that it was enough, and that he should call his people to cross the river in safety and sit around him and Agothyathik." To those who arrived first, "Aiwel Longar gave fishing-spears to pray with . . . . With the spears, Aiwel gave to these men the power to invoke effectively with them (*lam*), and the power of his spittle to bless and of his tongue to curse, and the divinity Flesh, which was his originally." These men with the fishing-spears became the founders of the priestly clans. To the others who came later, Longar gave his war spears, and these men became the founders of the common or warrior clans. Longar thereby established the ritual authority of the priests of the fishing-spear and the dual organization of Dinka society under the leadership of the priestly and warrior clans.[8]

In the course of every Dinka sacrifice, the priests of the fishing-spear repeat Longar's deadly spearing action. Holding a sacred fishing-spear in the right hand, they thrust downwards over the head of the sacrificial animal, emphasizing every phrase of the invocation (*lam*) with a vigorous thrust of the spear. In repeating Longar's archetypal act, the Dinka project into the present moment of the sacrifice the original power of Longar's mythical deed. The spearing gesture is an integral part of the verbal act of invocation whose purpose is not only to invoke the gods but also to "kill" the sacrificial animal for the benefit of the community. "In the act of *lam*," Lienhardt tells us, "men think themselves to be actually *doing* something to the object of their invocation. . . . Therefore, to cut the throat of a sacrificial ox is merely the necessary physical conclusion of a sacrificial act of which the most important part has already been accomplished by speech." [9] In this ritual Longar's original destructive action is thus repeated by the spear masters with creative effect; it "kills" the sacrificial victim whose death gives life to the community. As Lienhardt observes, this action repeats the movement from death to life in the myth:

> The darting of the spear, which in the myths, originally brings death to human beings, is re-enacted in the sacrificial rites but directed against the animal victim. It is amply clear that this beast dies in the place of men. . . . In the boldest terms, then, both myth and rite represent the conversion of a situation of death into a situation of life. In the myth the spear is deflected from men and handed on to them as a source of life. In the rite the death of the victim is explicitly the source of life to the people.[10]

In this way the Dinka are constantly able to renew their world through the repetition of a mythical paradigm.

CONCEPTS OF TIME

Before turning to more historical forms of African mythology, we may stop for a moment to look at how the concept of "time" is represented in the myths and rituals we have examined thus far. As we have seen, mythical time is basically cosmogonic time, the time of creation, when the world came into existence. There is a major division in this time represented by the separation between the sky world and the human world and the shift from the one to the other. Cosmogonic time moves from a state of cosmic eternity and perfection to a state of worldly temporality and imperfection. The "fall" from Sky to Earth, from divinity to humanity, is a "fall" from eternity and pure being to temporality and becoming. These two time states and realms are the inverse of each other and are represented in terms of opposition: divine/human, sacred/profane, immortality/mortality.

But although these time states are vividly and dramatically separated, the cosmogonic myth itself provides a model for their unification. Eternity can be joined to temporality by repeating the creative acts of the gods (who span both dimensions) in ritual action. This is possible because of the special nature of ritual time. It is cyclical, not linear, In this respect, ritual time is an interruption of ordinary linear time, a time-out-of-time, when man may reestablish contact with the creative events of the cosmogonic period. In ritual, the mythical past is thus constantly recoverable. It is not, as Mbiti suggests, an irretrievable "graveyard" of time, but rather a constant source of new beginnings, of ontological renewal.

For this reason, traditional African thought turns to the past for redemptive and soteriological power: it does not look to the future. This does not mean that the African view of time lacks a genuinely prophetic dimension, as Mbiti and others have claimed.[11] Divinely inspired leaders often projected visions onto the immediate future, and these visions sometimes carried millennial overtones, as we shall see in subsequent chapters.

What African thought did not conceive of was an *indefinite* future, stretching beyond the *immediate* future of the next two or three years. The African view of time is local and foreshortened, microcosmic not macrocosmic. It stretches back only a few generations, except in centralized kingdoms whose dynastic traditions go back several centuries. The Nuer, for example, could still visit their Tree of Creation until it was destroyed by the British in the 1930s. In this respect, Mbiti has rightly observed that "according to traditional concepts, time is a two-dimensional phenomenon, with a long *past,* a *present* and virtually *no future.* The linear concept of time in western thought, with an indefinite past, present and infinite future, is practically foreign to African thinking."[12] Instead of a linear, unitary conception of time, there are a variety of "times" associated with different kinds of natural phenomena and human activities. Time is episodic and discontinuous; it is not a kind of "thing" or commodity. There is no absolute "clock" or single time scale. Time has multiple forms, coordinated in different ways, each having a different duration and quality, e.g., mythical time, historical time, ritual time, agricultural time, seasonal time, solar time, lunar time, and so on.

This does not mean, however, that Africa lacks a "sense of history" or of historiography, as Europeans once believed. Writing almost a century ago, Hegel declared that "What we properly understand by Africa, is the Unhistorical, Undeveloped Spirit, still involved in the conditions of mere nature." [13] Unfortunately, this view is sometimes echoed today. In the opinion of the British historian Hugh Trevor-Roper, "there is only the history of the Europeans in Africa. The rest is darkness . . . and darkness is not a subject of history." [14]

On the contrary, African oral traditions reveal an intense interest in the development and preservation of complex renderings of the past. What Africa did not develop is the modern, Western notion of a purely factual history for-its-own-sake, apart from norms of culture and the changing realities of the present. In traditional Africa, as in the classical and ancient world, historiography was never considered to be a separate enterprise unrelated to cultural values and contemporary socioreligious conditions. Even in the case of kingdoms which developed the institution of the court chronicler-historian, history was made to conform to changing political circumstances and to ideal models of action and behavior. As an oral phenomenon, African historiography is therefore very much a normative and living record which grows and changes in relation to contemporary life.

To be sure, oral history always gives the appearance that things have remained unchanged. This is important, for history provides not only a chronicle but also, like myth, a set of normative patterns or archetypes for interpreting the past and the present. Only thus could a solid basis be given to the present in the face of the otherwise overwhelming contingency, the state of "becoming" of the world. Myth, as Levi-Strauss has said, is "a machine for the suppression of time." It does this by interpreting the chaotic flux of history according to symbolic paradigms, thus giving meaning and form to otherwise meaningless events. For this reason, there was a continuous application of the myth-historical past to contemporary situations and everyday life. In the following discussion I shall focus upon this "mythic" dimension in the historical traditions of the Yoruba and Shilluk. Here again, we shall see how binary structures and archetypal patterns are used to give structure and meaning to the world.

MYTH-HISTORY

Yoruba Mythic-Historical Drama

The oral traditions associated with the founding of the Yoruba town of Ife reflect the Yoruba conquest of the indigenous Igbo peoples (in the fifteenth century) and the assimilation of their mythology. Though the Igbo no longer exist as a separate or identifiable group among the Yoruba, Yoruba traditions preserve the memory and meaning of the conquest. The Yoruba hero Odudua is represented in these traditions as the son of the supreme god Olorun and as the father and leader of the Yoruba people. Odudua personifies the conquering Yoruba. In the creation myth he takes over the cosmogonic role of Obatala, the sky-creator god of the indigenous Igbo. The legendary opposition between these two gods and the ritual dramatization of it interprets the history of the Yoruba conquest in cosmological perspective and establishes the Yoruba right to rule the ancient kingdom at Ife, the "center of the universe." It shows that the kingship of Ife rests upon a reconciliation between Odudua's superior force and Obatala's original right to the land.

In the beginning, Olorun, the "Owner of the Heavens," sent his son Obatala to establish the earth upon the primordial waters. Obatala did so by tossing some soil upon the waters and by letting loose a five-toed hen to spread it out over the surface. The place that Obatala created was reported by a chameleon to be "wide wide," so it was named Ile-Ife, meaning "wide earth." Then Olorun told Obatala to people the earth by fashioning men from pieces of clay. In this way Obatala made the Igbo. While performing his task, Obatala grew tired and thirsty, and drank too much palm wine. He became intoxicated and began to make misshapen people, whereupon Olorun relieved Obatala of his duties and sent Odudua to complete the job. Odudua created his own kind of people, the Yoruba. He then set about organizing Ile-Ife and founded his kingdom there, from which all other Yoruba kingdoms derive. Jealous of Odudua's superiority, Obatala and his people, the Igbo, turned against Odudua and tried to reclaim the kingdom which they felt was rightfully theirs, but they failed.

Today, at Ife Obatala's yearly festival commemorates Obatala's rebellion and defeat at the hands of Odudua and his many years of forced exile. According to Ife tradition, the two gods were eventually reconciled, and Obatala returned to Ife to become its fourth king. During the ritual reenactment of this story, the images of Obatala and his wife Yemowo, the goddess of the waters, are taken out of the city to the town where Obatala was exiled. Then the Oni (king) of Ife, described in the ceremony as the "divine ruler, second to the god (Obatala)," sends gifts to Obatala as "Chief of the Igbo," and in return the Oni receives Obatala's blessing for the ensuing year. Obatala remains the rightful owner of Ife and guards its destiny, even though his political powers (and those of the Igbo) have passed to the descendants of Odudua. For this reason, the priests of Obatala also crown the Onis of Ife in recognition of Obatala's moral right over the land as the original sky-creator whose land and people were conquered by the invading Yoruba.[15]

At Ede, Obatala's annual festival dramatizes a later conflict between Obatala's grandson, Alaiyemoore, and Odudua's grandson, Oranmiyan, over the throne of Ife. Also taking part in this ceremony are the members of the secret Ogboni (Earth Cult) Society, which was formed by the followers of Obatala in order to defend the land against the invading Odudua and his forces. The ceremony begins with a prologue, commemorating Obatala's original position as the supreme god of the Igbo:

> Obatala,
> The Oba [king] that we praise,
> The truly king,
> Who was born in the city of Igbo,
> And went to become king in the city of Iranje.
> The great Orisa,
> The divinity of Igbo.
> They showed him ingratitude,
> They tricked him with palm wine,
> They then deserted the divinity from heaven.
> When they had all vanished,
> Then they asked where else could the secret be found?
>
> Whom shall we worship annually?
> The Igbo divinity,
> You shall we worship annually.
> You, who proposes and disposes,
> You shall we worship annually.[16]

The ceremony itself takes the form of a Passion play in which the priest of Obatala, portraying Alaiyemoore, is beaten, captured, and imprisoned by another priest representing Oranmiyan. The Timi (king) of Ede ransoms and frees the Obatala priest, who is carried back triumphantly on the shoulders of his followers and hailed by all as "Orisha, the Immovable" and "The Noble One." As at Ife, this dramatic conflict and reconciliation between Obatala and Odudua is a public recognition of Obatala's prior historical and legal supremacy over the Igbo land now ruled by the Yoruba invaders.

Another festival at Ife celebrates the final defeat of the Igbo and commemorates their assimilation into the kingdom. It dramatizes the legend of Moremi, the Yoruba heroine, whose daring and cleverness led the Yoruba to victory over the marauding, masked Igbo warriors, whom the Yoruba were unable to defeat. In return for this victory, the gods demanded the sacrifice of Moremi's only son Ela, whose name means

"Preserver" and "Savior." After Ela's death, his spirit rose to the sky, from whence he promised to return one day to reap the full reward of his good deed. (Since the coming of Christianity, Moremi has been identified by some Christian Yoruba with the Virgin Mary and Ela with Jesus Christ.) Despite her great loss, Moremi declared that the Igbo should be allowed to return and settle in peace in a quarter of Ife which still bears their name. Moremi's intervention on behalf of the Igbo thus effected a permanent reconciliation between the conquered and the conquerors. This legend is reenacted each year at Moremi's festival at Ife. It is part of a larger agricultural festival and includes a mock combat between two men representing the Yoruba and Igbo forces. In the course of this "battle," the masked Igbo leader finally flees before a flaming torch carried by the Yoruba warrior, for this was Moremi's successful strategem against the Igbo troops. Later, the Igbo warrior appears before the Oni and expresses his loyalty to the king.[17]

Through these traditions and ceremonies, the Yoruba symbolically relive their history in the recognition that the past continues to define and legitimate the present political order.

Myth-History of the Shilluk Kingship

On the other side of Africa lies the small Nilotic kingdom of the Shilluk of the southern Sudan. Like the Yoruba, the Shilluk have developed an impressive set of historical traditions centered on the institution of divine kingship.

Shilluk history begins with the birth and wanderings of Nyikang, the culture hero and founder of the Shilluk nation.[18] Nyikang was a prince who lived in his father's kingdom, the original homeland of the Shilluk. This homeland is said to have been located far to the south of present-day Shillukland, "at the end (or head) of the earth." It was a paradisal land where no one died. When people grew old, they were trampled upon by cattle until they became small infants again.

Nyikang and his followers left their homeland because of a quarrel between Nyikang and his brother Duwat over the succession to the throne. For the Shilluk, this original conflict explains an essential political feature of the kingship: the absence of any rule of succession and the rivalry between princes for their father's throne. At the death of the king, it is announced, "there is no land—Shilluk country ceases to be." The kingdom temporarily dissolves into anarchy and separates into two ritually opposed divisions, one northern and one southern. The leaders of these divisions must choose a new king from the rival princes, who are supported by different political factions. In the past, the outcome was often decided by fighting. In Nyikang's case, his brother Duwat was elected the successor, so Nyikang left with his followers to found a new kingdom of his own.

As Nyikang and his party were leaving, Duwat threw after them a stick, saying they should use it in digging their graves. Thus death came into Shilluk experience as a result of their separation from the source of creation and their desire to venture forth and found a new world of their own.

The traditions then tell how Nyikang and his followers came into contact with other migrating Nilotic peoples. In these stories, Nyikang emerges as the primary symbol of "Shillukness," differentiating the Shilluk from other branches of Nilotes, the Dinka, Anuak, and Luo. Wider relationships to non-Nilotes, especially Europeans and Arabs, were established by the supreme god, Juok. It was Juok who created mankind and made the white race more powerful than the black by giving the whites swords, guns, and writing.

As Nyikang and his people approached their destination, their path was blocked by a river covered with floating vegetation. One of Nyikang's followers came forward and offered himself as a sacrifice, so that his blood would clear the way across the river. These acts have now become ritual archetypes in the installation ceremonies; they are repeated by the new king and his party of followers. After journeying through the southern division of the kingdom, the king-elect and his party stop before a river which separates the two divisions. The leader of the king's party sacrifices a sheep and a bull before the king crosses over to the opposite side, where the concluding phases of the ceremonies take place.

Shilluk traditions also tell how Nyikang and his warrior son Dak conquered the original inhabitants of the land, whose leader was the Sun. While Dak defeated the Sun's son and his armies, Nyikang drove the Sun back into the sky and revived his own armies by sprinkling them with water. Today, royal temples situated across the land commemorate these battles, and Nyikang, who is called the "bringer of rain," still revives his people with the rains after the dry season. The royal installation ceremonies also repeat the combat-opposition theme. After the king-elect and his party cross the river, they encounter another party belonging to the northern division. This party bears the effigies of Nyikang and Dak, which represent the kingship. The two groups engage in mock combat, until the party of Nyikang defeats the party of the new king. At this moment, the kingship symbolically "captures" the new king, as Nyikang originally captured the kingdom for his people.

This original act of conquest has become paradigmatic for subsequent Shilluk kings, whom the Shilluk regard as the defenders of the land from foreign enemies. The spirit of Nyikang guided by Juok is present in all of them, ensuring the military prowess of the nation.

> Nyikang is the Father of the Shilluk
> And he has united with Juok,
> Who rules the world.
> Nyikang himself wants the battle against the foreigners.

> He [the Arab] has taken our land;
> But where is the help of the ancestors?
> Juok sends him (Dak) to battle.[19]

Once in the land, Nyikang and his successors established the Shilluk clans. Nyikang is said to have made the commoner clans from the insects, fish, and animals he found in the land, obliterating the previous social structures of original inhabitants and grafting them onto the course of Shilluk history. The royal clan derives from Nyikang himself, while two other clans derive from offices associated with the kingship.

For the Shilluk, these historical traditions provide not only a political charter, legitimating the kingship, but also a cosmological and ritual charter that structures their entire world. In these stories, Nyikang is variously linked to the sky, the land, and the rivers that constitute the ecological ambience of the Shilluk universe, and he mediates between them. The stories also provide symbolic categories which have become the archetypal symbols of Shilluk ritual space and time. Finally, they firmly anchor the Shilluk to an historical past whose events provide both continuity with the present and a framework for conceiving the future.

NOTES

1. In addition to the anthropological sources noted in this chapter, my discussion of mythology draws upon the work of MIRCEA ELIADE, *Myth and Reality,* trans. Willard Trask (New York: Harper & Row, Publishers, 1968) and CLAUDE LÉVI-STRAUSS, "The Structural Study of Myth," in *Structural Anthropology,* trans. Claire Jacobson and Brooke Grundfest Schoepf (New York: Basic Books, Inc., 1963). For an informative exposition of Lévi-Strauss's thought, see E. R. LEACH, *Claude Lévi-Strauss* (New York: The Viking Press, Inc., 1970).
2. MARCEL GRIAULE and GERMAINE DIETERLEN, *Le Renard Pale* (Paris: Institut d'ethnologie, 1965), chaps. 1-3. A brief outline of Dogon cosmology and social organization appears in MARCEL GRIAULE and GERMAINE DIETERLEN, "The Dogon," in *African Worlds,* ed. Daryll Forde (London: Oxford

University Press for the International African Institute, 1954). Illustrations of the egg of the world are from *African Worlds,* pp. 84, 85, 88. Used with permission.

3. J. P. CRAZZOLARA, *Zur Gesellschaft und Religion der Nueer* (Vienna-Mödling: Missionsdruken für Anthropos-Institut, 1953), pp. 67-68; V. H. FERGUSSON, "The Nuong Nuer," *Sudan Notes and Records* 4, no. 3 (1923), 148-49. Cf. EVANS-PRITCHARD, *Nuer Religion,* p. 10.

4. P. LOUPAIS, "Tradition et legende des Batutsi sur la creation du monde et leur establishment au Ruanda," *Anthropos* 3, no. 1 (1908), pp. 5-6. [Passage quoted in text translated from the French by the author.]

5. On Nuer social organization and religion, see E. E. EVANS-PRITCHARD, *The Nuer* (Oxford: The Clarendon Press, 1940), and EVANS-PRITCHARD, *Nuer Religion.*

6. An outline of Tutsi religion and social organization appears in J. J. MAQUET, "The Kingdom of Ruanda," in *African Worlds,* ed. Daryll Forde.

7. JOHN MIDDLETON, *Lugbara Religion* (London: Oxford University Press for the International African Institute, 1960), pp. 230-38. Used with permission.

8. R. G. LIENHARDT, *Divinity and Experience: The Religion of the Dinka* (Oxford: The Clarendon Press, 1961), pp. 173-75. © Oxford University Press 1961. By permission of the Oxford University Press, Oxford.

9. *Ibid.,* p. 236.

10. *Ibid.,* p. 296.

11. JOHN S. MBITI, *African Religions and Philosophy* (New York: Frederick A. Praeger, Inc., 1969), p. 190.

12. *Ibid.,* p. 17.

13. GEORG FRIEDRICH HEGEL, *Philosophy of History,* trans. J. Sibree, rev. ed. (New York: The Colonial Press, 1900), p. 99.

14. Broadcast lecture by HUGH TREVOR-ROPER, reprinted in *The Listener* (London), November 28, 1963. For a response to Trevor-Roper's remark, see J. D. FAGE, "On the Nature of African History," in *Africa Discovers Her Past,* ed. J. D. Fage (London: Oxford University Press, 1970).

15. PHILLIPS STEVENS, "Orisa-nla Festival," *Nigeria Magazine,* no. 90 (1966), 187; cf. IDOWU, *Olodumare,* Chap. 3. On Yoruba oral tradition and ceremony, see OYIN OGUNBA, "Ceremonies," in *Sources of Yoruba History,* ed. S. O. Biobaku (Oxford: The Clarendon Press, 1973), chap. 7.

16. JOEL ADEDEJI, "Folklore and Yoruba Drama: Obatala as a Case Study," in *African Folklore,* ed. Richard M. Dorson (New York: Doubleday & Company, Inc., 1972), pp. 329-30.

17. ADEDEJI, "Folklore and Yoruba Drama," pp. 325-27; MICHAEL J. WALSH, Edi Feast at Ile-Ife," *African Affairs* 48, no. 186 (1948).

18. Shilluk traditions have been summarized by R. G. LIENHARDT in "The Shilluk of the Upper Nile," in *African Worlds,* ed. Daryll Forde.

19. WILHELM HOFMAYR, *Die Shilluk* (Modling by Vienna: Administration des Anthropos, 1925), pp. 421, 426.

2

Divinity and Man

MONOTHEISM, POLYTHEISM, PANTHEISM

It is generally recognized that there are two fundamentally different types of divinity in African religions: the one creator god, who is usually remote from daily religious life, and the many lesser gods and spirits which are constantly involved in everyday religious experience. This contrast between the one universal god and the many local gods has raised an important question about the unity and structure of African religions. Does the widespread belief in a universal creator mean that African religions are fundamentally monotheistic? Or does the more predominant everyday concern with the lesser gods and spirits mean that African religions are essentially polytheistic? Or do African religions consist rather in a kind of pantheism, based on an underlying notion of sacred "force" or "power" which permeates and controls even the gods themselves?

Most writers have tended to adopt one or another of these inter-pretations and thus to reduce African religions to a Westernized religious scheme.

However, recent studies suggest that African religions are better understood as involving elements of each of these schemes (monotheism, polytheism, and pantheism) at different theological levels and in different contexts of experience. In connection with Nuer religion Evans-Pritchard has observed that

> A theistic religion need not be either monotheistic or polytheistic. It may be both. It is a question of level, or situation, of thought rather than of exclusive types of thought. On one level Nuer religion may be regarded as monotheistic, at another level as polytheistic; and it can also be regarded at other levels as totemistic or fetishistic. These conceptions of spiritual activity are not incompatible. They are rather different ways of thinking of the numinous at different levels of experience.[1]

J.D.Y. Peel has noted a similar pattern in Yoruba religion.

> Yoruba paganism is a very discrete religion, with many varied theological elements (a Supreme Being, subordinate deities, ancestors, sacred kings, all sorts of local spirits and an elaborate system of divination), and the whole system looks different from different social standpoints.[2]

As Peel points out, the highly contextual nature of Yoruba religion has given rise to different models of unity, reflecting different internal socio-religious perspectives. Thus, Professor Idowu views Yoruba religion in terms of a hierarchical model drawn from the political sphere. He makes the supreme god, Olorun, a king (Oba) and the other divinities his ministers. Peter Morton-Williams uses a different model which reflects the Sky-Earth dualism of the Ogboni earth cult society at the Yoruba city of Oyo. He interprets Oyo cosmology as a bounded Sky-Earth system with the gods, spirits, and cult groups mediating between the Sky-Earth poles. Emphasizing a ritual orientation, Pierre Verger has proposed a pantheistic model based on the Yoruba notion of *ase,* or ritual power, as the underlying principle. For Verger, "the various powers are only particular manifestations and personifications of it: each of them is this power seen under one of its numerous aspects." [3]

Another question which has puzzled Western scholars concerns the nature of African supreme gods. Why are they generally remote and unworshiped? Some scholars believe they see a contradiction: How can the creator god be supreme yet withdrawn and ignored? A recent statement puts it this way:

> There is an apparent contradiction between the supremacy of the high-god and his withdrawal from concern with the world. The attributes assigned to him heighten this effect of contradiction. He is said to be at the origin of things, often as a creator, he is all-knowing and all-powerful, he introduces order into the chaos of the universe, he is the final arbiter of right and wrong. . . . But in spite of these attributes the high-god is not usually directly worshipped, he has no priests and no shrines dedicated to him; people may make a token offering to him in every sacrifice but hardly do they ever offer a sacrifice exclusively to him.[4]

One way of resolving this problem is to adopt a perspective which makes the supreme god the underlying core of the religious system. From this point of view it is possible to unify African religions around the concept of monotheism.

This interpretation was first proposed by Father Schmidt, who wished to prove that monotheism was the earliest form of religion. In Schmidt's view, the polytheistic gods were nothing but functional "differentiations" which split off from the original supreme god.[5] This interpretation was adopted by Evans-Pritchard, who regarded Nuer divinities as "hypostases" or "refractions" of the supreme god, Kwoth.[6] This view has also been taken up by contemporary African theologians. Professor Idowu suggests that Yoruba divinities are "no more than conceptualisations of some attributes of Olodumare [Olorun]," the Yoruba supreme being. Thus he believes that Yoruba religion is best regarded as a "Diffused

Monotheism." [7] Dr. Mbiti also finds that African divinities "often stand for His [the Supreme Being's] activities or manifestations . . . as personifications." [8]

While it is clear that African religions cannot be numbered among the monotheistic religions of the world (Judaism, Zoroastrianism, Christianity, and Islam), it is true that all religions possess what Paul Tillich has called an "element of ultimacy." [9] In Africa this element is clearly expressed in the notion of supreme being. Hence most scholars have used a hierarchical model in describing the structure of African religions: the supreme being at the top, followed by a graded order of subordinate divinities, then the ancestors and local spirits.

But, as we have seen, there are other elements which tend towards polytheism or pantheism. What, we may ask, accounts for these different tendencies? As Evans-Pritchard and Peel suggest, they do not derive so much from different observers' standpoints as from different standpoints *within* the religious systems themselves. This, of course, does not mean that African religions consist of conflicting "systems" (monotheism, polytheism, pantheism, totemism), which lack any inherent unity. Rather, the totality of elements in each religious system can be viewed from different internal perspectives according to different contextual alignments. What is misleading is to seize upon one perspective or tendency and make it the dominant framework. This may satisfy the observer's own theological preferences, e.g., monotheism, but only at the expense of over-systematizing the contextual diversity of African religious thought.

THE MORPHOLOGY OF TRANSCENDENCE: OLORUN AND NHIALIC

The debate about African "monotheism" might have ended long ago if both sides had recognized that African supreme beings are *like but unlike* Western concepts of God. By taking sides on this issue scholars have allowed the Western concept of God to control the study of African supreme beings.

It is possible, however, to exercise theological restraint and to "bracket" the Western idea of God, permitting a more objective and descriptive approach. In this connection, Robin Horton has suggested that we should distinguish between "constant" and "variable" features, in order to lay bare the basic structure of African supreme beings.[10] A similar method has been used by historians of religion in investigating the morphology of supreme beings in other religions. Raffaele Pettazzoni has suggested that the notion of supreme being involves a "two-sided" structure, one cosmic and the other human: some supreme gods are distant, inactive creators rooted in the primordial past and in the cosmic background; others are active, morally omniscient sky-gods that directly intervene in human affairs and supervise the world order. Pettazzoni also finds that these two types may combine to form a third type that is both a primordial creator and an active judge.[11] Other historians of religion, such as Van der Leeuw, Eliade, and Long, have identified a more constant structure of transcendence, symbolized by primordial creativity and celestial remoteness, underlying the different historical forms described by Pettazzoni.[12] In Africa supreme beings are perhaps best understood in this fashion as variations upon a constant religious structure of transcendence and ultimacy.

A number of salient features of transcendence can be shown by comparing two prominent supreme beings, Olorun of the Yoruba and Nhialic of the Dinka. Like other African supreme beings, they are part and parcel of particular socioreligious systems which have shaped them in very different ways.

Several centuries ago the Yoruba developed a highly urbanized society organized around large city-state kingdoms located in what is now the western state of Nigeria and in neighboring areas of Dahomey and Togo. Yoruba religion is centered on the worship of a variety of divinities, called *orisha*, each having its own priesthood, temples, cult community, and special section of town. People serve different orisha, but everyone shares a common belief in a personal destiny determined by Olorun, and everyone practices a common method of divination (Ifa) which reveals the destinies and the will of the orisha.

Unlike the Yoruba, the Dinka are a noncentralized, pastoralist society. They live dispersed in villages on both sides of the White Nile in the southern Sudan. Dinka religion is centered upon prophet-led cults of a few major sky-divinities, which are closely related to the supreme god Nhialic, and upon totemic clan spirits. As we shall see, neither Olorun or Nhialic can be classified as entirely transcendent or entirely immanent. Both gods exhibit certain common features of transcendence in different ways according to the general configuration of the cosmologies to which they belong.

Yoruba myths say that Olorun (whose name means "Lord or Owner of the Sky") delegated the task of creating the world to one of his sons, Obatala. He gave Obatala the necessary supplies, some earth and a five-toed hen, to spread the earth over the primordial waters. In some versions Obatala became intoxicated by palm wine and failed to perform his mission. So Olorun appointed his younger son Odudua to do it. Obatala also became drunk while fashioning men from clay and Odudua intervened and completed the job. To each human being, Olorun gave the breath of life, as he still does today, in addition to an allotted destiny. Yoruba traditions also include stories about the separation of the sky from the Earth. According to one version, mankind originally took his food from heaven until some greedy people took too much, whereupon Olorun pushed the heavens away from the earth. Another version states that a woman soiled the sky with her dirty hands, and it withdrew. But these stories appear to be only etiological, explaining why the sky is distant from the earth, without relating the separation to other aspects of the human condition, as in the "lost paradise" myths described above. The major events of Yoruba history are accounted for by the orisha. After creating the world, Odudua established the institution of kingship at Ile-Ife, and his sixteen sons founded the other major kingdoms across the land. Many Yoruba towns also recognize a special tutelary deity who intervened and "saved" the town from historical calamities, such as military invasions, drought, or infertility. Olorun has never been known to have directly intervened in Yoruba history or to have sent saviors or heroes to assist the people. In this respect, Olorun has remained aloof from the course of history, after originally delegating the care of the world to the orisha.[13]

By contrast, Nhialic (whose name means "Above") is a more prominent mythological and historical figure. In the beginning Nhialic fashioned the first people from clay or created them in a river or tree. Today he continues to act as the sole creator of human beings by shaping them in the womb and by giving them life. According to some traditions, Nhialic also created certain sky divinities.

The Dinka thus attribute the primary acts of creation solely to Nhialic, whereas the Yoruba appear to have divided these acts among different powers, ascribing them partly to Olorun and partly to the orisha as secondary figures.

The Dinka also believe that the world took shape in the course of a series of divine/human encounters in which man played a significant oppositional role.

The central theme of Dinka mythology concerns the separation between the earth and the sky and between man and Nhialic. A widely known myth tells of a primordial time when Nhialic and man were close together and people could climb up to the sky by means of a rope. It was a paradisal time when there was no death or illness and a minimum of labor was required to produce the necessary food. Nhialic is said to have stayed with his people and was good to them. However, the proximity of the sky eventually proved too confining. From the beginning, Nhialic permitted the first couple, Garang and Abuk, to sow only one seed of millet a day. They had to take care during their planting and pounding of the millet not to strike Nhialic and the sky with their hoe and pestle. At last the woman decided to plant more than the alloted single grain. She took one of the long handled hoes which the Dinka now use, and raising it upwards she struck the sky. Whereupon Nhialic withdrew, offended, to his present distance above the earth, and he sent a small bird (a finch) to sever the rope. Thereafter, the country was spoiled. People had to labor for food and they suffered sickness and death, and "Nhialic became irritated in his heart and hated mankind."

According to another myth, Nhialic created the first people and placed them in a world of darkness. When one of the ancestors, named *Aruu* ("Dawn"), asked Nhialic to make an opening in the world so that people could see, Nhialic refused. Then Aruu cleaved the world in two with an axe, dividing the sky and the earth and allowing light (dawn) to appear. Nhialic responded by pushing the people down into the ground so they could not see, and he began to spear anyone who tried to escape. Still determined, Aruu put a stone on his head and deflected Nhialic's spear, bending it so that it was useless. Nhialic seized Aruu by the neck and said, "Why are you like a man?" [14]

Other traditions tell how Nhialic hindered the Dinka from following Longar to the "promised land" of fertility and immortality by placing mountains and rivers in their path and by trapping them in a fishing dike. Again, the Dinka asserted their independence against the will of Nhialic, and parried the spears of Longar. [15]

Yet despite this oppositional relationship the Dinka desire Nhialics's personal protection and presence, for only he can alleviate major misfortunes. When the Dinka suffer widespread sickness and death—the consequences of their separation from Nhialic—they try to reunite the separated parts of their world and to restore their relation to Nhialic by ritual means. In this context the separation theme is frequently alluded to. The following ritual song refers to the disruptions caused by colonialism, and expresses a desire for reunification:

> . . . the strangers came with muskets
> and the aeroplane flew and evil followed
> Does Nhialic laugh and injure? Alas, the ants of the earth (human beings)
> Nhialic laughs, Creator, alas!
> Deng brings the rope of the finch
> That we may meet on one boundary
> We and the moon and Nhialic
> Give the rope of the finch
> That we may meet on one boundary with the moon. . . . [16]

It appears that the Dinka recognize that their original union with Nhialic was fundamentally ambiguous. It was beneficial but restrictive. For this reason, the Dinka view the woman's role in causing the separation indulgently, even approvingly, despite the tragic consequences. As Lienhardt suggests, the separation from Nhialic had to occur if the Dinka were to be free to follow their own path.[17]

The Yoruba look upon the situation quite differently. Their original relationship with the creator was distant and benign, and the process of creation was carried out by intermediaries. Though the responsibility for breaking contact with Heaven lay solely with man, the consequences were much less severe. Separation did not bring death, illness, and suffering, and the Yoruba are not forced on occasion to wonder whether the creator is essentially vindictive or kind. In Yoruba mythology, man and Olorun never meet face to face and disclose themselves to each other in a personal way. This conforms to the Yoruba view of Olorun as a secluded, impersonal monarch, a Lord of the Heavens, whom people rarely see, and then only at a distance.

By contrast, the Dinka conceive of their creator in a more personal way. He is a father who exercises a rather stern will towards his children. In Dinka experience the father/son relationship develops from an initial stage of filial dependence and submission to a later stage of conflict and opposition as the son grows up and strives for independence from the restrictive authority of his father. As Lienhardt points out, it is a striving for separation within a framework of conjunction.[18] It is in this light that the Dinka view their relation to Nhialic. For the Yoruba the relation to Olorun is more distant and impersonal and requires the help of intermediaries between an inaccessible supreme ruler and his people.

The Dinka also experience Nhialic as an historically active force. He enters directly into the course of events through certain outstanding prophets, called "men of Nhialic," or "creators." Such men, who have not been numerous in Dinkaland, are specifically chosen by Nhialic to be the vehicle of his spirit under special names, e.g., Cyer Did, or Ariandit (Great Meteor, Great Ariath). In the past these prophets provided unusually wide-ranging political and religious leadership, as befits the wider image of community that Nhialic represents. During the disturbances of the colonial period, they worked for peace and unity among otherwise divided and hostile tribal sections and between the Dinka and the colonial government. On one occasion in 1921 a minor prophet aroused great excitement by proclaiming that Nhialic would rejuvenate the aged and bring the dead to life as soon as the British forces left the country. An uprising was averted only when Nhialic showed his acceptance of a peace offering by a British District Officer.[19]

While Olorun lacks Nhialic's prophetic and historical character, both divinities exhibit similar ritual characteristics. In keeping with their universal and transcendent status, they have no temples, images, priesthoods, or cult groups; and they have no regular cults or festivals.

In comparison to the orisha, which are essentially local, cultic, personal, active, and vocal, Olorun is universal, non-cultic, impersonal, inactive, and silent. His relation to mankind is generally indirect and unilateral; he transcends the ritual mechanisms of mutual reciprocity and exchange. He is not directly involved in man's relation with the gods, but stands above that relation as its ultimate condition or sanction. As the "Architect of Destinies," Olorun determines the overarching framework of destinies in the world affecting both men and gods, and he determines the pattern of their intersection at any point. Olorun is thus the ground of all transactions between men and the gods. Offerings to the orisha therefore conclude with prayers acknowledging Olorun's indirect involvement: "May Olodumare accept it," "Olodumare will accept it," "May Olodumare send blessing upon it." [20]

Olorun is also involved in the system of divination, called Ifa. On many occasions, when no orisha or ancestor is specifically named in the divination process, the messenger god, Eshu, takes the sacrifice directly to Olorun. He is exhorted by the supplicants' prayer, "Please tell Olorun to accept my sacrifice and relieve my suffering." [21] The purpose of the offering is not to induce Olorun to change the person's given destiny, but to request Olorun to protect it, so that it will come to pass as originally ordained, untainted by the destructive acts of human or superhuman agents.

Olorun is invoked outside ritual contexts as well. In situations of sudden personal crisis when no other power is available or deemed effective, the Yoruba appeal directly to him: "May Olorun save me!" "Olorun have pity!" "Deliver me Olorun!" [22] As the most universal category of divinity, only Olorun can intervene on someone's behalf without regard for ritual circumstances or the need for vows and offerings. These ejaculations express a strong belief in Olorun's readiness to intervene in human affairs. But the Yoruba also realize that Olorun will not necessarily respond. He is unfathomable and unpredictable.

Yet everyone is ultimately in his care. Hence the Yoruba commonly refer to Olorun's providential character in their everyday greetings: "Thanks to Olorun," "Praise Olorun." Similar expressions are prominently displayed on buses and trucks, with the added meaning that only Olorun can insure protection against the dangers of motorized travel. Evening greetings also make reference to Olorun's providence: "Until morning, may Olorun wake us well." As these expressions indicate, Olorun's relation to man is not limited to the confines of ritual space and time or by the usual inducements of offerings. He is essentially beyond the ritual mechanism of the gods, and deals with men in a uniquely providential way.

In the same manner, Nhialic transcends the conventional ritual framework as a god of providence. He has no shrines, priesthood, special rituals, or groups of devotees, all of which are typical of the other divinities. Although Nhialic is more frequently involved in ritual affairs than Olorun, this is a difference of degree, not of kind. Like Olorun, Nhialic is the ultimate sanction of man's relation to the gods. When prayers and sacrifices fail to bring help from the gods, the Dinka say "Nhialic has refused." If Nhialic is the cause of an illness or some other misfortune, the situation is beyond ritual control, and the Dinka resign themselves to Nhialic's will.[23]

The Dinka also consider Nhialic to be the ultimate ground of divinity; they assert that each of the major gods "is" Nhialic, though they do not identify Nhialic with any one of them. What this means, according to Lienhardt, is that the specific fields of action of each of the gods—for example, rain, lightning, sun, fertility, health—are recognized as belonging to the total field of experience ultimately controlled by Nhialic. Affirming that "Nhialic is one," the Dinka believe that Nhialic embraces the multiplicity of experiences which are more specifically associated with the other major divinities.[24] He is the ultimate ground of man's relation to the gods.

Another distinguishing feature is Nhialic's relation to his prophets. Unlike the other gods, he does not speak through them by means of ritual trance or possession. Nhialic's prophets speak entirely outside of ritual circumstances in a normal and deliberate manner with words that are considered universally effective and true. Nhialic may also be invoked in times of personal distress by short petitionary phrases: "Nhialic, Father, help me!" "Creator, Father, Nhialic, help me! I ask you, my Father!" This sense of Nhialic's providence is appropriately expressed in the consoling words spoken to a person in despair, "Nhialic is here and cares for you." [25] But the Dinka recognize that Nhialic does not always choose to intervene. In these respects, Nhialic and Olorun are basically similar. They care for the general welfare of men outside as well as inside the ritual context. Their relation to mankind is universalistic and absolute; it transcends the mechanisms of ritual exchange.

In the sphere of ethics Olorun and Nhialic play a similarly transcendent role. They are neither the guardians of morality nor are they entirely removed from the moral sphere. Paradoxically, they both transcend the moral order and undergird it as the ultimate guarantors of truth and justice.

When the Yoruba feel they have been wronged but cannot avail themselves of any official means of retribution, they may be advised, according to a well-known proverb, "to allow Olorun revenge and stand aside." For Olorun is "He who sees both the inside and outside (of men)." He is an all-seeing and all-knowing judge. Hence the Yoruba say, "Those we cannot catch, we leave in the hands of Olorun." When misfortune strikes a known offender, it is said, "He is under the judgment of Olorun." The Yoruba also believe in a final judgment, when everyone must account to Olorun in the afterlife. With this in mind, someone may say to his offender, "As to this thing or this wrong you have done to me, I say, both you and I will have to relate it before Him (Olorun) who sees us." [26]

Equally fundamental is the concept of destiny, which is assigned and maintained by Olorun independently of the moral sphere. Accordingly, the wicked may prosper and the just may suffer, for success and failure ultimately derive from Olorun's predetermined plan, not from human striving. Similarly, when Olorun intervenes in crisis situations and when he chooses to favor someone with social or financial success, it is not because of the individual's moral worth. Moral character and initiative are highly prized in Yoruba society, but they alone are not enough. Ultimately, all personal success comes from Olorun, either because of his arbitrary favor, which no one comprehends, or because of the destiny which he has assigned before birth.

Olorun therefore exhibits a subtle and paradoxical combination of attributes as part of his transcendent nature. He is both supremely moral and supremely amoral, both an active administrator of justice and an arbitrary determiner of destinies.

Nhialic, too, is the source of truth and justice. But he is also the source of irrationality and disorder. As the ground of reason and morality, he transcends both. Nhialic is not the immediate guardian of public morality. This is the responsibility of the clan-divinities and sky gods. But Nhialic is the sole guarantor of truth and justice outside specifically legal and kinship contexts. Thus the Dinka use the expressions "like Nhialic" or "as Nhialic" to guarantee the truth of an assertion where no formal authority can be brought to bear. Similarly, the expression "Nhialic will see" is used when someone suspects another of wrongdoing but cannot prove it or take any further action. If misfortune subsequently befalls the accused, this is taken to be Nhialic's judgment. In other words, in situations when serious legal and moral confusion are likely to occur, Nhialic intervenes in order to make the truth appear. In more formal legal and ritual contexts, the Dinka also refer to the objective truth of things as the "word of Nhialic." [27]

Nhialic is therefore regarded as the ground of truth, justice, peace, and community in the widest sense. For this reason, he is frequently called upon to act like a father and protect his household, and to establish harmony and order within. When things go wrong, the Dinka feel it is because Nhialic has forsaken them. One hymn expresses this attitude in the following words:

Our home is called "Lies and Confusion."
What is all this for, O Nhialic?
Alas, I am your child.[28]

As these lines suggest, Nhialic stands beyond the reach of Dinka understanding. As the final explanation of both fortune and misfortune, luck and disaster, Nhialic is regarded as the incomprehensible source of the fundamental ambiguities and paradoxes of life. His will transcends moral reasoning, and the Dinka are sometimes forced to say "Nhialic has no heart," or "Nhialic's eyes have no tears," meaning that he lacks understanding and that the Dinka cannot justify his ways.[29] When Lienhardt asked why the hero, Aiwel Longar, initially tried to kill off the Dinka, and why he later bestowed blessings upon them, the usual reply was, "Is it not Nhialic?"[30] Lienhardt was also told by a young man whose father willfully allowed him to go to jail,

Why, is not your father like Nhialic? Does he not bring you up and look after you? And if he injures you or helps you, is it not his affair? How should you be angry about it?[31]

Here again, we encounter the paradox of simultaneous conjunction and opposition, which is the Dinka way of expressing the transcendent nature of Nhialic. With this paradox in mind, the Dinka compare Nhialic to the violent spring rains which bring both life and death, fertility and destruction:

Spring rain in a dry spell, strikes the ants [human beings] in the head with a club [lightning]
And the ants say: My father has seen
And they do not know whether he helps people
And they do not know whether he injures people.[32]

As transcendent Gods above the gods, Nhialic and Olorun also stand beyond the particular components of the social structure. Yoruba kingdoms, towns, cult groups, and lineages are sociologically correlated with specific orisha, ancestor spirits, or with the Earth goddess. Yoruba national identity is attached to Odudua, whose "children" the Yoruba conceive themselves to be. As we have seen, Olorun's involvement in the social order occurs primarily on the individual level through personal destiny and morality. For this reason Olorun can be regarded as the very ground of the sociopolitical process, for everything which happens in the social sphere ultimately derives from the interaction of personal destinies determined by Olorun. Thus, the Yoruba see a certain correspondence between Olorun, the "King of the Heavens," and the traditional ruler who is a "King of the World." Both are remote from everyday life, both administer the world through intermediaries, and both are "absolute" monarchs in the sense that they are ultimately responsible for everything that happens. While these parallels cannot be used to support a rigidly monotheistic interpretation of Olorun's position within Yoruba religion (for Olorun, like Yoruba kings, merely reigns but does not directly rule), they do express the central idea that Olorun, like the Yoruba king, constitutes the ultimate principle of unity without which the coordination of the cosmos and world cannot exist.

Nhialic also stands above particular social structures. The ancestors, clan-divinities, and sky divinities are correlated with more specific levels of society (families, lineages, clans, tribal sections), whereas Nhialic is correlated with the Dinka experience of community as a whole. The Dinka also believe that Nhialic sets the limits of individual lives and governs their general course. Although the Dinka do not have a concept of destiny equivalent to that of the Yoruba, they generally affirm that Nhialic determines both the births and deaths of men in a way that transcends the influence of the other powers. In this respect, both Nhialic and Olorun can be said to be directly related to the two fundamental extremes of the social structure: to the total life of the individual and to the total life of the community. As the ultimate agents of birth, destiny and death, these supreme gods account for the general course of both personal and collective experience.

MORPHOLOGY AND HISTORY

Our understanding of the morphology of Olorun and Nhialic would be significantly improved if we also knew how these two divinities developed over the course of time. Unfortunately, we know too little about the Yoruba and Dinka religious past to provide anything but the most tentative reconstruction.

Judging from Yoruba oral traditions, it is plausible to suppose that Olorun was the supreme creator god of the invading Yoruba who conquered the indigenous forest dwelling peoples in the eleventh and fifteenth centuries. During this period much religious and cosmological assimilation seems to have occurred. Yoruba traditions suggest that Obatala, the sky-creator God of the indigenous Igbo, probably had to forfeit his preeminent role to the conquering Yoruba hero, Odudua. As the victorious founder of the new Yoruba kingdoms, Odudua may also have usurped some of Olorun's cosmogonic functions after establishing the Yoruba "new world." Thus traditions may have developed making Odudua not only the first king but also the creator of the world and the fashioner of men. These attributes may originally have belonged exclusively to Olorun, now superseded and pushed into the background by Odudua and his royal orisha. This line of development would support Professor Idowu's conviction that Olorun was formerly worshiped to a far greater degree than in recent times. But there remains little evidence for this theory. Olorun may never have been the focus of primordial Yoruba "monotheism," as Idowu believes.

We know even less about Dinka religious history. The Dinka themselves say that they originally knew only their supreme god Nhialic and the sky divinity Deng (often equated with Nhialic) and their clan divinities. Lienhardt suggests that other sky divinities may have arisen later in response to Dinka contact with foreign peoples. In Father Schmidt's view, Dinka religion was originally "pure monotheism" in its early pastoralist stage. Under the pressure of agriculturalist "animism," Dinka monotheism become more polytheistic when certain attributes of its pastoralist supreme being split off into separate sky, earth, and clan gods, thus causing the withdrawal of the supreme god from his dominant position.[33] In line with this view, Charles Long has drawn attention to the fact that it was an agricultural act, the planting and pounding of millet, which drove away the Dinka supreme god.[34] This suggests that Nhialic was closer to the Dinka world in its purely pastoralist stage before the assimilation of agriculturalist economic and religious forms. But too little is known about Dinka cultural history to support this hypothesis.

We are fortunate, however, in having more information about the historical development of other supreme gods. One of these is Mwari, the sky-god of the Shona of southern Rhodesia, whose history has been described by M. L. Daneel in *God of the Matopo Hills*. Originally, Mwari seems to have been a remote, creator rain God, associated with the fertility of the fields. He was invoked only in connection with oath-taking and during rain ceremonies when elders asked the senior ancestor spirits to intercede for them with the distant Mwari. After the Shona migrated south of the Zambesi River, the Mwari cult began to develop into a centralized institution linking the scattered Shona groups to a common rain cult-center under the leadership of a priestly clan, the Mbire.

In the fifteenth century, the new Shona monarchy, developed under the Rozvi dynasty, brought the Mbire priests and Mwari cult to the royal city of Zimbabwe and used it to help unify the loosely confederated Shona tribes. As a celestial god, Mwari was a logical choice because he was unbounded by particular local ties. Through the royal Mwari cult, vassal chiefs showed their allegiance to the monarchy by sending special deputies to the capital with requests for rain and by sending temple servants to the royal temple. The cult itself resembled a chief's court, with intermediaries and senior priests serving as the "Eyes," "Ears," and "Mouth" of Mwari. By controlling the office of the "Eyes" which was the link between the temple and the people, the kings were able to keep constant surveillance over their sub-chiefs, combining political sovereignty with ritual authority. In addition, the Rozvi kings augmented the Mwari cult with an oracular function taken from the ancestor cult. In this way Mwari acquired a medium and a "Voice" superior to that of the tribal ancestors. Mwari not only received messengers, he sent back his replies to the subject states, thus exerting direct influence over local events.

When the Ndebele conquered the Shona in 1830, Mwari's influence diminished, and the Mbire priests were forced to give up all but local political powers. But with the coming of the British, priestly aspirations rose again as Ndebele rule began to collapse before the advancing settlers. Speaking on behalf of the Shona chiefs, the prophet of Mwari is said to have told the last Ndebele king:

> You are so busy killing people. You are a little man. Climb on top of a
> high hill and see these people who are coming up. See the dust rising in
> the south. My white sons whose ears are shining in the sun are coming
> here.[85]

Mwari was not only the Lord of the Shona, he was now the Lord of all men.

After the British defeated the Ndebele, the priests of Mwari assumed control of Shona political life. First they worked actively and effectively against the efforts of European missionaries. Then they helped to co-ordinate the Shona side of the Shona and Ndebele Rebellions of 1896–97, giving them the highest sanction of the supreme god.

After the rebellions failed, the Mwari cult continued to serve as a center for Shona resistance. Mwari also adapted to Christian theological ideas. He acquired increased importance as a personal God concerned with everyday life and he took on a more universal character as the Creator of all mankind, European as well as African. By classifying Europeans as his "sister's sons" Mwari ranked them below his own African sons, thus indicating his support for Shona resistance to European domination.

Today, Mwari and the ancestors face yet another challenge. This time it is from within. The leader of the Zionist Christian Church, Bishop Samuel Mutende, has not only attacked Mwari and the ancestors but has also developed parallel religious institutions in an attempt to supplant the entire traditional system. The success of the Zionist Church and the resultant loss of political influence have led the traditionalists to doubt Mwari's concern for them. One of their hymns expresses their feelings of despondency:

Ay, the unburnt pot [the white man] has spoilt the world . . .
Yelele, the unburnt pot just handles the world, twisting it,
Yelele, we are troubled . . .
Yelele, the God who is in heaven has given us his back;
The God who is at the roof has thrown us away like dogs,
Yelele, the Mwari in heaven has given us his back.[36]

The outcome of Mwari's contest with Zionism remains to be seen. But his influence as a God of healing is growing in the urban areas and his message of passive resistance has recently gained ground with the rise of the Nationalist movement in the 1950s.

In the case of Mwari we can see how an obscure sky-god was drawn into increasingly closer contact with political life until he became the chief agent of history itself. The important factor here was the use of the Mwari cult by the kingship which cast him in a prophetic role, as the God of the nation and the Voice of its destiny. As Eliade has pointed out, only "a few sky gods [have] preserved their position in people's religious life, or even strengthened it, by being seen as sovereign gods as well." [37] Although Mwari was never a "sovereign" god, he became the Eyes, Ears, and Mouth of the monarchy and the ancestors, and thus the omniscient guide of the nation and the guardian of its values. Having his own institutional basis in a priestly clan, Mwari was able to function as the leader of the people, even when the monarchy collapsed under foreign rulers. When danger threatened again under European conquest, Mwari and his prophets were therefore in a position to effectively endorse the Shona struggle.

THE GODS AS SYMBOLS OF EXPERIENCE

While supreme beings generally remain in the background as objects of ultimate concern, daily religious life is given over to more concrete forms of divinity. Unlike the supreme gods, these powers are highly dynamic, communal, and vociferous. They are immanent, not transcendent, and their relationship to man is fundamentally reciprocal and interdependent. Indeed, their very nature is essentially bound up with human experience. Hence, they require many temples, shrines, priests, cult groups, images, rituals, and offerings to organize the frequent transactions between them and mankind.

These gods are known through personal encounter as living agents directly affecting people's lives. But since we cannot personally experience the gods in this way, we can try to understand them as images or symbols of psychological and sociological realities which are more accessible to us. Such an approach is, of course, highly interpretive, but it may help us to understand the significance of the gods in relation to experiences of the self and society.

Dinka Sky-Gods

Among the Dinka, the major sky divinities make themselves known by possessing people and causing illnesses and by announcing their names and demands in this way. Lienhardt describes a typical case of possession which occurred to a young Dinka named Ajak.[38] Ajak had left home to work in a town. When Lienhardt first became acquainted with him, the young man was anxious and upset about his family at home. His father, who objected to Ajak's leaving, had died before his son could become reconciled with him. The family affairs were left in the hands of a brother whom Ajak thought incompetent. News from home confirmed Ajak's fears that things were not going well, but he preferred to stay away and earn money rather than return home and take charge of the matter.

Late one night it was suddenly announced that Ajak had become possessed by a divinity or ghost. Ajak was seen running around in circles outside a hut and panting heavily. He did not respond when addressed and seemed unaware of the crowd of spectators gathering around him. After about twenty minutes of violent running about, he fell to the ground, and then jumped up intermittently with bursts of frenzied movements, singing unintelligible songs.

Eventually a priest of the fishing-spear came up to him and demanded that the spirit which was troubling Ajak tell its name and say what it wanted. The priest used various forms of address—"You power," "You Divinity," "You ghost"—in an effort to elicit the identity of the spirit. But he was unsuccessful, and Ajak continued rolling around on the ground. Then the priest chastized the unknown spirit: "You, power, why do you seize a man who is far away from home where the cattle are? What can he do about it here?" His point was that if the spirit wanted a sacrifice, Ajak was unable to make it, because he was away from home and had no livestock of his own to offer.

Getting no answer, the priest started to admonish Ajak himself, apparently assuming that Ajak was not completely possessed, and could hear him. Why had this happened? What had Ajak done? What had he failed to do that he should have done? Ajak gave no reply.

Ajak became possessed on two other occasions, but it was not discovered which divinity was afflicting him. On the last occasion, Ajak ran into the forest at night and nearly wandered into a crocodile-infested river before he was rescued. Afterwards, everyone, including Ajak, concluded that something was trying to kill him. Ajak suggested it might be the divinity Deng, because his brother had carelessly parted with one of the family's cows dedicated to Deng. Some disagreed with this interpretation, saying that Deng would never kill anyone, but instead would seize the person at home where a sacrifice could be provided. Others thought it might be just a power of the forest or the evil divinity Macardit, both of whom might kill people away from home out of sheer malevolence.

No solution was reached. But Ajak returned home and participated in sacrifices for the supreme god, Nhialic, for his clan-divinity, and for his father's ghost. Lienhardt did not observe these ceremonies, but from what he tells us of other sacrifices, it is evident that there would have been considerable moral reflection upon the family's social circumstances in the course of the ritual. All of this would have helped to restore the broken family bonds. Afterwards, Lienhardt tells us, Ajak became well and remained untroubled by the possessing spirit.

This example illustrates how the Dinka use their ideas about the gods to link personal suffering to moral and social causes. What had Ajak done? What had gone wrong at home? In Dinka experience, the gods often serve as diagnostic media, pointing up problems in domestic and family relations. If Ajak had been at home, his suggestion that Deng was avenging his brother's negligence would have been an effective protest against his brother's irresponsibility and probably would have been taken up by Ajak's other kinsmen as well. For they would have shared in the brother's guilt, making them liable to suffer Deng's revenge. Steps would have been taken to resolve these conflicts.

As for the state of possession itself, we would say that Ajak had temporarily become mentally unbalanced as the result of his anxiety about his family and his intense feelings of guilt towards his deceased father. In our view, these mental factors made him momentarily psychotic. Given the cultural availability of spirit possession and its diagnostic role among the Dinka, Ajak's psychotic tendencies manifested themselves in this form.

The Dinka, of course, do not look at it this way. As Lienhardt observes, they do not have our conception of a "mind" which mediates and stores up external experiences and transforms them into internal drives and impulses affecting human behavior. What we regard as internal psychic factors, the Dinka regard as external spiritual beings. Thus, from our point of view the Dinka spirits represent aspects of the self which are personified and symbolically projected onto external spiritual agents.[39]

In Ajak's case, his frenzied thrashing about, unintelligible singing, and his running precipitously into the bush are typical of possession during the initial stages. Ajak's behavior was spontaneous, but it was not at all arbitrary or invented. Nor was it extremely pathological (hysterical, mad) or uncontrollably physiological (epileptic), as possession behavior was formerly assumed to be. In Africa, as elsewhere, possession behavior is culturally patterned and highly symbolic. It is an integral part of society and has a well-defined meaning within it. Such dramatic reversals of normal human behavior are signs of sacred "presence." Humanity is temporarily abolished by contact with divinity. In this situation, an individual's normally controlled movements, intelligible speech, and socialized behavior become the frenzied gyrations, meaningless utterances, and antisocial actions of the divinely possessed person. For the Dinka, who regard possession as an affliction (except in the case of professional diviners and prophets), the aim is to expel the intrusion of divinity and adjust the social situation so that the suffering person may fit back into society without further affliction.

Before the process of treatment can begin, it is first necessary to isolate and identify the particular spiritual power which has attacked the patient. This Lienhardt calls the process of making manifest an "image" or "representation" of the affective state of the sufferer. The diviner must discover the reason for the spirit's attack on the patient by disclosing some human sin of omission or commission. In Ajak's case the irresponsible parting with a beast of Deng is such a reason. Other reasons include neglect of the gods, or acts of injustice committed by or against other kinsmen.

When these reasons are made public, often in the form of a confession, the healing process can begin. The assumption is that the illness is ultimately caused by a moral problem, and the process of healing requires a full examination of it. Lienhardt summarizes this procedure:

> The patient is led to focus upon one among possibly many latent elements in his experience or the experience of his kin which give rise equally to bodily sickness and uneasy conscience. Confession, by which the wrongful acts of the self are made present to it and to the community, is therefore often part of the Dinka way of dealing with sickness. When the affective condition is imaged in a Power, both its grounds and the reason for it become manifest not only to him but to those who care for him, and his experience is represented in a form in which it can be publicly understood and shared.[40]

In other words, Dinka gods are external, symbolic realities representing internal psychological states, such as anxiety and guilt, which, when identified, enable men to link them with moral situations that can be examined and adjusted. The final step then becomes one of ritually "separating" the intruding divinity from the person, thus ending his affliction. In Lienhardt's words,

> The theme of separation of an image [divinity] . . . from the self is carried further in the symbolic action taken by the Dinka to deal with suffering once its grounds are recognized. . . . the Power is said to be "cut off" or "separated" from the man, and his suffering and guilt placed "upon the back" of the sacrificial victim . . . to be carried away in its death.[41]

Since possession is an unwelcome intrusion, expelling the divinity thus restores the sufferer to his normal condition.

Yoruba Orisha

The Yoruba look on possession in a different way. Generally they desire a close association with the orisha, which at times verges upon personal identification with them. Usually an individual worships the orisha of his or her father, but if some illness or other serious problem arises, this may reveal that another orisha wants the person as his special devotee.

Pierre Verger describes the following case which occurred in a village in the region of Ilodo.[42] A woman lost her children, one after the other, each dying a few days after birth. One day while crossing the village square, she began to make uncontrollable gestures and staggered to the front of Ogun's temple, and fell stiffly to the ground. It was said that Ogun had chosen her and had taken her under his protection. She then began the process of initiation. Three weeks later, she appeared at the festival of Ogun, ready to be his medium and "wife" in service to the people of the village. During the festival, one of Ogun's mediums announced that Ogun had acquired a new medium:

> See the new *iyaworisha* [medium]; it is *Ogun* that chose her.
> Is it not good? It is because I have seen the death on her that I took her.
> Now she is not going to die; no more danger for her;
> She is going to have a lot of children; boys and girls.
> I am going to tell her father and her husband what they must do now.
> Because she is not the same any more; the husband must not beat her any more,
> He must leave her in peace.
> If the husband has anything to say, he must tell it to me.
> It is *Ogun* now who is the father. Everybody must hear, men and women.

The woman's father then acknowledged Ogun's authority over his daughter.

Ogun:
Is that said with a good heart?
The father:
Yes, it is with a good heart. I am too young to say no in front of the *orisha*. The *orisha* is my father.

The dialogue continued.

Ogun:
I knew before choosing her that it would be for her happiness.
The father:
Yes, it is *Ogun* who knows the good and the evil. May he save my daughter for me. I shall do whatever *Ogun* may ask me. If necessary, I shall give him all my children and myself.
Ogun:
If you are always at my side, I shall do everything that you ask me for your happiness. Your daughter will be in good health. She will have a lot of children, boys and girls, and all will live.
The father:
Please give me a young girl to bring me water to drink.
Ogun:
If you are obedient, you will have all this. But if you are not obedient, I shall know it.

The woman's uncle and her husband's father and brother then came forward to express their gratitude to Ogun for taking the woman into his protection.

At this festival the mediums also sang the orishas' praise songs and in this way they strengthened the power of their gods:

I have come, we say, I have come.
I have come, I have come.
. . . .
I have come, I have come today.

One of the ritual functionaries asked the mediums, "what do you want to do?"
They sang in chorus:

We worship the *orisha*.
If we worship the *orisha*
We will always have money,
We will always have children.

Then each of the mediums in a state of trance sang aloud the praise of his orisha and gave the orisha's blessing to the people.

Shango sang:
  Everything is going to be all right.
  They are going to get wealth.
  . . . .
  If the rain does not fall,
  People say it is because of *Shango*.
Ogun sang:
  You will not meet death on your road.
  No sudden death, the country will be full of people.
  There will not be enemies.
  I am the enemy of everybody.
  I kill everyone the *orisha* tells me to.
  Nothing bad will happen.
  Happiness, long life to everybody.

Commenting on this and other orisha festivals, Verger observes:

These festivals give the impression of a theatrical performance or even
operetta. Their cast, costume, orchestral accompaniment, solo and chorus
differ little in spirit from the Mystery and Passion Plays enacted in
medieval Europe in the forecourts of the cathedrals. The salient difference
is that in the present case the actors, if we may so call them, are in a
state of trance.[43]

In this way the Yoruba welcome the orisha and cultivate their presence.

On the psychological level, the orisha also serve as images of the
self, integrating and completing unrealized dimensions of the personality.
In the case just described, Ogun promised to fulfill the woman's longing for children and to protect her from her husband's beatings and her
father's stern authority. Like all orisha, Ogun brings children, but he
also wields a threatening sword in defense of his devotees. Hence,
the Yoruba recognize a direct correlation between the devotees and the
orisha who choose them. Judith Gleason has expressed it this way: the
orisha "are like immense magnifying mirrors in which we behold ourselves as potentialities. To those who believe in them, the orisha are
guardians through whom one lives a more intense life vicariously, guides
whose excess of energy leads their devotees to a more placid, a more
balanced existence." [44]

For the Yoruba devotee, the orisha is thus a magnified symbol of
him or herself. It enables the devotee to express certain unconscious
aspects of the self and to channel and integrate his or her total personality. Since this psychological correlation is culturally explicit, we
can perhaps understand what would otherwise appear to be bizarre and
unintelligible features of the orisha themselves.

→ Shango is an appropriate example because of the unique violence
and tragedy of his character and the elaborateness of his cult. According
to tradition, Shango was the son of Oranyan, the powerful son of

Odudua. He became the fourth king of Oyo and used his special powers over lightning to protect the kingdom from its enemies and to punish disloyalty among his subjects. Some say that Shango's reign was so cruel and destructive that he was deposed from the throne and hanged himself in disgrace. But Shango's priests and devotees believe otherwise. They agree that Shango had an inherently violent disposition and that he was born to destroy himself, but not until he had mastered his own destructive impulses. In later years, Shango feared that his constant efforts to control his faction-ridden kingdom were wearing him down. He felt he was losing his vital powers and his manliness. In an attempt to convince himself that his strength and virility were intact, he took up his double-headed thunder axe, climbed up a hill, and hurled the axe violently towards the ground. But it slipped from his hands and crashed into the palace, killing everyone in a flaming cataclysm. In despair, Shango immediately abdicated his throne and hanged himself from a tree. Reports spread that the king was hanged. But his followers discovered that he had ascended into the heavens and ruled from above as a god. Some denied this, whereupon lightning struck and they were killed. To this day, Shango kills liars and frauds with his lightning bolts, and his followers proclaim their famous motto, "the king did not hang."

Shango's devotees exhibit a personality that strongly resembles the violent, antisocial, and sexually unbalanced character of Shango himself. A study by Wescott and Morton-Williams shows that many devotees have tendencies toward aggression and violence.[45] Others are boisterous or highly temperamental. When Shango's spirit enters his priests, they display unusually violent and erratic possession behavior, and appear to be venting aggressive impulses. They also dress in women's clothes and have their hair braided in a feminine style. Since Shango often appears to his priests in dreams, Shango's praise hymns repeat the characteristic phrase, "the dream is the father of the god." From a psychoanalytic point of view, the connection between personages in dreams and psychic complexes suggests that Shango represents certain unconscious needs for violent, antisocial, and transvestite behavior. In allowing these tendencies full expression, the Shango cult appears to have a therapeutic character. In this respect, it resembles other African and Afro-American possession rituals in which, according to Lewis,

> everything takes on the tone and character of modern psychodrama or group therapy. Abreaction is the order of the day. Repressed urges and desires, the idiosyncratic as well as the socially conditioned, are given full public rein. No holds are barred. No interests or demands are too unseemly in this setting not to receive sympathetic attention. Each dancer ideally achieves a state of ecstasy, and in a stereotyped fashion collapses in a trance from which he emerges purged and refreshed.[46]

The symbolic behavior of the Shango priests carries over outside the cult as well. When lightning strikes a house, the priests appear on the scene to "dig up" and recover Shango's virile lightning symbols (stone celts). These they place in their sacred satchels, which are decorated with female symbolism. As men who must keep strict control over themselves, they abhor any form of changeable or deviant behavior in others. In the name of Shango they punish the "offender" whom the orisha has singled out by looting his house.

Ashanti Obosom

Another way in which the gods symbolize forms of experience can be seen in the mediumship seances of rural Ghana. Here it is not a question of the therapeutic value of possession itself, for the client seeking help does not become possessed. Rather, the god's advice to the client has a psychiatric function. The client has his problems diagnosed by a god who symbolizes superhuman knowledge and authority. By speaking through a priestly medium, the god, called an *obosom,* diagnoses illnesses and social problems and prescribes remedies for them. My account here is taken from Margaret Field's pioneer study, *Search for Security,* which provides extensive information about the gods and mediums of rural Ghana in the 1950s.

According to Field, people visit the obosom shrines for several reasons: to allay anxieties about personal success, to give thanks for the god's protection during the past year, to discover the cause and remedy for illnesses, and to ask for children. But the most frequent type of supplicant is the frustrated and despairing person whose complaint is "I am not prospering." This includes men who are repeatedly fired from their jobs, people who cannot manage money, farmers whose crops are diseased, and alcoholics.

At the shrine, the priest, while possessed by his obosom, questions the client about his complaint and particularly about his family situation. If he discovers family strife and anxiety, he renders advice about it. One area of questioning concerns the supplicant's spouse. If a man is on good terms with his wife, he usually brings her with him. If she does not come, the priest asks about her absence. A goldsmith whose wife refused to come along was finally told, "She is the cause of your plight, leave her and take a better woman."

Most clients who complain of economic and social failure tend to feel socially threatened and readily project their fears onto other persons (witches) or onto things ("bad medicine"). The shrine priest usually goes along with this and assures the client of the deity's protection. But the priest does not go so far as to identify the suspected witch or the medicine. He simply says, "The cause is among your own kinsmen," or "There are witches in your house." [47]

The kind of advice given to unprospering people is usually sound and practical. The client himself may have thought of it or it may have been suggested to him by others. But coming from the god, it has added authority and validity. A man who couldn't hold onto his wages complained that witches made his hands into a sieve. He was assured that he would have the god's protection, but he was also told that he should lock up half of his wages in a box every week. A woman trader who was unable to make a profit was advised that she had better give up trading and go back to farming. She may have considered this alternative herself, but now she could do it without suffering embarrassment in the community.

People complaining of physical ailments receive different kinds of advice. Most do not, in fact, appear to have anything physically wrong, though some are clearly suffering from actual organic diseases. These cases are often referred to the hospital. But regardless of the nature of the illness, the priests' and their clients' understanding of its primary causes is always the same: it has a supernatural origin linked to a particular moral problem. Illness involves the total moral person and the family to which he or she belongs. It is unthinkable as a purely physical or bodily matter. Hence successful treatment always requires some form of ritual procedure, either to atone for the person's sins or to symbolically ward off the malevolent influence of others.

The majority of physical complaints concern generalized symptoms such as "pains all over," headache, trembling, giddiness, or temporary loss of vision, all of which are indicative of psychological stress and anxiety. In these cases, the priest (or, rather the obosom speaking through him) immediately inquires into the person's moral and social situation, usually by leading comments: "There are [moral] troubles in your sickness," "You are sick because you are keeping things in your head." These comments are intended to elicit a confession about a particular anxiety. If this approach fails, the priest may become more aggressive: "What about a certain man?" "What about a certain woman?" "What about a certain quarrel?" People often make confessions without such probing. However the information is gained, the point of the dialogue with the divinity is always to establish a connection between the illness and certain misdeeds and anxieties.

Most often, confessions refer to marital conflicts and to kinship disputes. Field describes some typical examples:

One said, "I have pains all over ever since the day I cursed my nephew."

Another man with pains all over came with his wife confessing that they had together been to a Kramu [a Moslem medicine-man] and made bad magic against the wife's mother. For this they were fined a cow each, the wife also being ordered to give a sheep to her mother. Another uneasy man said, "I brought a bad *suman* to use against my uncle, and I have been sick and miserable ever since the day I bought it." Another said, "I have been sick ever since I did my kinsmen out of their share in a cocoa-farm," and yet another said, "I used a bad *suman* to protect my cocoa-farm against my neighbors." A woman who had not reached the point of bad magic against her husband said that she had felt ill ever since she made up her mind to injure him. Among other sick people who came bringing their own diagnoses one said he had reviled the *obosom,* another that he had eaten tabooed food, several that they had omitted to bring their promised thank-offering and another that he had flouted the *obosom's* advice.[48]

In such cases, religious and moral dimensions are closely fused together; hence the obosom may give moral advice together with ritual prescriptions. One man was told, "Make a sacrifice to your dead brother's ghost, but also keep an eye on your envious sister." Usually the obosom merely provide moral and psychological solutions. A man who was becoming emaciated because he was unable to eat anything after hearing of his wife's infidelity, was told, "Stop worrying about your wife's adultery. There are plenty of better women in the world." Afterwards, Field tells us, the man began eating again and regained his health.

In general, the Ashanti obosom serve as authority figures. Like advice columnists in Western newspapers, Ashanti mediums dole out much needed moral and religious counsel. Their effectiveness does not derive from any special revelations they give, but from the authority which possession bestows upon the medium's words. This sets the medium apart from the rest of society. It is not he who advises, but the deity who speaks through him. Consequently, the priest is removed from the social intrigues of the community and his advice is considered impartial and absolute.

NOTES

1. Evans-Pritchard, *Nuer Religion,* p. 316.
2. J. D. Y. Peel, *Aladura: A Religious Movement Among the Yoruba* (London: Oxford University Press for the International African Institute, 1968), p. 29. Used with permission.
3. Pierre Verger, "The Yoruba High God," *Odu* 2, no. 2 (1966), 38.
4. James O'Connell, "The Withdrawal of the High God in West African Religion: An Essay in Interpretation," *Man* 42, art. no. 109 (1962), 67, as

quoted in CHARLES H. LONG, "The West African High God: History and Religious Experience," *History of Religions* 3, no. 2 (1964), 328.

5. SCHMIDT, *The Origin and Growth of Religion,* pp. 262-63.

6. EVANS-PRITCHARD, *Nuer Religion,* pp. 48-52, 118-122.

7. IDOWU, *Olódùmarè,* p. 63.

8. MBITI, *African Religions,* p. 76.

9. PAUL TILLICH, *Systematic Theology* (Chicago: University of Chicago Press, 1951), 1: 218-20.

10. ROBIN HORTON, "The High God: A Comment on Father O'Connell's Paper," 42, art. no. 219 (1962).

11. RAFFAELE PETTAZZONI, "The Supreme Being: Phenomenological Structure and Historical Development," in *History of Religions: Essays in Methodology,* ed. Joseph M. Kitagawa and Mircea Eliade (Chicago: University of Chicago Press, 1959).

12. GERHARDUS VAN DER LEEUW, *Religion in Essence and Manifestation,* 2 vols., trans. J. E. Turner (New York: Harper & Row Publishers, Inc., 1963), 1: chap. 18; MIRCEA ELIADE, *Patterns in Comparative Religion,* trans. R. Sheed (Cleveland: The World Publishing Company, 1963), chap. 2; CHARLES H. LONG, *History of Religions* 3, no. 2 (1964).

13. IDOWU, *Olódùmarè;* PETER MORTON-WILLIAMS, "An Outline of the Cosmology and Cult Organization of the Oyo Yoruba," *Africa* 34, no. 3 (1964); PEEL, *Aladura,* pp. 19-36.

14. Both versions appear in LIENHARDT, *Divinity,* pp. 33-35. © Oxford University Press 1961. By permission of the Oxford University Press, Oxford.

15. See above, pp. 39-40.

16. LIENHARDT, *Divinity,* pp. 37-38.

17. *Ibid.,* pp. 37-43.

18. *Ibid.,* pp. 39-45.

19. V. H. FERGUSSON, "The Holy Lake of the Dinka," *Sudan Notes and Records* 25, pt. I (1942).

20. IDOWU, *Olódùmarè,* p. 52.

21. WILLIAM BASCOM, *Ifa Divination: Communication Between the Gods and Men in West Africa* (Bloomington: Indiana University Press, 1969), p. 60; cf. J. OMUSADE AWOLALU, "Yoruba Sacrificial Practice," *Journal of Religion in Africa* 5, fasc. 2 (1973), p. 93.

22. IDOWU, *Olódùmarè,* p. 37.

23. LIENHARDT, *Divinity,* p. 271.

24. *Ibid.,* pp. 156-60.

25. Texts collected by P. A. Nebel and published in WILHELM SCHMIDT, *Der Ursprung der Gottesidee,* 12 vols. (Munster-in-Westphalia: Aschen-dor-fische Verlagsbuchhandlung, 1912-1955), 8: 127, 142.

26. IDOWU, *Olódùmarè,* pp. 189-201; ISSAC O. DELANO, *Owe l'esin Oro: Yoruba Proverbs* (Ibadan: Oxford University Press, 1966), p. 22; JAMES JOHNSON, *Yoruba Heathenism* (Exeter: James Townsend and Sons, 1899), extracted in RICHARD E. DENNETT, *At the Back of the Black Man's Mind* (London: Macmillan & Co., Ltd., 1910), p. 269.

27. LIENHARDT, *Divinity,* p. 47.

28. *Ibid.,* p. 45.
29. Francis Mading Deng, *The Dinka and Their Songs* (Oxford: Clarendon Press, 1973), p. 54.
30. *Divinity,* p. 210.
31. *Ibid.,* p. 42.
32. *Ibid.,* pp. 54-55.
33. Schmidt, *Ursprung,* 8: 169.
34. Long, *History of Religions* 3, no. 2 (1964), 333, no. 20.
35. M. L. Daneel, *The God of the Matopo Hills* (The Hague: Mouton, 1970), p. 30.
36. *The God of the Matopo Hills,* p. 35.
37. Eliade, *Patterns,* p. 110.
38. *Divinity,* pp. 57-62.
39. *Ibid.,* p. 149; cf. Francis Mading Deng, *The Dinka,* p. 49. n. 1.
40. *Divinity,* pp. 152-53.
41. *Ibid.,* p. 153.
42. Pierre Verger, "Trance and Convention in Nago-Yoruba Spirit Mediumship." Copyright © Pierre Verger. From *Spirit Mediumship and Society in Africa,* ed. John Beattie and John Middleton (New York: Africana Publishing Corporation; London: Routledge & Kegan Paul Ltd., 1969).
43. "Trance and Convention," p. 64.
44. Judith Gleason, *Orisha: the gods of Yorubaland* (New York: Atheneum Publishers, 1971), pp. 112-13.
45. Joan Wescott and Peter M. Morton-Williams, "Symbolism and Ritual Context of Yoruba Laba Shango," *Journal of the Royal Anthropological Institute* 92, no. 92 (1962).
46. Lewis, *Ecstatic Religion,* p. 195.
47. Margaret J. Field, *Search for Security: An Ethno-Psychiatric Study of Rural Ghana* (London: Faber and Faber Ltd.; Evanston, Ill.: Northwestern University Press, 1960), p. 107. Used by permission.
48. *Ibid.,* pp. 113-14.

3

Ritual Expression and Control

In Africa, as elsewhere, ritual behavior is a way of communicating with the divine for the purpose of changing the human situation. As such, ritual has two important dimensions: what it "says" and what it "does." What ritual does, or is believed to do, is a variety of practical things. Rituals are performed to cure illness, increase fertility, defeat enemies, change people's social status, remove impurity, and reveal the future. At the same time, ritual words and symbols also say important things about the nature of what is being done—for example, how and why men communicate with the gods, expel illness, settle moral conflicts, manipulate sacred power, make children into adults, control and renew the flow of time. The dimensions of "saying" and "doing" are thus closely related. What is "said" in symbolic terms is what is "done" in ritual terms to modify experience in accordance with what men desire.[1]

Ultimately, we may wish to go beyond what the participants themselves may say and do, and find the meaning of rituals in their psychological and sociological functions—the way in which they reintegrate personalities and groups. To a certain extent, all rituals promote psychological and sociological integration, and it would be odd if they did not. But before we explore such functions, let us examine the internal verbal and symbolic structure which gives ritual its basic unity and coherence.

In Africa, two of the most common types of rituals are animal sacrifices and rites of passage. Both types follow virtually universal patterns, and both exhibit characteristically African forms of ritual "saying" and "doing."

ANIMAL SACRIFICE

Ritual Structure: Ogun Sacrifice

In general, ritual sacrifice accomplishes a two-way transaction between otherwise separate and partially opposed realms: the world of man and the world of the gods. In this transaction, the animal victim is the mediating symbol because it partakes of both worlds. It lives in the human world, but its life belongs to the spiritual world. Furthermore, it combines certain symbolic features which link the human with the divine so that the divine is subject to human control. In this way, the ritual manipulation of the sacrificial victim helps men mediate their relation to the gods. The verbal component of the sacrifice, the "word," also serves to control this transaction by influencing the gods through prayer and song to act on man's behalf. Equally important are the preparatory and concluding phases of the sacrificial process. Before it begins, the participants must sacralize the time, place, and victims of the sacrifice and all those who participate in it. Afterwards, the sharing of the victim's flesh confirms the spiritual bond between the worshipers and the god or spirits to whom a portion is also given. Acts of desacralization and purification may also take place in order to safely return the participants to the normal human world. Ritual sacrifice thus has a basic threefold structure: consecration, invocation-immolation, communion-purification.[2] As for its social function, public forms of sacrifice bring people together and reinforce the moral and social bonds that bind them as a group.

Among the Yoruba, the annual Ogun festival usually takes place in the dry season, when there is good hunting. Since Ogun is the patron deity of hunters, fresh bush meat is required for his festival. Although the festival is sometimes the affair of a whole town, it is more often celebrated by individual family compounds whose members are devotees of Ogun. The festival date is determined through divination in accordance with Ogun's wishes. Prior to the event, the Ogun priests (Oloode) and the officiating family heads prepare themselves morally and physically, so that they may be acceptable servants of Ogun. They must abstain from cursing, fighting, sexual intercourse, and eating certain foods. The day before the festival begins, the men undertake a hunting expedition in the surrounding bush to gather fresh game. In the evening, an all-night vigil is kept near the compound's Ogun shrine, which consists of a stone column and a tree. Palm fronds decorate the tree on this occasion, for palm wine is Ogun's favorite drink. Throughout the night large quantities of palm wine and beer are consumed by the family members and their guests, and Ogun's special praise chants are sung in honor of the divinity. These songs not only entertain the people, but also attract Ogun's attention and induce him to shower his blessings upon the assembled congregation.

The sacrifices of the next day begin with an offering of kola nuts brought by each family head on behalf of his wives and children. The kola nuts themselves signify friendship and reconciliation. Presenting them to Ogun at the beginning of the sacrifice establishes an initial bond between the worshipers and the divinity. Setting them before the Ogun stone, each family head, or the Oloode in his stead, asks Ogun for blessings and protection during the year. Since Ogun is the god of iron and steel, he asks especially for Ogun's protection from things made of metal, e.g., from automobiles, bicycles, knives, axes, or guns:

> Ogun, here are Ebun's kola nuts:
> He rides a bicycle,
> He cultivates with a matchet,
> He fells trees with the axe.
> Do not let Ebun meet your anger this year;
> Take care of him.
> He comes this year,
> Enable him to come next season.[3]

The next phase of the ceremony is the presentation of the sacrificial victims before the shrine. Each god has his own special tastes, and Ogun is especially fond of snails, palm oil, pigeons, and dogs. These offerings are also appropriate because they symbolically mediate and control Ogun's relations with mankind. Since Ogun has a notoriously wild and arbitrary temperament, he is as much opposed to mankind as he is disposed towards him. Snails are therefore offered to calm his anger; they symbolize "softness" and "smoothness," this being the literal meaning of *ero*, "snail," in Yoruba. Palm oil is also offered because it signifies the calming down and soothing of otherwise wild and uncontrollable things. Pigeons, too, represent serenity and, as domestic pets, they signify docility and closeness to man. Above all, it is the dog which is especially noted as Ogun's sacrifice. The dog appears to be uniquely appropriate because it combines in itself both the wildness and ferocity of its natural state and the friendliness and protectiveness of its domestic state. In this respect, the dog symbolically corresponds to Ogun's dualistic, destructive/protective nature and is therefore a most suitable medium for establishing and controlling intimate contact with him. In a wider sense, as elements of nature transformed by human contact into elements of culture, the offerings are appropriate mediating symbols between nature and culture, divinity and humanity.[4]

Special bearers present these offerings to Ogun and place them in direct contact with his shrine, which consecrates them as sacred media. The snail is set at the base of the stone, the pigeon is held aloft in front of it, and the dog is tied to Ogun's cudgel or to the shrine's sacred tree. The Oloode dedicates these victims in the following manner:

> Ogun, here are the festival kolanuts for you from all of us.
> Ogun, here is your festival snail from all of us.
> Ogun, here is your festival pigeon from all of us.
> Ogun, here is your festival dog from all of us.
> Spare us so that we can do this again next year.
> Ward off death and sickness from us.

Ward off accidents from us.
Ward off untoward incidents from the young folk.
Ward off untoward incidents from the elderly ones.
Ward off untoward incidents from the children.
Ward off untoward incidents from all pregnant women.[5]

Then the Oloode takes the offered kola nuts, splits them into four lobes and casts them before the shrine to ascertain Ogun's will. If a favorable result is obtained, the nuts are gathered up and eaten by the worshipers as an expression of their common bond with Ogun. The sacrifices follow immediately.

The Oloode cracks open the snail's shell with Ogun's cutlass and pours its slime onto the Ogun stone. Next, someone wrings off the pigeon's head and the Oloode drips its blood on the stone. Lastly, the dog is beheaded with the cutlass and its blood sprinkled on and around the stone.

In each case, the immolation of the victim completes the process of consecration. By this act the victim becomes fully separated from the profane world and fully transferred to the spiritual world as its life-force flows with the blood into the sacred realm. In return, the divinity bestows his spiritual benefits of life and health onto the celebrants of the rite, completing the transaction.

Later, the participants share the consecrated flesh of the dog and partake of Ogun's special "bush" meat while singing his praises. In this way they renew the bonds of unity among themselves and, at the same time, reinforce Ogun's relation to them.

When the festival involves a whole town, it serves an even broader social purpose.[6] People return to the town from outlying farms and renew old friendships; sons and daughters return to rejoin their families. The town quarters organize dancing groups and engage in general competition. Motor trucks passing through the town are decked out with palm fronds, and those which are not decorated are halted by the townsmen and urged to properly display themselves. Socially despised individuals are also singled out and ridiculed in songs and lyrics. A general carnival atmosphere prevails. People chalk their faces, men wear women's clothing, dogs are indiscriminately killed, and property is occasionally damaged. It is a liminal period when people reverse their normal behavior, expressing the exceptional nature of sacred time before returning to the normal social order. As we shall later see, in connection with rites of passage, this liminal phase is a time of heightened social integration. It is a time when the people of the town come together face-to-face, free from the social constraints of normal life in an intense form of social communion and solidarity.

Lugbara Ritual and Social Process

Among the Lugbara, the social function of sacrifice is more specifically linked to particular social processes. The same general pattern of consecration, invocation, and communion appears, but as Middleton's analysis shows, each of these phases is closely coordinated with the underlying dynamics of the social context.[7]

A certain elder, named Ondua, was both old and ill, and he realized that he would soon die.[8] Unable to leave his compound, he sent his half brother Ogdua to consult an oracle priest about the cause of his illness. The priest said that Ogdua and another man, named Olimani, had invoked the ghost of Ondua's father, Dria, because they were dissatisfied with Ondua's behavior. Ogdua felt that Ondua had neglected to sacrifice to his ancestors, and Olimani felt that he had been greedy at the sacrifice which he (Olimani) had offered to his own ancestors. Upon hearing this verdict, Ondua tried to test it by consulting his own rubbing stick oracle, but he was unsuccessful. Again, he sent his half brother to consult the oracle. This time the oracle revealed that Dria's ghost was the sole cause of Ondua's illness and that Ogdua and Olimani were not responsible. But the reason for Dria's vengeance remained the same: Ondua had failed in his religious duties to his ancestors and he had behaved improperly at Olimani's sacrifices. This judgment was subsequently confirmed by Ogdua, who consulted a chicken oracle in the presence of Olimani.

Although Ondua was forced to accept this interpretation, he harbored strong misgivings. He had recently quarreled with his half brother and with Olimani, and he suspected that both of them were challenging his authority as lineage head. He knew that Ogdua would try to usurp the lineage headship from his son when he died, and he knew that Olimani was striving to break away and become an independent elder of his own lineage segment.

After hearing and confirming the second verdict of the oracle, Ondua decided to sacrifice a sheep to the supreme god, Adro, and to his father's ghost. This was contrary to accepted practice, because ordinarily a sheep can be offered only to Adro and not in conjunction with another spirit. Furthermore, the oracle had spoken only of his father's ghost, not of Adro. Nevertheless, Ondua was still within his rights because the client, not the oracle, determines the kind of sacrifice to be offered. In making this type of sacrifice, Ondua wished to partly override the oracle's verdict of ghostly vengeance, which implicitly supported Ogdua's and Olimani's claims, and to stress his nearness to death, over which Adro has sole prerogative. Though a sacrifice of this kind can never compel

Adro to prevent death, it can indicate the person's recognition that he is involved, whereupon Adro may decide to postpone death to some later time. By emphasizing his nearness to death, Ondua could implicitly stress his old age and eldership, and thus focus the ritual on his authoritative status against the younger men.

Ondua then performed the act of consecration which begins the sacrifice. He took a sheep and placed his hands on its back, telling it that its meat would be laid on the ancestral shrines. In this way the sacrificer identifies himself with the victim he offers. Next, Ondua paraded the sheep round his homestead, "showing" it to the people of his lineage (both living and dead) and to Adro. Encircling the people creates a further bond between the victim and the sacrificer, and between the sacrificer and his immediate kinship group. The elders and important men of other lineage groups also placed their hands on the back of the sheep to show that the groups they represented joined in and supported the sacrifice. If the animal urinates while being led around or immediately afterwards, it is a sign that Adro and the ancestors have accepted it and the patient will recover. If not, or if the animal defecates or becomes stubborn, it is a sign that "Adro refuses." No sacrifice is made, for the matter concerns only Adro, not the dead, who are interested only in breaches of lineage ties. In Ondua's case, the sheep urinated. It was then taken back to the herd to await Ondua's recovery. The purpose of Lugbara sacrifice is not to appease the ancestors but to restore the moral ties between the members of the lineage. If the afflicted person dies, showing that Adro has intervened, the breach may still remain and the animal will be sacrified for another patient. If the person recovers, the animal is sacrificed to "welcome the ancestors" and to "thank" them for curing the patient whom they have punished. The person is thought to have atoned to the ancestors by his own suffering and illness. Sacrifice is a sign that the lineage stands ready to re-create the moral bonds weakened by the offender's misdeeds.

The next phase of the sacrifice consists of the acts of invocation and immolation. Ondua performed the sacrifice on the day following the consecration because he was feeling better and wished to show Adro that he had accepted his illness as a sign of his impending death. All the men of Ondua's lineage were present in addition to the representatives of coordinate lineages. Before coming, they had purified themselves by ritual washing, so that they might meet together in communion with one another and with the ancestors. They had also laid aside the animosities which initially gave rise to the intervention by the ancestors.

As the officiating elder, Ondua made the first speech. This is called "showing the words." Its purpose is to announce the sacrifice to the living and dead members of the lineage and to state the main facts of the case; it implies that the social conflict within the community is now resolved. In addressing the people, Ondua said that he was offering the sheep because Adro had sent him an illness to show he was approaching death. He also indicated that his father's ghost was involved. But he deliberately refrained from saying why the ghost had intervened, thereby avoiding any admission of Ogdua's and Olimani's claims against his authority.

When Ondua finished, the sheep was immediately slaughtered, portions of its meat were placed on the ancestors' shrines, and some of its blood was poured out onto the ancestral stones. Beer was also offered to the ancestors. Killing the animal marks the culmination of the sacralization process which began with the act of consecration. It releases the most sacred part of the animal, its life substance, as food for the ancestors, and it makes the animal's meat available for the human community. As mentioned above, the offering of the victim is not a propitiation or bribe to induce the ancestors to act on the patient's behalf. The ancestors have already acted by lifting the illness after the patient's recognition of his misdeed. Rather, the sacrifice is an act of communion between the lineage members, who have previously identified themselves with the victim, and the ancestors. Sacrifice is a way of reestablishing communication and solidarity with the ancestors and with the moral values they uphold. Responsible members of the lineage want to reaffirm their corporate union with the world of the ancestors so that their lineage and its ancestral "words" do not become "lost and destroyed." The offering thus symbolizes the return of the lineage to the values of order and right relationship and behavior, that is, to the immortal "words" of the ancestors, which are its guiding norms. The sacralized victim is the mediating vehicle par excellence between the profane and imperfect world of men and the sacred and ideal world of the ancestors. The consecration of the victim is a sign of a renewed relationship, and immolation is the instrument of its realization.

The victim also serves as a means of communication and communion within the human world as well. But before this occurs, more speeches are made about the particular purpose and circumstances of the sacrifice. These invocations speak more directly to the human community than to the ancestors themselves. People representing different groups and viewpoints arise and state what they see to be the truth of the matter.

As each man speaks, he holds in his hands a small bunch of sacred leaves which symbolizes his ritual role and the truth of his words. The leaves signify that the speaker is putting the interests of his lineage above his own personal feelings and that he is not telling lies. If he speaks falsely, the ancestors will know and the sacrifice will be voided in their eyes. In the course of the speeches, men emphasize their words by spitting on the leaves. When a speaker is finished, he passes the leaves around to the other elders so that they may spit on them and thereby ratify his words.

Ondua was the first to speak. He stressed his legitimacy as the lineage elder and said that his father's ghost, as the supreme lineage head, was disturbed at the hostility within his lineage, especially since he (Ondua) was so near death. He went on to point out that although Adro had a hand in his illness, the oracles showed that his father's ghost had made him ill in order to demonstrate the seriousness of the tensions within the lineage. He appealed to the congregation to cool their ill feelings and to show Adro and the ancestors that they had "closed their hearts against evil words." He concluded by saying that the members of Olimani's lineage segment had "strong" hearts, an oblique reference to witchcraft, and told them to forget their past actions and to eat together with their kinsmen in renewed solidarity. With these words Ondua thus turned the verbal dimensions of the sacrifice to his own purposes, away from those of Ogdua and Olimani, while at the same time performing the religious act of joining the world of men together with the world of the ancestors. In effecting this unity, he was attempting to smooth over the moral cleavage which threatened to divide the lineage.

Olimani then took up the sacred leaves and spoke, but he was visibly upset and said only a few words. He brought the dispute over the lineage authority out into the open by saying that Ondua's illness had been sent by Adro and Dria's ghost because of Ondua's ritual negligence and greed. He also referred to a past dispute over land between the ancestors of his own segment and the ancestors of the whole lineage and indicated that Adro and Dria were angry about it. But he avoided saying this dispute had been resolved, and called upon everyone to cool their hearts.

The elders of other lineages then spoke briefly. They stressed the harmonious history of the clan and, by implication, deplored the present disputes between the lineage segments.

In his own way, each speaker declared what he perceived to be the truth of the situation, and in different ways each tried to relate the social problems of the community to the ideal norms sanctioned by Adro and the ancestors. At the same time, the speakers were representing their own interests as well.

The sacrifice concluded with the purification of the patient and with the corporate sharing of the meat. The sacred leaves held by the speakers carry their own mystical power, and added to this is the power of the speakers' "true" words and spittle, which blesses the leaves and enhances their efficacy. Placing the leaves on the patient's sacrum and insteps of his feet "cools" his emotions and purifies his body, and insures against his committing further offenses. This was done to Ondua. It was an outward expression of the moral effect the ceremony and "words" of the congregation had had upon him.

As the meat was distributed, each elder and representative received a portion appropriate to his social rank. In this way the moral lines of authority were once more emphasized; at the same time the eating of the common flesh also emphasized the moral unity and wholeness of the lineage. On this occasion it was significant that Ondua invited his rivals, Ogdua and Olimani, to sit with him and the other lineage elders, instead of with the lower ranking men, thus temporarily raising their status. With this gesture, Ondua hoped to avoid further disputes and hence to make the eating and drinking on this occasion an act of genuine reconciliation and corporate unity.

Myth and Word in Dinka Sacrifice

In the preceding account I have drawn attention to the relation between ritual process and social dynamics. Dinka sacrifice follows the same ritual pattern and performs a similar social function of unifying the worshiping community. But in Dinka sacrifices invocation plays an even more important symbolic role, and the dimension of myth, which is absent in the Lugbara rite, assumes major significance. However, it may be that these differences are partly a function of the approaches of Middleton and Lienhardt. Middleton emphasizes the sociological side of Lugbara sacrifice, while Lienhardt emphasizes the verbal and symbolic side of the Dinka rites.

The Dinka act of invocation is, first of all, a repetition of the central event of Dinka mythology: the deadly spearing action of the hero Aiwel Longar. As we have seen in Chapter 1, this myth describes an archetypal action which the Dinka appropriate in the ritual context. It converts the death of the sacrificial animal into a vehicle of life for the total community. Among the pastoralist Dinka, cattle are in many ways symbolically "equivalent" to men. The archetypal spearing action which was once directed at men is now directed at the sacrificial ox, converting this animal into a substitutionary victim. Its life is given to the afflicting powers in exchange for the lives of the human beings on whose behalf it is offered. The enactment of the myth establishes this equivalency in the ritual and makes the substitution possible.

Equally important are the invocations or "words" of the sacrifice, for they effect a moral transaction among men, paralleling the spiritual transaction between men and the gods. In their invocations, the speakers confess their immoral acts and reaffirm their commitment to the moral values of Dinka society. Like the Lugbara invocations the Dinka speeches must be true to be effective. They are filled with genealogical detail and with references to past quarrels and disputes. But, unlike the Lugbara addresses, the purpose of the Dinka invocations is not only to set forth the moral circumstances of the sacrifice but also to serve as a means of confessing past wrongs. In the course of their invocations the speakers state what they wish to be recognized as their true intentions and attitudes about the past, even if they have previously acted wrongly. Indeed, the speakers often deny that they have committed certain acts (even though everyone knows they have) as a way of confessing to what their behavior should have been. In this way the speakers attempt to create a new moral picture of the circumstances underlying the sacrifice, and thereby to re-create the moral bonds of the community which have become divided by personal disputes.

At a sacrifice for a young man who was suffering from pulmonary tuberculosis, his maternal uncle, named Akol Dit, revealed in his invocation that he had quarreled in the past with his nephew's father who was now dead.[9] Fearing that this quarrel might have contributed to his nephew's illness, Akol began his speech by calling upon his clan-divinities and telling them his true intentions about the matter. As he spoke, he emphasized each phrase with thrusts of his fishing-spear towards the sacrificial ox. Each phrase was also taken up and repeated by the gathered group of kinsmen:

> Repeat this, son of my sister. You of my father I call upon you because my child is ill. And I do not want words of sickness and I do not want words of fever.
> And you of my father, if you are called, then you will help me and join yourself with my words. And I did not speak [in the past] that my children should become ill; that quarrel is an old matter.

When Akol Dit finished, several masters of the fishing-spear made their invocations. The last was made by a priest who was also the maternal uncle of the sick man. He indicated that he was concerned about some incident in connection with his own father's death and about a quarrel with his nephew's family.

> And you of my father, I did not neglect you (treat you lightly) on the occasion in the past when my father died, it is not so, it is not true that I caused confusion in the descent group of my father.
> You my own father, and you my grandfather and you my grandmother and you my mother, I have called upon you that you may help me when I pray about sickness, the sickness of my sister's child. My sister's child shall be well. I did not quarrel with the family of your

daughter, I stayed in peace with them, and I meant no malice against my sister's children. If I call upon you, then you will agree [to accept my prayer.]

In denying past acts, the speakers are not trying to deceive the divinities or their kinsmen. What they are denying is that their past actions represent their permanent and true dispositions. Their denials are implicit confessions of past wrongs and at the same time expressions of renewed acceptance of the social norms which hold the community together. These acts of confession and commitment receive their authenticity from the ritual context, and they are further endorsed by the congregation, which repeats the speeches phrase by phrase. In the world of the ceremony, the speakers and the community re-create the true meaning of the moral circumstances surrounding the sacrifice by blotting out transitory wrongs and by reaffirming social norms through ritual expression of true and lasting dispositions.

In addition to this expressive dimension, the words of the invocation are deemed to have important instrumental force. They are said to "do" something. Through the power of ritual language, the masters of the fishing-spear command the agents of illness to "separate" themselves from the sick person and to take possession of the sacrificial animal. Having converted the living beast into a submissive victim, the act of invocation transfers to it the malevolent spirits of illness and destruction. In effect, the words of the invocation create an exchange of the life of the animal for the life of the patient, offering the victim to the spirits and imposing upon its flesh the destructive forces that have caused the illness. Thus, in Lienhardt's words, "to cut the throat of a sacrificial ox is merely the necessary physical conclusion of a sacrificial act of which the most important part has been already accomplished by speech."

In the rite just described, one of the priests told the sacrificial ox, named *malith*, "You *malith* we have given you to the Power," that is, to the illness. This recalls the act of consecration in which the animal was originally dedicated to the responsible divinity and identified with it. The priest then added, "You *Macardit* [a destructive divinity] they say that you kill people. I have separated you [from the patient], cease! Thus!" Another priest, senior to the first, made a similar declaration, "You *malith,* it is not for nothing that we have tethered you in the midday sun, but because of sickness, to exchange your life for the man, and for the man to stay on earth and for your life to go with the Power." He, too, commanded the Power of illness to depart from the sick man and to enter the ox. "You Power I have separated you from the man. I have spoken thus: 'You leave the man alone, you have been given to the ox called *malith*. Thus!' "

The authority of the ritual Word does not derive from the priests alone; it stems from the divinity Flesh, which Longar gave to them. As the tempo of the invocations increases, Flesh makes himself manifest in the bodies of the masters of the fishing-spear, causing them to tremble slightly in a mild form of trance. Their words are his words. It is Flesh who helps to make the priestly invocations "true" and effective against the malevolent powers.

As the invocations draw to a climax, the congregation begins to sing hymns in honor of the divinities who have been asked to lend their assistance. In these praise hymns, the Dinka not only propitiate the gods, but also seek to coerce them into acting on their own behalf by favorably disposing them toward the needs of the congregation. The hymns are aggressively sung at the divinities so that the divinities are made propitious by the praises which the singing renders to them.

For the Dinka, then, the act of sacrifice is an act of the mythical and the living Word. In their invocations the speakers confess their wrongs and, together with their assembled kinsmen, reaffirm the moral values of the social order. Through the mythical authority and sacred power of the invocation, the priests expel the agents of illness from the community and transform the living animal into a substitutional victim. The words of the hymns also compel the gods and ancestors to render assistance. As we have seen, the sacrificial victim is the essential focus and mediator between the human and spiritual world, but it is the Word which makes this transaction possible and articulates its meaning.

The Vital Word of the Dogon

For the Dogon, the sociological dimension of sacrifice has little if any importance, at least in Griaule's account of it. According to Griaule, Dogon sacrifice is a purely metaphysical act, unrelated to particular sociological circumstances.

Every Dogon sacrifice is ultimately a reenactment of the creator Amma's primordial sacrifice of Lebe for the fructification of the earth. In this act, Lebe's sacred life-force was infused within the earth so that it could bring forth the fruits of life. This is the essential meaning of every Dogon sacrifice: the redistribution of *nyama*, or "life-force," for the benefit of mankind. Nyama permeates all things both animate and inanimate as the power behind their existence. But the gods and ancestors have nyama in greater abundance than does mankind, who stands in constant need of replenishment. In the Dogon language, the word for sacrifice comes from a root meaning, to "renew life," and sacrifice is the primary means for this renewal. As described by Griaule, sacrifice is a system of exchange which is manipulated and controlled by the ritual

Word. This Word has the same properties as the Word originally spoken by Amma which fertilized the Cosmic Seed at the beginning of creation. As spoken by the priest, it consists of poetic praise formulae, rich in nyama which is conveyed by the priest's breath. Alerted by the invocation and infused with its verbal nyama, the supernatural beings are irresistibly drawn to the sacrifice. The killing of the sacrificial victim, usually a chicken, releases a quantity of nyama which is transmitted to the altar by its blood. This augments the supply of nyama already contained within the altar from previous sacrifices. As the spiritual beings come into the altar to drink, they also deposit some of their own nyama within it, adding to its accumulated potency. Some of their newly infused nyama flows back via the blood into the victim's liver (the seat of nyama), which is consumed by the person making the sacrifice. The circuit of exchange is complete, and the sacrificer has become recharged with a new supply of life-force.[10]

In a public sacrifice, the circuit of exchange is further extended to the rest of the community through the vehicle of the Word. Since the liver is both the source of the Word and the seat of nyama, everything said by the priest who has consumed the liver imparts a flow of life-force to the people, strengthening and renewing their existence. Even in private sacrifices for personal welfare, the meal of the sacrificer benefits all by virtue of his words. In the seasonal sacrifices for Lebe, the liver is consumed by a special category of persons called the "Impure," who represent the ancestors. By eating the liver, the "Impure" people become infused with Lebe's life-force and identified with Lebe himself, who died and rose again for the restoration of the world. Everything said by the "Impure" is as though it were said by Lebe, and their words communicate the redemptive Word and life-force of Lebe to the rest of the community. According to Ogotemmeli, the Dogon philosopher, "The effect of every sacrifice is the same as that of the sacrifice of Lebe. First one feeds and strengthens oneself, and then by means of the Word, gives strength and life to all men." As the vehicle of nyama, the Word of the sacrifice is for all. "The Word," observed Ogotemmeli, "is for everyone in this world; it must come and go and be interchanged, for it is good to give and to receive the forces of life." [11]

RITES OF PASSAGE

We have seen that ritual sacrifice creates a bond between man and divinity in order to restore the human condition. Rites of passage create a similar bond between temporal processes and archetypal patterns in order to give form and meaning to human events. This is done according to a threefold ritual pattern consisting of rites of separation, transition, and reincorporation. The specific object of rituals of passage is to create fixed and meaningful transformations in the life cycle (birth, puberty, marriage, death), in the ecological and temporal cycle (planting, harvest, seasonal changes, New Year), and in the accession of individuals to high office.

The important phase in these rites is the middle or liminal phase of transition.[12] In this phase people are metaphysically and sociologically remade into "new" beings with new social roles. Newborn infants are made into human persons, children are made into adults, men and women are made into husband and wife, deceased people are made into revered ancestors, princes are made into kings. Seasonal transitions are also marked and celebrated in this way; thus the old year is made into the new, and the season of drought is made into the season of rain.

This remaking of man and time involves the symbolic destruction of the old and the creation of the new. It is a dual process of death and rebirth involving symbols of reversal, bisexuality, disguise, nakedness, death, humility, dirt, intoxication, and infantilism. These symbols of ritual liminality have both negative and positive connotations representing the paradoxical situation of the womb/tomb, the betwixt and between period when people and time are both abolished and renewed. At this critical period people are neither what they were nor what they will become. Initiates are neither children nor adults, male nor female, human nor animal. They are momentary anomalies, stripped of their former mode of being, ready to become something new. Similarly, the time between the seasons and the time between the years belongs neither to the old nor the new, but to both. It is a time out of time, when the usual order of things is reversed and thrown back to primordial chaos, ready to become reestablished and renewed in a new order of temporality.

Bambara Kore

The most elaborate rites of passage usually concern the initiation of the young into adulthood. In this way a society not only socializes its young by outwardly moving them into new roles of social responsibility, but also transforms them inwardly by molding their moral and mental disposition towards the world. This is what African societies consider to be the primary purpose of initiation rituals.

Among the Bambara of Mali, who are neighbors of the Dogon and resemble them culturally, the complete initiation of boys into manhood takes several years and involves six distinct states, each having its own initiation group or "society." From beginning to end, the goal of this series of passages is the complete social and metaphysical transformation of the boys from childhood to adulthood and, ultimately, from mortality to immortality. This process culminates in the rites of the Kore, which is the sixth and last initiation phase. As Dominique Zahan has shown in a masterful study, *Société d'initiation Bambara,* the purpose of the Kore is to create "new" men who are both morally and intellectually enlightened, and metaphysically endowed with immortal souls.[13]

The rites of the Kore are divided into two phases, performed a year apart, each lasting fifteen days. The first phase separates the initiates from the world and concludes by transforming them into perfect humanity. The second phase takes this transformation one step farther, changing their humanity into divinity and incorporating them into the adult world of similarly transformed men.

The dominant theme of both phases is rebirth through the acquisition of knowledge. The initiates must first be taken out of their normal profane world and ushered into the sacred world of the initiation grove, where they will be spiritually transformed. There they will be separated from their former mode of being and reduced to passive *prima materia* so they can be made into perfect human beings. Wearing white gowns and reduced to common anonymity, the boys are led out of the village single file and into the initiation grove. The grove is situated to the west of the village. The westward journey of the initiates leads them towards the setting sun and towards the symbolic death they must experience. Squatting down with their arms extended forwards, they enter the grove by its eastern gate, which represents commencement and rebirth. Thus contorted and shrunken in stature, the initiates begin the painful process of dissolution and rejuvenation. Inside, the elders whip them with thorn branches and flail them with burning torches. The thorns signify the pain of leaving their former life and the difficulties of acquiring new knowledge. The grove itself is also made of thorn bushes, symbolizing its impenetrability by all except the initiated. The flaming torches represent the searing illumination of divine knowledge which the initiates will acquire. Scourged and beaten, they move painfully toward the center of the grove, where there is a cleared space. This place, called the "sky," is where the initiates will be enlightened. At the center is a tree, an *axis mundi,* signifying the Creator in his role as the Supreme Sage. The grove is the dwelling place of Divinity within which the initiates will live. It symbolizes the sky come to earth and Divinity come to man.

This initial stage of the Kore is called the "return of the dry excrement." The name signifies the reversal of the bodily processes and ultimately the regression to the womb. The initiates are regarded as "dead" and entombed at the place where the sky meets the earth. Hidden at the center of the cosmos, the initiates are thus invisible to the outside world in a manner befitting their anomalous social and ontological status between normal social categories of childhood and adulthood. Mothers bring food to the grove but do not see their sons, who remain completely passive and helpless and must be fed and dressed by the elders. During the first day's rites, one of the elders presents the initiates with two knives, one made of iron, the other of wood. "Master of the Kore," he announces, "I kill the children of the Kore in accordance with the gift of their fathers and mothers." He adds, "To die in the Kore is the resurrection of the dead by the living." He then puts the knives to their throats, and says, "The iron makes an entrance, the wood makes an exit," meaning, "iron kills" while wood "revives." Then the initiates sit down in the center of the grove, eyes closed and heads lowered. In this position, they are covered by a large blanket of animal hides sewn together; it is the "sky" enveloping them. An elder invokes, "If the sky is curved, then it will rain. Let the millet be abundant, let births multiply, let sickness go, let the "dead" [the initiates] return to life, forever, forever, forever." The initiates are "entombed" at the juncture of the sky and the earth, where they will eventually be reborn into immortality. Using various means, the elders attempt to stimulate in the initiates an attitude of reflection and contemplation about the symbols involved, encouraging them to seek the meaning of ritual words and behavior and to draw comparisons and analogies within the ritual context. Now that the initiates have been reborn, direct teaching takes place. In this phase the elders use both objects and words to open the "eyes" of the initiates' minds.

The chief instrument of instruction is the *kala ni*. It is a long horizontal pole on which are suspended 240 objects representing the totality of things and beings in the Bambara universe. The initiates learn the symbolic meaning of each of these objects and the correspondences between them. As represented on the kala ni, all things in the universe—animals, plants, minerals, stars, household utensils—are symbols signifying the fundamental principles of Bambara philosophy. In this way the initiates learn that things are not simply what they appear to be on the material and natural level. They learn that the ordinary things of their world are also things to think with, things arranged in a cognitive system. The purpose of the kala ni is to put the novices in a philosophical frame of mind so that they can perceive the underlying ontology of Bambara culture. A spoon, for example, is not only an eating utensil, it is also a symbol of Woman, Winter, Transmission of Knowledge, and Death. A gourd suspended from the kala ni represents Stomach, Humanity, Secret Knowledge, World; the moon represents Calmness, Water,

River, Lightning; a piece of black cloth represents Obscurity, Beginning, Secret Transformation, Original Word, Primordial Knowledge. Until now, the initiates have been aware only of practical and immediate meanings. They have been ignorant of the system of symbolic meanings which comprises their culture. The objects of the kala ni are arranged in pairs of opposed and complementary items in order to emphasize dominant distinctions and relationships, thus exhibiting the basic logic of the Bambara world-view:

Black Cloth	*White Cloth*
Obscurity, Beginning, Secret, Transformation, Original Word, Primordial knowledge	Explication, Demonstration, Revelation, Truth, Spoken Word, Language, Work
Small Wooden Spoon	*Large Wooden Spoon*
Mixture, Heartiness, Spoon, Taste, Breath, Word, Tongue	Creator, Creation, Mind
Calabash Fragment	*Calabash (Whole)*
Elders, Deference, Respect, Arcane Knowledge	Continuity, Woman, Knowledge
Bow	*Arrow*
Curvature, Beginning, Comprehension, Progress, Courage, Domination, Womb, Difficulty, Sky and Earth	War, Attack, Criticism, Poison, Hunt
Nude Figure	*Clothed Figure*
Myself, Self-Knowledge	World, Society, Marriage, Tree, Knowledge of Man and Culture

These oppositions and relations constitute the conceptual building blocks, the symbolic archetypes, of Bambara cosmology, and the objects suspended from the kala ni are its exegesis. They demonstrate to the initiates that the basic elements of the world lie beyond its tangible, everyday realities in the sphere of abstract principles and symbolic relations. In this way they learn to see beyond the common-sense empirical world to the ultimate meanings and values of their culture. A series of maxims also teaches them that this knowledge will raise them above the material level of existence and even make them superior to death itself. It is divine knowledge emanating from the Creator himself. "Listen!" say the elders, "What one learns [now] existed before, what happens [now] existed already: the rhythm." The "rhythm" refers to the teaching of the Kore. It is the "Word" of the Creator that existed before all time, immortal and unchanging. By learning the "Word" the initiates themselves become immortal. "I let myself be carried by the current (of the rhythm), this is the transformation."

Having been thus instructed, the initiates reenter the world as fully enlightened men. The ritual of the fourteenth day leads them through a hole in the earth towards sunlight at the end. This hole is the burrow of the hyena, regarded as the incarnation of wisdom. During their "entombment" in the burrow, the novices have acquired the characteristics of the hyena. On the fifteenth day, their resurrection and reincorporation into the world is complete.

The second phase of the Kore, performed a year later, transforms the enlightened initiates into immortal men. The main episode in this series of rites is the bestowal of an immortal soul, called *ni,* which comes from the Creator. At the conclusion of these rites, all the broken and discarded items of the ceremonies are collected and burned, the entrances of the grove are carefully closed and sealed off, and the initiates return to their village amid joyful celebrations.

Throughout their initiation, the initiates have been divided into eight ranks representing the ancient hierarchical class structure of Bambara society: priests, famous men, nobles, captives, warriors, mercenaries, common men, and women. At the conclusion of the Kore, these distinctions are symbolically abolished. Though the initiates will, in fact, take up different roles in life which will socially divide them, they know that they form a single "family," and that they will be reunited at the celestial court, where all humanity will meet as one "kingdom" after death.

Installation of the King of Buganda

The rituals that installed the Ganda king on his throne follow the same "passage" structure of separation, transition, reincorporation.[14] Their purpose was to make the king-elect into a fully legitimate monarch. In doing this, they also expressed the ideological premises on which the Ganda kingship was founded.

The installation procedures began with the announcement of the previous monarch's death. This was proclaimed by the euphemistic expression, "the fire is extinguished." The sacred fire which symbolized royal vitality was put out and its official attendant was strangled. Bereft of its ruler, the whole kingdom immediately entered into a state of symbolic and political transition. Mourning prevailed, work stopped, and political anarchy threatened to disrupt the kingdom until the chosen successor could secure his position as the official heir to the throne.

The main installation rites took place at the shrines of Budo hill, about twelve miles from the present capital of Kampala, Uganda. The rites began with a mock combat between the king with his party of electors and the priests of Budo. Both sides fought with elephant grass reeds until the king "conquered" the defending priests and ascended the hill. This expressed the conquest ideology of the kingship and demonstrated the king-elect's right to obtain the spiritual resources of the kingship from the priestly guardians. The "combat" re-enacted the original fight between Kintu, the legendary first King of Buganda, and Bemba, the mythical "snake-chief" who ruled the land before Kintu's arrival. Kintu's victory marks the origin of the Ganda kingship and embodies the principle of succession by conquest, not by inherited or elected right. Though election by the ministers of state frequently occurred, conquest by rival princes was, until recent times, the dominant pattern. As King Mwanga was told at his installation ceremonies in 1884, "Fight your enemies and conquer Buganda." Ritual conquest thus displayed the new king's legitimacy in accordance with the conquest traditions as revealed in the archetypal myth of origins.

The installation ceremonies then moved into the liminal phase in which the new king and his queen sister were humbled and exhorted to carry out the duties of their office. Stripped of their regal dress, the royal pair was led to the crowning mound where Kintu originally killed Bemba. After crawling to the mound on their knees, the couple was pulled to their feet and invested with new bark cloths signifying their accession. The chief priest gave the king a royal spear, saying "Go and conquer your enemies," and the queen sister was given a knife with the exhortation, "Go and prepare food for your husband." Grasping the spear, the new king repeated the vow, "I am the king to live longer than my ancestors, to rule the nations, and to put down rebellion." Then the king, supported by his priests, played a ritual board game against his ministers of state and "defeated" them, thus demonstrating his superior wisdom as the supreme judge and arbiter of the law.

The new king then went into mourning for a period of six months while awaiting the mummification and burial of his predecessor. For the king, this was an anomalous time between the initial phase of his installation and the concluding phase wherein he would acquire the full rights of the kingship. The significance of this period was expressed through symbols of reversal, indicative of the king's liminal status. He lived in seclusion in a special hut (called a "prison"), wore old clothes, ate burnt food, and was prohibited from washing, cutting his hair and nails, and from engaging in sexual relations.

When his predecessor had been fully entombed and buried, the king ordered the drums to be sounded and declared the end of national mourning. The period of mourning was brought to a close by a royal hunting party in which the king "hunted" and killed a gazelle. Afterwards he washed and shaved in order to remove all traces of mourning. The hunting party reenacted the legendary return of King Kimera, the third king of Buganda, who was born in the foreign kingdom of Bunyoro and returned to Buganda to reclaim the throne, hunting as he came. In a symbolic sense, this rite also signified the "return" of the king-elect from his "imprisoned" state of mourning "outside" the sphere of the kingship to the final ritual stage which would fully incorporate the new king into his kingdom.

Standing upon the enthronement stool of his ancestors, the king was told, "You are king, rule over your people well, and always do what is right." The king responded with the vow, "If I am the real king, I will conquer my enemies." Then he was presented with the royal sword and told, "With it cut judgment in truth, and anyone who rebels against you, you shall kill with this sword." When the king beat upon the royal Mujaguzo drums, the installation was complete. Immediately afterwards he was carried aloft on the shoulders of his bearer to receive the salutations of his people. Taking up a bow and arrow, the king wounded a man from Bunyoro, Buganda's rival kingdom, and sent him forth to be killed at the border of this kingdom, together with the ashes of the sacred fire of the previous reign. Later, the king journeyed throughout his kingdom and accepted the homage and gifts of his chiefs, displaying to all his legitimacy and authority.

Through this series of rites, a Ganda prince was thus transformed into the king of his country, and the political and symbolic unity of his kingdom was thereby restored. At the conclusion of the rites the king acquired the symbolic and political authority to rule and the power to face his enemies and preserve his realm.

Ashanti New Year

African rituals of passage are concerned not only with transforming individuals in different ways, but also with transforming whole societies, and even time itself.

In marking a passage from one time period to another, New Year's ceremonies create a special interval "between the years." This interval is a liminal phase often characterized by the reversal or suspension of normal behavior. It separates people from the old year so that they may enter the new year refreshed and morally refortified.

The new year ceremony of the northern Ashanti of Ghana is called *Apo*. The word derives from a root meaning "to speak roughly or harshly." Another name for the ceremony means "to wash" or "to cleanse." It is a time when grudges and hostilities can be openly expressed, especially against the king. For the Ashanti, like other peoples, believe that harbored grudges and pent-up resentments can eventually injure both those who hold them and the people against whom they are held. Since powerful officials are more likely to offend the common people, rather than the other way around, it is they who bear the brunt of the accusations during the Apo celebrations. In this way people free their hearts of dangerous feelings which might otherwise lead to witchcraft and to physical illness. According to an old Ashanti priest,

> Our forbears knew this to be the case, and so they ordained a time, once every year, when every man and woman, free man and slave, should have the freedom to speak out just what was in their head, to tell their neighbors just what they thought of them, and of their actions, and not only to their neighbors, but also the king and chief. When a man has spoken freely thus, he will feel his *sunsum* [soul] cool and quieted, and the *sunsum* of the other person against whom he has now openly spoken will be quieted also. The King of the Ashanti may have killed your children, and you hate him. This has made him ill, and you ill, too; when you are allowed to say before his face what you think, you both benefit.[15]

The Apo takes place "when the cycle of the year has come round." This is an appropriate liminal time when the normal rules and structure of society can be suspended and even reversed so that people of high rank may be humbled and brought down to the common level and chastised by ordinary members of society. Whether or not this ritualization of social criticism actually relieves all the social tensions, it does express the moral ideal that all personal grudges, especially against authority, should be laid to rest for the future well being of society as a whole. A carnival atmosphere prevails, and people congregate in the streets to greet each other. Normally forbidden sexual advances are publicly permitted, and the gods come out of their sanctuaries to mingle with the people and to greet one another through their mediums. On the last day of the ceremonies, the shrines of the gods are taken to the river to be washed and purified. They, too, have become polluted by the accumulated sins of the past year and need to be renewed. Finally, on the first day of the new year, the king performs an animal sacrifice which marks the return of the normal social order. Cleansed by this experience of communitas, the structure of society is reestablished until the cycle of the year comes around again, when archetypes of order and disorder will once more be momentarily reversed.

Gogo "Reversal" of Time

The use of ritual to demarcate and control the passage of time is the central theme of Gogo rituals of purification. The Gogo are a semi-pastoralist people living in central Tanzania, and cattle are the main focus of their economic, social, and religious values. When their cattle show signs of a disease called *masaho* (thin milk, lethargic behavior, loss of vigor in bulls, growing thin), the men ask the women, who are normally excluded from herding cattle, to take charge of the herds and to "dance away" the illness. No special medicines are used; the dance is the primary "cure."

In this ceremony, described by Peter Rigby, the men and women reverse their normal ritual roles.[16] The women put on men's dancing bells and beaded belts and tie on their clothes in the male fashion over the right shoulder. They also carry the men's herding sticks, knives, machetes, and war spears. As the women drive the cattle out of the homestead to the pastures in the bush, the men remain behind at the homesteads with the old women and girls. If the women should happen to encounter a herdsman in the pastures, they "attack" him with their switches and "steal" his herd. During the day the women take their meals in the bush outside the homestead occupied by the men. In the evening, the women return with the cattle and sing songs praising themselves as marauding Masai warriors. They engage in mock combat with the men, beating them with their switches and "attacking" them with knives and spears. On the second and final day, the women again herd the cattle and bring them home. Afterwards, they dance and sing at the western boundary of the village, where they "throw away" the cattle disease into the swamp.

According to Rigby, the role reversal of the women is logically correlated with the rest of Gogo cosmology, so as to create a "reverse" ritual state and thereby change the "bad" conditions affecting the cattle. Ordinarily, women are in charge of the fertility of the land and crops, while the men control the health and fertility of humans and animals. When things go well in both these spheres, the Gogo say that things are in a "good ritual state." But when something goes wrong, in this instance with the cattle, they say that the cattle are in "bad ritual state." This means that despite the efforts of men, who are responsible for the health of the cattle and for maintaining them in a good state, time has somehow become reversed and a bad state has occurred. The remedy is not to apply medicines to the cattle nor for the men to perform their usual rituals of health. The remedy is to effect a reversal of the already reversed ritual state of the cattle, in other words, a "re-reversal" which will restore the diseased cattle to their proper ritual condition. Since the men have failed in their normal ritual role, the women must bring about the change. They can do this only as "men." The women's reversal of roles is thus a symbolic "re-reversal" which parallels the desired re-reversal of the ritual states. By taking over the ritual sphere of the men, the women's performance symbolically restructures and reverses the inauspicious alteration of time which has affected the cattle. Disordered time is reordered and the temporal situation is restored according to its proper archetype.

As we have seen, the primary function of African ritual is to "control" the world according to symbolic archetypes. In this way, the world is repeatedly renewed by bringing it into conformity with reality as imaged in symbolic paradigms. Sacrifice does this through the mediation of an animal victim which links the divine with the human in the way men desire. Rites of passage establish a similar linkage between temporal processes and eternal paradigms which give these processes order and meaning.

NOTES

1. On these two aspects of ritual, see J. H. M. BEATTIE, "Ritual and Social Change," *Man*, n.s., 1, no. 1 (1966), and BENJAMIN RAY, " 'Performative Utterances' in African Rituals," *History of Religions* 13, no. 1 (1973).

2. Here I have utilized, with slight modification, Hubert and Mauss's classic analysis of the "nature and function of sacrifice" in H. HUBERT and H. MAUSS, *Sacrifice: Its Nature and Function*, trans. W. D. Halls (London: Cohen & West, 1964).

3. JOSEPH OMOSADE AWOLALU, "Sacrifice in the Religion of the Yoruba" (doctoral thesis, University of Ibadan, 1970), p. 222. See also AWOLALU, *Journal of Religion in Africa* 5, fasc. 2 (1973).

4. See PETER RIGBY, "The Symbolic Role of Cattle in Gogo Ritual," in *The Translation of Culture*, ed. T. O. Beidelman (London: Tavistock Publications, 1971).

5. S. A. BABALOLA, *The Content and Form of Yoruba Ijala* (Oxford: Clarendon Press, 1966), pp. 12-13.

6. AWOLALU, "Sacrifice," pp. 305-7.

7. JOHN MIDDLETON, *Lugbara Religion* (London: Oxford University Press for the International African Institute, 1960), pp. 88-128. Used with permission.

8. This account is taken from *Lugbara Religion*, pp. 134-46.

9. This account, including Lienhardt's own interpretations, is taken from LIENHARDT, *Divinity*, chap. 6 © Oxford University Press 1961. By permission of the Oxford University Press, Oxford.

10. MARCEL GRIAULE, "Remarques sur le mecanisme du sacrifice dogon (Soudan francais)," *Journal de la Societe des Africanistes* 10 (1940).

11. MARCEL GRIAULE, *Conversations with Ogotemeli* (London: Oxford University Press for the International African Institute, 1965), pp. 136-37. Used with permission.

12. See Victor Turner's important discussion of rites of passage and of liminality

in "Betwixt and Between: The Liminal Period in *Rites de Passage*," in *The Forest of Symbols*, and in "Liminality and Communitas," in VICTOR TURNER, *The Ritual Process* (Chicago: Aldine Publishing Company, 1969).

13. DOMINIQUE ZAHAN, *Société d'initiation Bambara* (Paris: Mouton, 1960), I, 280-371.

14. JOHN ROSCOE, *The Baganda* (London: Macmillan & Co., Ltd., 1911), pp. 103-13, 189-204; AUDREY I. RICHARDS, *The Changing Structure of a Ganda Village* (Nairobi: East Africa Publishing House for the East African Institute of Social Research, 1966), chap. 4.

15. ROBERT S. RATTRAY, *Ashanti* (Oxford: The Clarendon Press, 1923), p. 153.

16. PETER RIGBY, "Some Gogo Rituals of 'Purification': an Essay on Social and Moral Categories," in *Dialectic in Practical Religion*, ed. E. R. Leach (Cambridge: Cambridge University Press, 1968). Reprinted in abridged form in *Reader in Comparative Religion*, 3rd ed., ed. William A. Lessa and Evon Z. Vogt (New York: Harper & Row, Publishers, 1972).

4

Religious Authorities

In most African societies, there are certain types of religious authorities, such as diviners, prophets, priests, and sacred kings, who perform specific ritual functions. Although these authorities operate in different contexts and in different ways, they serve a common religious purpose: the mediation between man and the sacred.

DIVINERS

Moral Analysts

Among the Ndembu of northwestern Zambia, a man becomes a diviner only after he himself has suffered the afflictions of the divination spirit Kayong'u. In this manner a diviner is "chosen" for his profession. Henceforth, the spirit of Kayong'u comes to him when he divines and assists him in his practice.

Much of what Victor Turner has written about Ndembu divination he learned from a skillful diviner named Muchona.[1] Muchona related that when he was about thirty-five years old, he became so seriously ill that people thought he was going to die. Eventually a diviner diagnosed his illness as coming from Kayong'u. It was a "heavy" sickness which caused severe asthmatic attacks and fits of trembling. For Muchona, the only cure was initiation into the diviner's profession. Later, when Muchona became a diviner, the symptoms would return, revealing Kayong'u's presence, but then they were under his control. As the spirit of hunters, Kayong'u is very "strong" and "knows everything"; hence he is a suitable helper for diviners who must track down elusive and dangerous witches and spirits.

During the night of his initiation, Muchona was put in a hut and washed with water and medicines. Towards dawn, as the drums began to sound, he was suddenly seized by violent spasms of shaking and fell to the ground. Kayong'u had seized him. Muchona's body was marked with red clay, denoting Kayong'u's power as the destroyer of witches. The drums played again, and Muchona fell into another seizure. This time a red cock, signifying the awakening of Kayong'u, was held out before

Muchona, and he bit off its head. A goat was beheaded and Muchona found himself lapping up its blood, another sign of Kayong'u's power within him. Muchona was then taken outside and tested to see if he could demonstrate the skills necessary for divination. He was put astride a clay alligator in which several symbolic objects had been hidden and told to divine their location, which he did with remarkable success. Muchona spent several months thereafter learning the techniques and symbolism of basket divination.

The Ndembu diviner's task is the practical one of disclosing the causes of misfortune and death. His job is not to foretell the future, but rather to scrutinize the past in order to identify the spiritual and human agents responsible for personal misfortunes. Since all human problems, such as infertility, illness, and trouble in hunting, are ascribed to moral conflicts within the human community, the diviner's task is to disclose acts of immorality which have provoked the vengeance of the ancestors, and to reveal the destructive hand of witches and sorcerers.

A typical case involving a village member's death begins with the assembly of kinsmen to discuss the probable causes. At this stage, people talk openly about various tensions within the community, and they proceed to select a diviner who is not associated with any particular faction. Once a diviner is chosen, the people go with their village headman to consult him. Members of neighboring villages also come along in order to defend their own interests, for their relations with the deceased may also be discussed, and the accused witch may be discovered among them.

When the group of clients arrives, the diviner seeks to impress them with his superior knowledge. He begins with a rigorous interrogation and attempts to establish the main facts of the case. His inquiry proceeds in terms of general and specific questions in a manner resembling the game of Twenty Questions. By listing alternatives to which the clients must respond unanimously "yes" or "no," the diviner eventually succeeds in identifying all the important circumstances of the situation. First, he determines how the person died:

> You have come (about) the fate of dead people? Is there death? Is it the death of a man or woman? If a woman died (may divination reveal) a woman. When you died, you person, did you die (of) diseases? Did you die (in an) accident? Or did you die (of illness after lying long) in bed? . . . Did illness catch you at night? Did you become sick in the day? . . . Did disease catch you in the head? Or in the arms? In the body or in the legs? [2]

He continues this line of questioning until he learns all the symptoms of the disease. He ends it by finding out whether the person was properly buried, for this is likely to reveal some of the conflicts within the community.

After eliciting the secret birth name of the deceased and thereby demonstrating his superior knowledge, the diviner proceeds to establish the exact kinship and social relationships between the deceased and everyone in the assembled group. Occasionally the clients try to throw the diviner off the track by giving wrong answers. But this is difficult to do since the answers must be spontaneous and unanimous, and the diviner is alert to deceptions. The diviner concludes by identifying the exact village to which the dead person belonged.

At the end of his inquiry, the diviner has reconstructed a detailed "map" of the social relationships between the clients and the deceased. The deceased was a kinsman to some, a neighbor to others, a subordinate to a particular village headman. Each of these relationships carries with it a specific set of moral responsibilities as well as potential lines of conflict, all of which are readily known to the diviner and to the people. Using his moral "map," the diviner proceeds to the important task of identifying the witch who killed the deceased, and the "grudge" or motive involved.

At this stage, diviners claim they already know the identity of the witch and the nature of his or her motivations. Their task is simply to make these "hidden" things known to the clients. The diviner is assisted by the spirit of Kayong'u and by the symbolic objects in his winnowing basket. Breathing heavily and trembling, he enters into a mild state of trance, signifying possession by Kayong'u. He shakes his winnowing basket and begins to "sift out" truth from falsehood. Slowly, he interprets the meaning of the various symbolic objects which rise to the top of his basket. These are his clues concerning the identity and motive of the witch.

The twenty-odd objects in the basket represent a variety of misfortunes, social categories, and malicious motives which are typical of Ndembu life. For example, a piece of red clay indicates "enmity" or a "grudge;" a piece of white clay indicates the absence of witchcraft; a piece of wood tied with a bark string, called *Mutu,* represents a corpse; a piece of clay, called *Chimbe,* represents a woman; a set of figures, called the Elders, indicates the members of a matrilineage or witches. Like all divination systems, these symbols constitute a diagnostic scheme. They classify personal problems and solutions under general principles and providing an authoritative framework for analysis and decision-making. If three or four objects repeatedly rise to the top of the basket after being pushed to the bottom, the diviner may reason as follows:

"The Elders" mean that someone has been bewitched—to death, for *Mufu* can mean a dead person. The red clay means that enmity or revengefulness led to witchcraft. And *Chimbu* tells me that the killer was a woman, a necrophagous witch. Now I must find out where this woman came from. Perhaps from the mother's side, perhaps from the father's of the victim? Or perhaps from a stranger residing in the village, or from a woman married into it? [3]

In the past, the person accused of witchcraft was either expelled from the community or killed.

If the diviner is investigating the cause of some other misfortune, e.g., illness or infertility, then he identifies the ancestor spirit that is seeking revenge for some breach of social norms by the patient or his family. In such cases, the diviner concludes by specifying the offering which will appease the ancestor, or some other appropriate remedy.

According to Turner, Ndembu diviners see themselves not only as physicians attending to the physical ills of their clients, but also as moral analysts of Ndembu behavior, holding up daily misdeeds and festering conflicts to the light of ethical scrutiny. Their clients, of course, already know all the facts of the case; indeed, they know much more than the diviner can ever discover. The diviner's task is not to reveal unknown facts but to combine all the known facts into a coherent picture, and from this to draw specific moral judgments. This process generally produces an acceptable result which helps to resolve varying interpretations into a single, encompassing solution. To be sure, the diviner consciously controls the winnowing basket (by means his clients do not perceive) so that certain symbols repeatedly appear, and thus he deliberately manipulates the opinions of his clients. But this is part of the total process of bringing people to moral awareness and of prescribing an otherwise unobtainable resolution for the conflicts involved.

In cases of illness, the diviner will succeed if his diagnosis is agreeable to the patient and to his kinsmen. Since many illnesses appear to be psychosomatic in origin, the moral and social features of the divination process have considerable effect. Even if the diviner's remedies fail and the afflicted person dies, the diviner will have performed the important service of raising the consciousness of the community about the moral issues surrounding the sick person, and he will have prepared their minds for further inquiry into the cause of death. Because illness and death are seen to be rooted in immoral acts, the diviner's role is to help the community in its constant efforts of moral judgment.

"Father of Secrets"

Unlike the Ndembu diviner, who is entirely concerned with analyzing the past, the Yoruba diviner is concerned with forecasting the future.

Yet both are functionally similar: they provide their clients with authoritative models for making difficult decisions.

As we have seen, the concept of predestination is one of the focal points of Yoruba religion. It is the ultimate explanation of success and failure in life. The task of the Yoruba diviner, called a *babalawo* ("father of secrets"), is to reveal his client's destiny and to show him how he may improve upon it in his life.

A person becomes a babalawo either by inheriting this ability from his father or grandfather or by being specially chosen by Orunmila, the orisha of divination. In either case, it is said that the person has been destined to be a babalawo from birth, for only such a person is properly fitted to disclose the mysteries of destiny to other people. Training begins between seven and twelve years of age. The novice goes to live with a master babalawo, whom he serves for ten to twelve years. During this time he must learn a prodigious amount of technical and oral knowledge.

The basis of Yoruba divination (Ifa) is a large repertoire of poems. These are correlated with a set of 256 divination figures, called Odu. The diviner selects one of these figures by a simple process. While shaking sixteen palm nuts in his loosely clasped hands (left hand below, and right hand above), he abruptly tries to lift all the nuts out of his left hand with his right. Because of the size of the nuts, it is virtually impossible to hold all sixteen of them in one hand; thus, one or two will remain in the left hand. If one nut remains, the diviner draws two parallel lines in the powder in his divination tray. If two nuts remain, he draws one line. He makes repeated casts and records his results until he completes a figure consisting of two parallel columns of four marks each.

For example:

```
||  |
 |  |
||  |
||  |
```

This arrangement of marks forms one divination figure, in this instance the figure called Ogbe Ika. Since each column has 4 x 4, or 16 possible combinations of marks, the two columns combined have a total of 16 x 16, or 256, possible combinations.

A shorter method involves the use of the divination chain, made from eight halves of seed pods. The chain is held in the middle and thrown in such a way that the eight pods fall in two parallel lines. Pods that fall with their concave side upwards are equivalent to one line on the tray; those that fall with their convex side upwards are equivalent to two lines.

Once the figure has been drawn on the tray, the diviner recites the poems associated with it. The poems refer to occasions in the past when the gods, ancestors, or animals consulted Ifa about certain problems. The poems describe the situation, its outcome, and the sacrifice that was made. For example, one of the shorter poems associated with the figure Ogbe

Ika (represented above) tells about the favorable outcome of a journey and the sacrifice prescribed:

> "Ogbe that we go home," King's child, Altar's child, the child of "He worships the God of Iron beneath a low, widespreading tree" was the one who cast Ifa for Orunmila on the day that he was going home to Olomo Ofe ward in the town of Ijero. Ifa says someone wants to go to a distant place; at that place the Sky God [Olorun] will give him many possessions and he will be king over the people there. Both the slaves and the townspeople will prostrate themselves before him and bow down before him. But he should sacrifice four pigeons and two shillings.[4]

A novice diviner should know at least four poems for each figure (i.e., 1024 poems) in order to begin his practice. An experienced diviner may know as many as eight for the major figures. Since the verses range from five to fifty lines in length, a diviner must commit to memory a vast store of oral knowledge.

The whole corpus of Odu poems refers to the anxieties, problems, and aspirations typical of Yoruba experience, e.g., death, long life, infant mortality, illness, bad medicine, witches, evil spirits, human infertility, the acquisition of wives and money and positions of authority, the proper location of a new house, the outcome of court cases and business transactions and travels, disputes with relatives, etc. In this respect, the Odu poems perform the same function as Ndembu divination symbols: they classify individual problems according to a set of typical situations. However, the Yoruba babalawo does not know the problem the client is investigating, nor does he concern himself with his client's moral behavior. The babalawo's sole object is to operate his divinatory apparatus faithfully and to recite the proper poems. The client whispers his problem to one of the diviner's ritual objects (usually a coin) so that the diviner himself cannot hear. Only Orunmila, the oracle divinity, knows the question. Having drawn the completed Odu figure on the tray, the diviner then recites the four or five poems which are associated with it.

After hearing the full set of poems, the client chooses the one that seems most relevant to his problem. Not knowing the client's case, the diviner has no way of manipulating his client's interpretation and choice of verse. What is at stake is not something open to public view, as in the case of Ndembu divination. It is rather the purely private relationship between an individual and his own destiny. If the diviner were to know the client's problem and try to choose a suitable poem for him, instead of letting the client's own "head" (*ori*) choose it, the diviner would stand between the client and his destiny, thereby preventing its full realization.

Some poems are highly prized by diviners because they are general and apply to almost any situation. But more highly prized are poems dealing with specific situations. The skill of the diviner lies in the number and type of poems he knows for any given Odu figure, and this increases the likelihood that that he will recite a poem appropriate to the client's problem. For example, the figure Iwori Meji ⫶⫶ has a set of seven poems which, as Bascom explains, covers a wide range of situations:

> Of these, the first one recited, though referring to a journey, is the most general in its prediction, stating only that "Ifa says he will not allow us to see evil in the matter for which we have divined." The second applies to several problems, with any of which the client may be concerned, implying good fortune not only in it but in others as well. "Ifa says he sees the blessing of visitors, the blessing of money, the blessing of children, the blessing of a title" for the client. The third specifies two problems, referring to something that has been lost and to someone who is about to become a chief. The fourth is applicable only to someone who is having trouble with his relatives, who do not allow him to have a home, a farm, or peace. The sixth refers to three children of the same mother, of whom the youngest is ill or is causing trouble because he is argumentative and the last refers to a group of six relatives, one of whom is ill or all but one of whom has died.[5]

The application of Ifa to life thus depends entirely upon the client's perception of his own situation. In this respect, Bascom has compared Ifa to a projection technique, like a Rorschach test, in which a person projects his own interpretation onto a given pattern. The Yoruba client makes his own diagnosis concerning his present and future circumstances from a set of typical models or archetypes given by the poems. They provide him with a framework for reflecting upon his own problem, for focusing his thought and narrowing down his field of choice. The final choice is not, in fact his, but his "head's" and Ifa's, and this serves to legitimize his decision and course of action. It gives the client far greater confidence than his personal decisions could ever achieve.

After choosing the appropriate poem, the client then departs and performs the sacrifice or other procedures prescribed in the verses. If he wishes, the client may inquire further about his case. He asks the diviner to cast the nuts (or chain) again to determine whether the outcome will be favorable or unfavorable. Of the two figures cast, the highest ranking figure will indicate the result. The client may also inquire about the particular kind of fortune or misfortune involved. Good fortunes are classified under five categories: defeat of an enemy, children, marriage, money, and long life. Bad fortunes are also classified under five categories: personal loss, want of money, a fight, illness, and death. Although these classifications appear to be specific, they admit of wide interpretation. As a final procedure, the client may ask what type of sacrifice will insure that a predicted good fortune will actually come to pass or, alternatively, what type will mitigate the worst effects of a predicted bad fortune.

Ifa does not, however, make absolute predictions about the future. What Ifa provides is advice about what can be done to secure the most favorable outcome within the limits of a person's given destiny. If an unhappy outcome follows, it is not because Ifa has failed, but because the person's destiny has not permitted a better result or because other powers have intervened. There is also considerable room for interpretation, for Ifa does not make specific predictions. If a woman wishes to have children, Ifa may tell her to join an orisha cult group or to make a certain sacrifice. Ifa does not tell her that she will actually have children or how many. A man who wishes to know whom he should marry submits a list of names, asking Ifa to decide among several alternatives. The situation is a relative one; it is not a matter of simple prediction. If a man is contemplating a journey, Ifa will tell him what he should do to make it turn out favorably. But Ifa will not tell him specifically what will happen beyond a general prognosis. Thus there is wide latitude for interpretation after the events have happened.

Without Ifa it is assumed that human affairs would turn out worse. Ifa provides confidence and certainty in a world of anxiety and doubt. Hence, Ifa is surrounded by images and symbols of Eshu, the Yoruba trickster-messenger of the gods, who brings irrationality and confusion into the world. As the opposite of Eshu, Ifa performs an important stabilizing function, which Robert Thompson has described in the following way:

> Man, in a state of anxiety, confronted by a universe of disordered energy presided over by Eshu, consults the diviner who brings him into a realm of vital confidence. Suddenly, the suppliant finds the universe is actually divided into sixteen segments, the Odu, and he is pointed in the direction of one of these segments where he finds his problem outlined with essential focus. . . .[6]

In this respect, Ifa and Ndembu divination are the same. Both interpret personal concerns according to meaningful, archetypal patterns, so that people may decide upon a plan of action amidst the uncertainties of life.

PROPHETIC LEADERS

Diviners are essentially the servants of society. Unlike prophets, they do not act on their own initiative, but upon the initiative of their clients. They are consultants, not leaders of men. By contrast, African prophets go directly to the people and inspire religious and political movements. Diviners and prophets alike are mediators of the divine, but prophets speak forth the divine word directly without reading it off a symbolic medium. For this reason, prophets are often sources of creative religious change. It is this directness of communication, scope of leadership, and tendency towards novelty which distinguishes the prophet from the diviner. However, these differences are not absolute. Under certain circumstances diviners and priests may develop prophetic powers and become leaders of religious and social change.

"Possessors of Spirit"

In modern times Nuer prophets have become the focus of major religious and political movements in the southern Sudan. But they were not merely the products of recent colonial upheavals. In the past Nuer prophets attracted large followings and initiated large scale action above the village level. They organized cattle raids against the Dinka, performed rituals to stem widespread epidemics, and introduced new divinities from neighboring societies. Later they led resistance movements against Arab slavers and British colonial power.[7]

The first Nuer prophet to achieve prominence in modern times was Ngundeng of the Lou tribe, who died in 1906. Ngundeng was born into the priestly leopard skin clan and was probably of Dinka origin. According to legend, he was a child prodigy, possessed of a powerful spirit even before his initiation into manhood. At an early age, he displayed his powers by imitating priestly invocations and by sacrificing other people's goats. One of his favorite pranks was to curse people so that they temporarily lost their voices. He is said to have caused such a disturbance that people moved away from the immediate vicinity of his village. After his initiation, he assumed the duties of the priest of the soil, blessing the crops and performing rituals for settling blood feuds. But he soon rose above the stature of an ordinary priest. His deeds of curing the sick and the crippled, of protecting his people and effectively cursing anyone who stood in his way spread his fame far and wide. Eventually he announced that a sky divinity named Dengkur ("Wrath of Deng," a Dinka god) was the source of his power, whereupon he shut himself up in a hut and refused to see or speak to anyone or to partake of food or drink for seven days. He is said to have lived for weeks alone in the bush, refusing food and eating human excrement, and to have seated himself on a cattle peg for hours at a time, letting it penetrate his anus. After falling into a trance for three days and nights, he summoned the people to hear the words of Dengkur. People came not only from Lou country, but also from more distant tribal areas, an unprecedented event, and numerous blood feuds between lineages and clans were forgotten. Ngundeng told the people to build a *luach kwoth,* "House of Spirit," in honor of Deng. For two years thousands of people labored to build a sixty-foot high mound of earth and ashes. When it was finished, it was unlike anything seen before in Nuerland. It became the focus of large-scale ritual assemblies, reaching far beyond local social boundaries.

After the completion of the shrine, Ngundeng appeared holding a special smoking pipe which he said was given to him by the supreme god, Kwoth. It would make him invulnerable and would eventually destroy the Arab slavers who were raiding the land. Nevertheless, Ngundeng avoided any direct confrontation with the Arabs. For many years he performed his acts of healing and continued to renew his powers with periods of fasting and seclusion in the bush. Nuer say that when Deng seized him, Ngundeng would rise into the air without any support and easily run to the top of his "House."

After his death, Ngundeng's spirit went to his son Gwek, whose peculiar behavior and physical deformities seemed ample proof of his selection by Deng. At night, Gwek would stand on his head atop the pyramid, shouting forth the words of Deng. Like his father, Gwek was successful in curing barrenness and stopping epidemics. For Gwek, possession was almost a daily occurrence. Trembling and shaking from every limb and foaming at the mouth, he would ascend the pyramid unseen at night and unexpectedly appear the next day on top, uttering chilling cries and prophecies of the future.

Like other Nuer prophets, Ngundeng and Gwek separated themselves from society in order to gain a measure of control over it. They conformed themselves as much as possible to the divine source of their power, according to the scope of their religious and political task. By acts of fasting, solitude, and living in the bush, the prophets communicated the fact that they were "outsiders" belonging to a separate and sacred reality. They also wore long and unkempt hair and beards, which are objectionable to ordinary Nuer. These "possessors" of spirits were, in turn, completely possessed by the spirits and transformed into superhuman bearers of the divine. This enabled them to become leaders of large intertribal groups which did not recognize any other political authority.

British administration, however, posed a serious challenge to Gwek's leadership. Government chiefs courts and police forces gradually began to undermine his juridical and military authority. At first, Gwek met this challenge by convincing the Nuer that these institutions were instruments for their own suppression, and they quickly fell into disuse. But later, things came to a head when the British proposed to build a road (with Nuer labor) across Nuerland to the border of their enemies, the Dinka. In full regalia and accompanied by a band of singing followers, Gwek appeared before a British official who was explaining the scheme to the government chiefs, and denounced the plan. Soon after, Gwek told his people about a forgotten prophecy of his father that the "Turk" (the Arabs and later the Europeans) would, at first, defeat them many times and then attempt to make a white "path" through their country. When the path reached the Dinka border, a plant would sprout on top of the pyramid, to the height of a man, and the Nuer would rise up and drive out the Turk forever. Then Gwek pointed to a small plant which could be seen growing on top of the pyramid. News of this prophecy spread rapidly around Nuerland, and Nuer began to assemble in large numbers at Luach Deng, while the Dinka along the border fled to the safety of the government stations. The government sent out an armed patrol and succeeded in scattering the Nuer warriors and in partially destroying Deng's pyramid with dynamite. Then the British forces concentrated on hunting down Gwek himself. Eventually he was discovered and killed in a brief skirmish. After the fight, one of his warriors, questioned about Gwek's alleged invincibility, scoffed at Gwek's claim. Asked why he followed, he replied, "Would you, if you have a master, turn on him in his hour of need?"[8]

As this statement implies, Gwek's significance did not lie so much in his exaggerated personal claims as in the charismatic quality of his leadership. Gwek, Ngundeng, and other Nuer prophets attracted followers primarily because they were successful spokesmen of the aspirations and ideals of their people. These aspirations, voiced in the divine words of Deng and other sky divinities, effectively reflected the needs of the people in times of sickness and political upheaval. In this way the prophets served to weld the Nuer together, enabling them to respond in a strong, innovative manner to the tides of history washing over them.

"A Man of God"

Not far to the South, the Lugbara of northwest Uganda were also affected by Arab and European intrusion, especially by slave- and ivory-raiding and epidemics of rinderpest and meningitis. Their response was the Yakan water cult. One of the leaders was a prophet named Rembe who came from the neighboring Kakwa tribe. In the early 1890s, Rembe brought some sacred water from the southern Sudan, where a water cult had proved effective against Egyptian, Mahdist, and Azande expansion. Those to whom Rembe sold his water formed a separate organization superseding local lineage authorities and established a kind of intertribal leadership previously unknown in Lugbaraland. It enabled the Lugbara to unite in large enough units to defeat troops of the German soldier-explorer Emin Pasha. Later, when the Belgians began to administer the area, they appointed some of the Yakan cult leaders as government chiefs because of their wealth and public standing. At the same time, other cult leaders became the center of opposition to the Belgian administration and led attacks on its mercenary forces. As the bearer of new spiritual power, Rembe and his organization gave the Lugbara a new social and ideological basis for dealing with the disturbing influence of European power. Rembe was regarded as the prophet and mediator of a new age of Lugbara independence. Middleton, who visited Lugbaraland in 1949 and again in 1951, was told by a man who knew Rembe well that,

> Rembe brought these things of the Europeans to us. He knew the words of the spirit. The Europeans came as clients. We did not know them and feared them. Rembe came to show us that the Europeans were people. He showed us how to fight against them and not fear them and their strength. Then later the people who became chiefs of the Europeans were those chiefs of Yakan water. They had learnt those words from Rembe and did not fear the Belgians.[9]

After the Belgians withdrew, the Yakan movement lapsed until the British took over in 1914. The British reappointed most of the Yakan chiefs and started an ambitious program of road building, taxation, and military recruitment. New outbreaks of meningitis, smallpox, and influenza also occurred, which the Lugbara attributed to the coming of the British. Rembe became active again. He traveled about the northern part of the country dispensing sacred water. He told the Lugbara that it would make them immune to rifle bullets (which would turn to water) and that it would save them from meningitis and protect their cattle from rinderpest. Rembe set up sacred poles, which he called *dini,* the Swahili word for "religion," and said that they were his "trees." They were planted on the elders' graves, whose authority Rembe was beginning to supplant. At the poles, men came to dance to the Yakan cult songs and to drill with rifles made of reeds and wood. These warriors, Rembe said, were training so that they could later drive out the British with real rifles obtained from the Germans. He also told the people that their cattle and ancestors would come to life again and that they should refuse to pay government taxes. Those who drank the water and became adherents of the cult would be preserved from death, while those who refused would become termites when they died.

Rembe was not concerned with restoring Lugbara society to its precolonial state, but with adapting it so that it could meet the changes bearing down upon it. The Yakan cult organization was a unifying institution whose leaders replaced local kinship authorities with a new countrywide institution that could compete with European power on equal terms. The result was a new era of peace among traditionally feuding Lugbara groups. The cult awakened in the Lugbara a sense of national identity. As one of Middleton's informants explained, "We took his [Rembe's] water because we wanted one chief (*opi*) to make up into one peaceful tribe (*suru*, 'clan'), without fighting." [10]

The cult spread rapidly and disturbances soon developed. In 1919 the government sent a police force to break up a large Yakan meeting, and a severe fight broke out. Another serious fight occurred a year later. As a result, most of the Yakan leaders were deported and Rembe was executed. This put an end to the movement.

Middleton was told that Rembe was "a man of God" and that people came to hear him because he spoke the "word of God." His power was recognized as coming from the Lugbara creator, Adro, who in his immanent form resides in pools and streams where Rembe got his sacred water. According to Middleton, Rembe appeared to the Lugbara as an emissary from the Creator, who was acting anew as he had in the beginning. "People were trying to get back to a pre-social phase when ancestors would live again and divine Spirit would rule men through the prophets," a return to an original, anarchic paradise out of which a new order would emerge.[11] But Rembe never had the chance to develop the full scope of his power. His life was cut short and his organization was too small.

Today, the Lugbara remember Rembe as a partly mythologized figure, bearing certain miraculous and "inverted" attributes of other Lugbara heroes. In 1951 Middleton was told:

> Rembe was a little man. But he was like a *Mukama* [king]. . . . When he sat here everyone would gather to hear his words. His words were great and many. He called men and all came to him.
> Is Rembe dead? Where is his grave? We have never heard how or where he died. Perhaps he is still alive. If he were locked up he would always escape. . . . We still look for him. Where did he go? [12]

Like Nuer prophets, Rembe's credibility had less to do with his political success or failure than with the mythical expression he gave to the fears and hopes of his people. As such, his memory lives on as a kind of messianic figure who tried to lead his people into a new political and ideological era.

PRIESTS

Though it is sometimes misleading to distinguish sharply between "priest" and "prophet," the distinctive mark of a prophet is his inspired sociopolitical leadership, while the distinctive mark of a priest is his ritual and symbolic authority. The main task of a priest is to sustain and renew the life of the community he serves. Often the priest contains within himself the life-force which he seeks to mediate to his people.

"Masters of the Fishing-Spear"

The Dinka say that their masters of the fishing-spear "carry our life." In the Dinka language the word "life" (*wei*) refers to the principle of vitality in all living beings, and it can be augmented or decreased by ritual action. Masters of the fishing-spear possess life in greater abundance than ordinary people, and for this reason they are able to sustain not only themselves but also the lives of the people and cattle for which they are responsible.

The source of their life-giving power is the divinity Flesh, which was given to the priests by Longar in the beginning. Flesh is said to be in the masters of the fishing-spear and in their spears, especially when they invoke the gods; and Flesh enables the priests to speak the "true" word. Flesh is said to "kindle the fire" and to be the source of the "light" by which the spear masters illuminate the world through their powers of truth-telling, knowledge, and vision. "Nhialic," said one of the priests, "made our masters of the fishing-spear thus to be the lamps of the Dinka." While invoking, the priests refer to the "words" of their spears "hitting" their mark, as Longar's spears originally hit their mark with deadly accuracy. As we have seen, in every sacrifice it is the efficacy of the "words" of the spear master which converts a situation of suffering and death into a situation of life and renewal. Like Longar, who led the starving Dinka across a river to green pastures, the masters of the fishing-spear lead the Dinka across situations of deprivation to sufficiency and life.[13]

Ideally, all masters of the fishing-spear are as effective as their mythical prototype, Aiwel Longar, whose herds were fat and sleek, whose pastures were perpetually green, and whose words were miraculously true and powerful. While the Dinka recognize that there are many inferior spear masters, everyone knows of some master whose cattle and crops flourish during times of drought, like those of Longar, and whose words bring rain immediately and cause some people to prosper and others to die.

When a master of the fishing-spear invokes at sacrifices, he is repeating the archetypal action of Longar's deadly spearing action and utilizing Longar's mythical power. By thus "weakening" and finally killing the sacrificial victim with his spear, the master releases its life-force for the benefit of the community which will partake of its flesh. The spear master himself receives the victim's heart, kidneys, liver, and certain other glands that contain the animal's "life." In taking them, the master consumes these organs of life for the people for whom he prays. His spears, the emblems of his office, also represent both destructive and creative power, for they kill to give life. They are objects of respect because they represent both the primordial authority of the spear masters, which stems from Longar, and the function of mediating life. Ultimately the spears represent the priests' ability to bring together in the ritual context the divided worlds of man and divinity for the benefit of the community.

Because the masters of the fishing-spear mediate and represent "life" to their people, they are not allowed to die in an ordinary way. In the past, when an aged and especially renowned spear master knew that he was about to die, he asked his people to bury him alive. Seated in his grave within an enclosure covered with the hide of a bull, the elderly spear master spoke his last words to his kinsmen. When he finished, the people covered over his grave with cattle dung. There was no mourning and no one said the master had died. Instead, the people rejoiced with songs and with warlike displays, saying "The master of the fishing-spear has been taken into the earth. It is very good." By thus contriving his death, the people symbolically ensured that his life did not depart but stayed among them to strengthen the community.[14]

The Hogon

Each Dogon district has a priest chief called a Hogon. He is the head of a council of elders who represent the eight original ancestors. The Hogon is also the head of the totemic priests, who represent the seven original cosmic seeds and govern the cultivation of the district. As the successor of the resurrected Lebe, the Hogon is the vehicle for the seed of the female sorgum, which represents all seeds and the source of their vitality. Since the seeds are also the images of the stars, the Hogon controls the cosmic rhythms. The Hogon thus unites in himself the social, ecological, and cosmic order, and as such he is the personification of the total universe.

As the high priest of Lebe, the ancestor who sustains life on earth, the Hogon is the mediator of Lebe's life-giving force. This is conveyed to him by a sacred serpent, the reincarnated Lebe, who visits him every night and licks his body, giving him the strength to live one more day. In this way the Hogon also acquires the power to speak, for Lebe's saliva carries the "moisture" of the "word." This vitality and power of speech is for the benefit of all. According to Griaule,

> the Hogon is, as it were, the representative of the serpent towards man; but he is also the representative of man towards the serpent. He is entrusted with all the life necessary for men and for the land.[15]

The Hogon's apparel, his household, and his daily activity further define his cosmic, life-giving function. The colors of his tunic and trousers represent the four cardinal directions and the four elements. Since everyone in the district contributes to the cost of making the tunic, it signifies both the total society and the total cosmos. The Hogon's sandals represent the ark of the Nommo which brought mankind to earth at the beginning of time. They also protect him from coming into contact with the earth, especially during the growing season, lest he "scorch" it with his radiant sun-like power.

The Hogon's cylindrical-shaped headdress is woven in a spiral pattern, corresponding to the path followed by the original cosmic seed. It can be worn only inside so as not to disturb the course of the moon and the rhythm of the seasons, which the Hogon controls. The headdress also serves as a means of direct communication with Amma. In times of severe crisis, the paramount Hogon of Arou places his headdress on the ground in an inverted position, symbolizing the world turned up side down. He speaks into it in the presence of the other Hogons, and invokes Amma's assistance to restore the world order.

The house of the paramount Hogon is an architectural model of the whole universe. Its front façade depicts the heavens and the stars; and upon it are represented the descent of the world, the sun, the twenty-two chiefships, and the solstices. On the right side stands the Hogon's staff, the "axis of the world," and on the left hangs his pouch of office, the "pouch of the world." In the dry season the position of the staff and pouch are reversed. Imbedded within the dais in front of the house are eight varieties of millet, the primary staple of life, and inside the house are eight storerooms containing these cereals. Leading into the house are eight stairs, representing the first eight chiefs and ancestors;

thus the Hogon treads daily in the steps of his predecessors. Eight stones representing the eight ancestors serve as seats when the Hogon sits in judgment with his council. These stones also symbolize the eight major constellations.

Against the background of this world in miniature, the Hogon's daily behavior expresses his participation in and control of the world's rhythms. At dawn he rises and sits facing east; at sunset he sits down, facing towards the west. His wider movements reflect the cycle of the seasons. When the crops are planted, he remains enclosed within his homestead so that he will not interrupt the growth of the millet, while his inner life-force helps it germinate in the fields. During the dry season, when the growing is stopped, the Hogon, like the master of the fishing-spear, serves to sustain the life of his people. In his person and office he represents the universe, by his movements he helps control the cosmic cycles, and through his mediational role he constantly infuses the land and the people with generative power.

SACRED KINGS

In many respects, African kings perform similar priestly functions, for they are often the ritual focal points of their kingdoms. Before looking at the ritual significance of African kingship, it will be useful to consider briefly the much debated question about its origins south of the Sahara.

Until recently, the question of Egyptian and "Hamitic" influence has dominated this discussion. Since Ancient Egypt was known to have developed the institution of kingship long before it appeared in black Africa, it was assumed that wherever kingdoms were found in tropical Africa they derived from Egyptian influence.

Ancient Egyptian and African kingdoms do exhibit some common traits: the divinity of the king, the practice of royal "incest," royal control over rain and fertility, royal bird symbols, the actual or ritual killing of the aging or dying king, the preservation of the deceased king's body, the cult of the royal ancestors. But most scholars now agree that a few similarities do not settle the question of direct historical influence. The above-mentioned traits can be found virtually all over the world, wherever sacred kingship exists. Convincing proof of Egyptian origins requires more specific parallels and these have not been found. It is also obvious that one motive behind the theory of Egyptian origins was the desire to link black Africa with an ancient and distinguished pedigree.[16]

Today, this motivation has virtually disappeared. African historians now believe they can explain the origins of sacred kingship south of the Sahara in terms of indigenous historical conditions. Using oral traditions and ethnographic materials, Professor Bethwell Ogot has suggested that Shilluk and other East African kingships developed on their own in the course of military conquest.[17] In response to the need for centralized leadership, one chief may have been elevated to prominence, making him the national leader. Similar developments may have occurred in Buganda and Rwanda. Of course, certain Egyptian and Near Eastern traits may have traveled south of the Sahara, but apart from occasional features it is likely that African kingdoms originated primarily from indigenous conditions.

Shilluk Regicide

For a considerable number of years Sir James G. Frazer's famous regicide theory dominated the study of kingship in Africa. Frazer's view is best described in his own highly imaginative language:

> . . . primitive peoples . . . sometimes believe that their safety and even that of the world is bound up with the life of one of these god-men or human incarnations of divinity. Naturally, therefore, they take the utmost care of his life, out of regard for their own. But no amount of care and precaution will prevent the man-god from growing old and feeble and at last dying. His worshippers have to lay their account with this sad necessity and to meet it as best they can. The danger is a formidable one; for if the course of nature is dependent on the man-god's life, what catastrophes may not be expected from the gradual enfeeblement of his powers and their final extinction in death? There is only one way of averting these dangers. The man-god must be killed as soon as he shows symptoms that his powers are beginning to fail, and his soul must be transferred to a vigorous successor before it has been seriously impaired by the threatened decay.[18]

As late as 1910 it was reported that the Shilluk customarily strangled their kings when they became old or ill. Frazer incorporated this information in the last edition of the *Golden Bough* and made it his primary ethnographic example. Subsequent authors collected further examples and illustrated the widespread "Frazerian" character of African kingship. Thus African kings were portrayed as incarnate gods who controlled the forces of nature, while being subject to periodic rites of physical or symbolic death for the purpose of renewing the kingship.

However, social anthropologists began to question Frazer's theory. Its central doctrine about the killing of the failing king had never been reliably verified; and Frazer's evolutionary, religious approach had long been rejected in favor of sociological explanation.

Evans-Pritchard proposed a new interpretation in his Frazer Memorial Lecture in 1948. Appropriately enough, Evans-Pritchard's theory was based on a re-analysis of Frazer's classic example, the Shilluk kingship. According to Evans-Pritchard, the sacrality of the Shilluk king derived from the sociological fact that

> a king symbolizes a whole society and must not be identified with any part of it. He must be in the society and yet stand outside it and this is only possible if his office is raised to a mystical plane. It is the kingship and not the king who is divine.[19]

In Evans-Pritchard's view regicide was not a mystical doctrine, as Frazer believed, but a political doctrine, justifying the rebellion of princes when the king became too closely identified with certain sectional interests. Since the king was responsible for the total welfare of the nation, any national misfortune—for example, a severe drought—could serve as a pretext for princes supported by their factions to raise a rebellion "against the king in the name of the kingship." In other words, the king was killed not to save a religious principle, the incarnate god, but to save a political principle, the universality of the office.

But Evans-Pritchard's political interpretation postulated a different kind of regicide from that claimed by Shilluk informants and was no better authenticated than the tradition that their kings were ceremonially strangled when they fell sick or grew senile.[20]

Yet Evans-Pritchard's interpretation is worthy of consideration, for it emphasizes the obvious fact that sacred kingship involves both political and religious dimensions.

This can clearly be seen among the Shilluk. The king (*reth*) was both a ritual and a political figure. Incarnated within the reth was the hero-divinity Nyikang, the founder of the kingship and the symbol of Shilluk national identity. As such, every reth was both a timeless image of the mythical past and an actual historical person around whom the country was politically united. This dual, sacred/political role was articulated in the process of electing and installing every new reth. The chosen candidate had to satisfy the political need to reunite the country and had to perform the symbolic act of rejoining its two opposing ritual divisions. The conflict and union between these two divisions represented the conflict and union between the political and ritual aspects of the kingship. Thus the king-elect and his party of kingmakers in the southern division were "defeated" and "captured" by the spirit of Nyikang and the bearers of his effigy from the northern division. The king-elect was then placed on a stool and the spirit of Nyikang took possession of him. In this act the king was united with the kingship and the nation with the king.

The reth's ritual powers were indissolubly linked to his political situation. As a divine personage, his chief ritual function was to mediate between the nation and the forces of vitality controlled by Nyikang. These included the coming of the rains, the change of the seasons, and the military defense of the country. At the same time, the reth was also the supreme judge and final court of appeals in cases of homicide, theft, incest, and violations of established custom—crimes which affected the foundation of the social and political order. Yet the king did not directly govern. Political decisions were made by the powerful settlement chiefs, not by the king. The king was primarily a priestly figure who, in Evans-Pritchard's phrase, "reigns but does not rule." Nevertheless, he was the focus of political harmony and he could be removed by rival princes who represented new alignments of political power. In this respect his position was not merely a ritual one but also a reflection of actual political realities to which his successes and failures in the ritual sphere were closely related. He was thus, as Evans-Pritchard suggests, a "double pivot," the political head of the nation and the center of its ritual expression.

Swazi Ncwala

Like the Shilluk reth, the Swazi king (*nkosi*) was both the ritual and political head of the nation. At the annual Ncwala ceremony both dimensions were dramatically expressed.

According to Professor Hilda Kuper, who witnessed this rite, one of the purposes of Ncwala was to show "the balance of power between the king, his mother, the princes, and commoners." [21] But its primary purpose was to "strengthen" the kingship and "to make stand the nation" at a time when the cosmic powers of the king had declined to their lowest point. This occurred at the end of the year when the sun's powers diminished as it approached the winter solstice. The Ncwala rituals were timed to end with the appearance of the full moon and with the rising of the sun on the day after the solstice occurred. The ritual renewal of the king was thus performed in conjuction with the "new" phases of these powerful celestial bodies. Like the Ashanti New Year ceremonies, the Ncwala was a rite of passage which took place during a time of liminality. It separated, renewed, and reincorporated the king into a revitalized cosmic and political order. As such, it was an occasion of national solidarity: "We see we are all Swazi; we are joined against outside foes."

The preliminary rites of the Little Ncwala begin when the "priests of the sea" treat the king with potent sea water. At this time, warriors sing about the people's hatred of the king: "You hate him, mother, the enemies are the people. /You hate him,/ the people are wizards." As the sun sets on the moonless night, the king goes into seclusion to be doctored by the priests. Then the royal councillors lead the people in the *simemo,* a mournful litany about the people's rejection of the king: "King, alas for your fate. . . . /King, they reject thee/King, they hate thee." This song is repeated again and again, until one of the "sea" priests abruptly shouts: "Out, foreigners!" and all non-Swazi and all members of the royal Dlamini clan are forced to leave. Surrounded by his most loyal supporters, the king spits sacred medicine to the east and west. In this way he "breaks" the old year in preparation for the new. Each time he spits the priest shouts "Eh! Eh! He stabs it with both horns." The people sing a final anthem, praising the king and beseeching his revitalization: "Our Bull! Lion! Descend/Descend, Being of heaven,/ Unconquerable./Play like the tides of the sea,/You Inexplicable, Great Mountain."

Then the rites of the Great Ncwala begin. Young warriors bring green acacia branches to the King, so that, according to one informant, he may be "reborn, revitalized, and . . . grow in prestige." The next day the warriors chase a black bull and throw it in a trial of strength, and pummel the life out of it. Certain "powerful" pieces of the bull are cut off and made into medicines for the king. The youths drive another black bull into the royal enclosure. The king mounts it, naked, while his blood-brothers wash his sides with foaming water to strengthen his personality and virility. The simemo is sung again: "King, alas for your fate," "King, they reject thee."

On the "great day" of the Ncwala, the king leaves his hut and appears before the people, naked except for a white ivory penis cap. The women weep in pity for the humbled king and sing the simemo in a melancholy tone. The king enters another hut, containing symbols of the nation's well-being, and the king spits some "medicine" through the holes in the side. As he spits, the king's new strength is said to penetrate "right through" and awaken his people. He is now strong enough to "bite" the most potent of the season's new crops, so that the people can perform their own "first fruits" ceremonies.

In the late afternoon the Ncwala enters its climactic phase. The members of the royal clan sing of their desire to leave the country and to give up their rule over the strangers whom they conquered long ago and still distrust. The princes weep for the king and force him into his hut. Then they lure him out again with taunting insults: "Come from your sanctuary. The sun is leaving you. You the High One."

Next, according to Kuper,

There emerges a figure weird as the monster of legends. He is *Silo,* a nameless creature. On his head is a cap of black plumes that cover his face and blow about his shoulders, and underneath the feathers is glimpsed a head-band of a lion's skin. His body is covered in bright green grass and evergreen shoots that trail on the ground. In his left hand he holds a shield smeared with fat of the sacred herd, the *mfukwane.* His right hand is empty and as he moves it gleams with lines of dark medicine. . . .
    In this powerful costume the king appears reluctant to return to the nation. He executes a crazy, elusive dance with knees flexed and swaying body. The movements are an intuitive response to the rhythm and situation, a dance that no ordinary man knows and that the king was never taught. . . . The people dance with vigour; here more than at any other stage they keep their king alive and healthy by their own movements. The mime goes on with increasing tension, each appearance of the king making a sudden startling and unforgettable impact. His eyes shine through the feathers as he tosses his head, his face is dark with black medicine, dripping down his legs and arms are black streaks—he is terrifying, and as the knife-edged grass cuts into his skin he tosses his body furiously in pain and rage.[22]

Amidst wild stamping of feet, frantic hissing, and thumping of shields, the king lunges at his warriors and throws them a sacred gourd taken from the region from which the royal Dlamini clan first emigrated to Swaziland. The king is then led away and his costume removed. He enters his hut for the night to cohabit with his chief queen. He spends the next day in seclusion, too potent to be seen by anyone. The people remain indoors to express their oneness with their powerful and secluded monarch.

On the following day, all the ritual paraphernalia containing the "filth of the king and all the people" are burned. The king is cleansed for the last time, and the drops of water falling from his body are said to make the rains come. The dirt and pollution of the old year are thus exchanged for the rain and renewal of the new. At the end of the Ncwala there is a feeling of general well-being as the rain falls and the people taste of their newly harvested crops. Once again the king and the nation are strong.

I have described the Ncwala at some length not only because it displays well the Swazi notion of sacred kingship but also because it has received considerable scholarly attention concerning its meaning and function. As Hilda Kuper has pointed out, the songs of the Ncwala may surprise Europeans who are accustomed to hearing royalty blatantly extolled at national celebrations. Far from extolling the king, the Ncwala songs express hatred and rejection. Yet Kuper believes that the songs express sympathy for the king and that they implicitly criticize his enemies. She suggests that the overall effect of the Ncwala is to strengthen the kingship and to unify the nation around the king.[23]

Developing this line of interpretation, Max Gluckman sees the Ncwala as a "ritual of rebellion." In his view, it "allows for instituted protest, and in complex ways renews the unity of the system." By dramatizing conflicts between the king and his subjects the Swazi release social political tensions which might otherwise lead to actual rebellion. In Gluckman's view, the Ncwala is more than a substitute for rebellion; it is ultimately an affirmation of an abiding commitment to the established political order, a commitment which is so strong that it confines public expression of political conflict to the safety of the ritual sphere.[24]

However, Thomas Beidelman has argued that Gluckman's analysis "focuses upon a very narrow [social-functional] aspect of ritual and in so doing diverts attention from the main [symbolic] themes and purposes of such rites." [25] Beidelman sees the Ncwala as a rite of passage whose initial purpose is to separate the weakened king from his kingdom so that he may be ritually "intensified" with renewed supernatural power. The climax comes at the height of the liminal phase, when the king charges forth as a fearsome, otherworldly monster, burgeoning with sacred power. The final phase "deintensifies" the king so that he may be safely reincorporated into his kingdom.

According to Beidelman, the simemo and other acts of ritual vilification are not merely social devices that relieve political hostility; they are ritual acts which separate the king symbolically from various groups which make overlapping and conflicting claims upon him. Thus the Swazi demonstrate their commitment to the idea that the strength of the kingship ultimately lies in its separation from the pressures of political factionalism.

Although Beidelman's analysis emphasizes the symbolic dimension more than Gluckman's, the two analyses are not mutually exclusive. Taken together, they show how the Ncwala serves a dual political and symbolic function in keeping with the dual nature of the kingship.

Kabaka and Modernity

The foregoing accounts have portrayed sacred kingships in traditional contexts. Today many of these institutions have been considerably changed and in some cases have been entirely abolished during the colonial period. Some have survived more or less intact, as in Nigeria and Swaziland. Until recently, the kingship of Buganda was one of these.

Contrary to what might be expected, the pressure of modern events strengthened the symbolic significance of the king (Kabaka) of Buganda. In 1953 Kabaka Sir Edward Mutesa II rebelled against the colonial government to protect Buganda from what was feared to be political extinction. When he was summarily deported to England, he suddenly became the focus of intense national feelings. Paradoxically, the kingship had never been weaker, but this threat to Buganda's national identity had the effect of transferring the symbolic values of the kingship directly onto the Kabaka himself. In him alone resided the hopes and aspirations of the nation; he became the focal symbol of Buganda's "ultimate concern." [26]

Immediately after his deportation, the sacred fire, symbolizing the life and vitality of the kingship, was extinguished at the palace and the royal drums were silenced as if the Kabaka had died. Public events were canceled; people wore barkcloth and men grew beards in mourning. The members of the Buganda parliament "gathered in tears" and refused to function. Newspapers began to use expressions of fealty which had lapsed and enthusiastically referred to the Kabaka as "our Lord," "chief of men," "our husband." People in the villages revived old songs about the glories of the Kabakas and made up new ones referring to Mutesa longingly as our "prince over the waters." [27] A year after Mutesa's departure, a vernacular newspaper published a "Mutesa Psalm," which aptly expressed Ganda sentiment at the time:

> We thank you, Oh Mutesa; everyone utters your name for your wonderful acts.
> The Country praises the honour of Mutesa. Uganda will follow his example.
> Mutesa is our rock and our everlasting strength;
> Mutesa is our shepherd;
> He has reared us in the pastures of the new Uganda and filled our minds with encouragement.
> He has guided us on the right path for the virtue of his name.
> Though we pass through the valley and the shadow of death we will not fear he is with us.
> His words and his education please us.
> He has prepared for us a new Uganda before the face of our enemies.
> Our self-rule is near at hand.
> His example will always be followed.
> We shall dwell in Mutesa's new Uganda for all our lives.
> May glory everlasting be to Mutesa II and his subjects.[28]

As the symbol of Buganda's national heritage, the Kabaka also became the focus of a revival of traditional religion. Royal ancestor spirits sent messages through their mediums to Mutesa in London via telegram, and worship of the ancient gods came out into the open. A diviner, possessed by the war god Kibuuka, foretold the return of the Kabaka and incited a crowd to kill a policeman as a preliminary sacrifice. Temples for the gods were also set up in the Kabaka's palace in preparation for his return.

When the colonial government resolved the political issues and allowed Mutesa to return, his homecoming was the most tumultuous event ever seen in Uganda. Crowds swelled the capital and lined the twenty-mile road to the airport. Festival banners proclaimed his praises, and the royal drums boomed out a welcome. Cathedrals and mosques offered services of thanksgiving. In the evening, Mutesa went to the royal shrine at Kasubi to take part in burial rites for members of his family who had died in his absence. Later, Mutesa made a complete tour of Buganda in the manner of a new king inspecting his realm, receiving the personal homage of the people. He also saw to it that all twenty-eight shrines of his dynastic ancestors were rebuilt and kept in repair.

With the Kabaka securely on the throne, the Ganda approach to the politics of independence was to support their king and his party, called the "Kabaka Alone," for the Ganda believed that their king and his realm should be second to no one. As independence grew nearer, it was openly said that the Ganda gods were returning to power to replace the God of the Christians in guiding the nation. Prior to the Buganda parliamentary elections in 1962, the following prayer was widely circulated:

> O Muwanga, who ordered this land, we kneel and pray Thee so to order it again as Thou didst order it in ages past. Guard our Kabaka and the Throne, together with the ancient traditions of our tribe, that they may again become as they were in the beginning. For ever and ever. Amen.
> O blessed Muwanga, have mercy upon us.
> O blessed Mukasa of the lake, have mercy upon us etc. etc.
> O all ye blessed ones of old [the royal ancestors], who disappeared, have mercy upon us, We beseech you.
> O all ye blessed ones of old, who fled because you feared the atrocities of the European, Arise and join with us that we may restore our land and establish it as it was of old.
> For ever and ever, Amen.[29]

The national elections of 1962 resulted in a coalition between Buganda's "Kabaka Alone" party and Milton Obote's United People's Congress party. In this way Buganda was able to secure for its Kabaka the Presidency of the newly independent Uganda, while Obote became the Prime Minister. Symbolically, at least, Buganda was thus able to maintain that there was no one above the "Lion" and "chief of men." More importantly, Buganda was also able to embark upon the independence era as a virtually autonomous state within Uganda.

However, this situation could not last. As Uganda's most advanced and prosperous district, long favored by the colonial government, Buganda's privileged position was a major political problem. In 1966

Prime Minister Obote forcibly expelled Mutesa and declared Uganda a Republic under his Presidency, thus abolishing the kingship and Buganda's special status. Mutesa fled to Britain and Obote's troops stopped the rituals at the royal shrines. The Ganda had no choice but to submit. In 1969 Mutesa died in London. At this time (it is said) one of the sacred trees in the coronation grove at Budo fell to the ground, a testimony to the demise of the kingship.

In 1971 President Obote was overthrown by the army leader, General Idi Amin. Although General Amin was not a Ganda, one of his first acts was to enlist Ganda support by arranging for the return of Mutesa's body for burial in the royal shrine at Kasubi. This gesture was welcomed by the Ganda with a massive outpouring of emotion. In the eyes of the royalists, Mutesa could now rejoin the ancestors, and his son, Prince Ronald, could accede to the throne. However, President Amin insisted upon Uganda's remaining a Republic and forbade full installation. Instead, Prince Ronald was made official heir and head of the clans, not the Kabaka. This created an anomalous situation, but it allowed the resumption of the rituals at the shrines, where the dynastic spirits could again speak to the people. If the future of the kingship was to remain uncertain, at least its links with the sacred past were fully restored and Buganda's historic identity thereby maintained.

NOTES

1. VICTOR TURNER, "Muchona the Hornet, Interpreter of Religion," in *The Forest of Symbols*; VICTOR TURNER, *Ndembu Divination: Its Symbolism and Techniques*, Rhodes-Livingstone Paper No. 31 (Manchester: Manchester University Press, 1961).
2. *Ndembu Divination*, p. 43.
3. *Ibid.*, p. 9.
4. BASCOM, *Ifa Divination*, p. 229.
5. *Ibid.*, p. 72.
6. ROBERT FARRIS THOMPSON, *Black Gods and Kings* (Los Angeles: University of California Los Angeles, 1971), chap. 5, p. 5. Here I have been able to present only the barest outline of this complex and fascinating system. In addition to the above-mentioned works by Bascom and Thompson, I have also benefited from two other important studies: WANDE ABIMBOLA, "An Exposition of Ifa Literary Corpus," (doctoral thesis, University of Lagos, 1969) and JUDITH GLEASON, *A Recitation of Ifa, Oracle of the Yoruba* (New York: Grossman Publishers, 1973).
7. As Thomas Beidelman has pointed out, there is considerable evidence against Evans-Pritchard's view of Nuer Prophets as a "recent development" (*Nuer*

Religion, chap. 12). See T. O. BEIDELMAN, "Nuer Priests and Prophets: Charisma, Authority, and Power among the Nuer," in *The Translation of Culture,* ed. T. O. Beidelman (London: Tavistock Publications, 1971), p. 377.

8. P. CORIAT, "Gwek the Witch-doctor and the Pyramid of Dengkur," *Sudan Notes and Records* 22, pt. II (1939), 237. My account of Ngundeng and his son Gwek is also based upon reports by Ferguson, who was an administrator in the 1920s, and upon reports by Alban and Willis. References to these authors appear in BEIDELMAN, "Nuer Priests and Prophets."

9. JOHN MIDDLETON, "The Yakan or Allah Water Cult among the Lugbara," *Journal of the Royal Anthropological Institute* 92, no. 1 (1963), 100.

10. *Ibid.,* 92.

11. *Ibid.,* 103.

12. JOHN MIDDLETON, *Lugbara Religion* (London: Oxford University Press for the International African Institute, 1960), p. 261. Used with permission.

13. LIENHARDT, *Divinity,* p. 141; cf. FRANCIS MADING DENG, *Tradition and Modernization* (New York: Yale University Press, 1971), pp. 46-51, 287-88.

14. *Divinity,* chap. 8.

15. MARCEL GRIAULE, *Conversations with Ogotomeli* (London: Oxford University Press for the International African Institute, 1965), p. 118. Used with permission.

16. For the relevant sources concerning the above discussion, see *Problems in African History,* ed. J. O. Collins (Englewood Cliffs, N.J.: Prentice-Hall, Inc., 1968), Part I.

17. BETHWELL A. OGOT, "Kingship and Statelessness Among the Nilotes," in *The Historian in Tropical Africa,* ed., Jan Vansina et al. (London: Oxford University Press for the International African Institute, 1964). Reprinted in COLLINS, *Problems in African History,* Part III.

18. JAMES G. FRAZER, *The Golden Bough,* abr. ed. (New York: The Macmillan Company, 1948), p. 265.

19. E. E. EVANS-PRITCHARD, "The Divine Kingship of the Shilluk of the Nilotic Sudan, The Frazer Lecture, 1948," in *Social Anthropology and Other Essays* (New York: The Free Press of Glencoe, 1962), p. 210.

20. See MICHAEL YOUNG, "The Divine Kingship of the Jukun: A Re-evaluation of Some Theories," *Africa* 36, no. 2 (1966).

21. HILDA KUPER, *An African Aristocracy* (London: Oxford University Press for the International African Institute, 1947), chap. 13. Used with permission. Subsequent references to the Ncwala ceremony are taken from this chapter.

22. *Ibid.,* pp. 217-18.

23. The Ncwala continued to be an important "resource" for strengthening the kingship during the colonial period as well. See HILDA KUPER, "A Royal Ritual in a Changing Political Context," *Cahiers d'Etudes Africaines* 12, no. 48 (1972).

24. MAX GLUCKMAN, "Rituals of Rebellion in South-East Africa," in *Order and Rebellion,* ed. Max Gluckman (New York: The Free Press of Glencoe, 1960).

25. T. O. BEIDELMAN, "Swazi Royal Ritual," *Africa* 36, no. 4 (1966), 374.

26. F. B. WELBOURN, *Religion and Politics in Uganda 1952-1962* (Nairobi: East African Publishing House, 1965), pp. 44-45.

27. AUDREY I. RICHARDS, "Authority Patterns in Traditional Buganda," in *The King's Men,* ed. L. A. Fallers (London: Oxford University Press for the East African Institute of Social Research, 1964).

28. D. A. LOW and R. C. PRATT, *Buganda and British Overrule* (London: Oxford University Press for the International African Institute, 1960), pp. 340-41. As quoted in WELBOURN, *Religion and Politics,* pp. 42-43.

29. J. V. TAYLOR, *The Growth of the Church in Buganda* (London: SCM Press, 1958), p. 207. As quoted in WELBOURN, *Religion and Politics,* p. 44.

5

Man, Ancestors, and Ethics

Until recently, Western scholars have failed to appreciate the extent to which African religions are founded upon a systematic anthropology and ethics. Heretofore, myths, gods, and rituals have attracted most attention, but they are far from being the sum and substance of African religions. They are only partial ingredients within a total world view at the center of which lies a moral conception of man. This conception is a complex one and involves notions of personal identity, freedom, destiny, ancestors, and social ethics.

THE CONCEPT OF THE PERSON

African views of man strike a balance between his collective identity as a member of society and his personal identity as a unique individual. In general, African philosophy tends to define persons in terms of the social groups to which they belong. A person is thought of first of all as a *constituent* of a particular community, for it is the community which defines who he is and who he can become. As Mbiti has aptly put it, "the individual is conscious of himself in terms of 'I am because we are, and since we are, therefore I am.' " [1] But African thought also recognizes that each individual is a unique person endowed by the Creator with his own personality and talents, and motivated by his own particular needs and ambitions. To this extent, African thought acknowledges the transcendence of individuals over their own sociocultural conditions. However, the emphasis upon a person's individuality and freedom is always balanced against the total social and historical context. It never approximates the Western notion of individualism—the idea that men are essentially independent of their social and historical circumstances. The traditional African world view is too systematic for such a doctrine, too logically and dynamically integrated. Freedom and individuality are always balanced by destiny and community, and these in turn are balanced by natural and supernatural powers. Every person is a nexus of interacting elements of the self and of the world which shape and are shaped by his behavior.

Different societies, of course, conceive of these elements in different ways, but the moral ideal is generally the same—the harmonious integration of the self with the world. This ideal is reflected in the Dinka concept of *cieng,* which means both "morality" and "living together." As explained by Francis Deng,

> On its highest level of abstraction, *cieng* is a guiding force above Dinka community process. It aims at an ideal social order in which people are united in full harmony with no quarrels or frictions and with mutual indulgences. On the lowest level, it requires and generally achieves conformity with the sum total of community expectations, which are in fact segments of the ideal.[2]

The result of *cieng* is well-being, which among the Dinka is intimately associated with *wei,* "life" or "soul." It is realized most fully when, in Deng's words,

> a Dinka strives to maintain unity and harmony between himself and the world outside. . . . Harmony is best achieved by attuning men's demands and desires to the mythicals [gods and ancestors], living superiors, and other fellow men.[3]

Man as Microcosm: the Dogon

As we have seen, the Dogon universe was created in the image of man. Man was prefigured in creation's first beginnings and he is the being around whom everything was organized. Man also contains in his own person the basic elements of the universe, the same primordial grains and words out of which the world itself was made. Man is the world in miniature. In his collar bones, he carries the four pairs of cosmic grains, representing the four basic elements, the four cardinal directions, and the eight original ancestors. The grains also determine his personality, sexuality, and social rank. At the same time they bring each person into dynamic relation with his community and the cosmos.

In this way the Dogon think of a person as participating in the general condition of his society and the universe; the condition of man and the condition of the cosmos reflect each other. If someone breaks the moral rules of life, this disturbs the cosmic grains in his body, prefiguring a wider social disturbance spreading from the individual to his kinsmen, his family, his clan, and his people. But the disorder may be corrected by the appropriate rituals, which restore the individual and preserve the general order. Conversely, to perform rituals modeled upon the original acts of creation helps to maintain and revive the world. The farmer plows his field according to the original spiral pattern of cosmic generation; the priest repaints the cosmic signs on the temple to renew the forces of life.

In some way all man's actions and all his circumstances are conceived as closely connected with the functioning of things in general.[4]

Because of these multiple connections, man is not thought to be a single or simple entity. In contrast to the Western notion of the soul as the "essence" of man, the Dogon think of man in terms of multiple "souls" or "selves," each reflecting a concrete relation between the individual and his social and cosmic environment. Unlike Western philosophers, the Dogon do not think of man as a static and unchanging being, but as a dynamically developing cluster of forces whose powers may be increased or decreased according to his moral and spiritual acts. They may also be influenced by other people and by supernatural and ritual acts.

Man does not come into the world "ready-made," bearing all his "souls" or bearing them in proper measure. In the Dogon view, a newborn child is only potentially a human being and must be given his own sexual, social, and spiritual identity by the human community into which he is born. Since every child is born with twin, male and female souls, it develops an unstable personality until circumcision removes the physical part (the prepuce or the clitoris) containing the soul opposite from the child's apparent sex. Until this is done, the androgynous soul is not stable and the child cannot act like a responsible being, nor can he be treated as such by the rest of society. Other aspects of a child's identity are conferred upon him in the course of several naming ceremonies. Usually four names are involved. If the child is a boy, his "secret" name is given by the clan priest. This endows the child with an "intelligent" soul, the capacity for knowledge and will, and conveys to him the cosmic grains linking him with the cosmic order. Often the secret name is the name of a patrilineal ancestor who has chosen the child as his special devotee, and in this way the child is brought into relation with the world of the family ancestors. The "customary" name, given by the patriarch of the joint family, confers another part of the intelligent soul upon the child and gives him a quantity of life-force. The maternal side of the child's identity is connected with the "shadow" soul conferred by the matrilineal patriarch. As a symbol of a person's ties with his home, the shadow soul resides in the lineage totemic shrine when he travels outside his immediate kinship area. Another aspect of this shadow soul is given to the child by the "nickname" that children his own age give to him.

In addition to these personal names and souls, every Dogon also inherits a set of family and regional praise names which belong to his clan, lineage, guardian ancestor, and village quarter. When relatives and friends shout out these names in times of personal trial or crisis, they give the individual social support and encouragement, strengthening his own life-force when he needs it most.

A person's soul powers can also be regularly strengthened in a ritual way at his own pair of personal altars. Here he performs rites which, more than any others, help to preserve his own life-force. Though they are initially constructed and maintained by the father, the child later assumes responsibility for them. The two altars represent the powers of the individual's "head" and "body." Rites performed at the "head" altar strengthen the person's "intelligent" soul, which controls his mind and will, while rites performed at the "body" altar strengthen his sex souls, which control his fertility and physical powers. After death, the person's sex souls continue to vitalize the life of the lineage through the life-force transmitted to its descendents. During his life time, a person's souls, life-force, and cosmic grains are in constant relation. Each can be ritually manipulated by the individual at his personal altars or by kinsmen and priests at public altars, both for the person's own well being and for that of the family to which he belongs.[5]

In the Dogon view, a person is therefore a multidimensional and dynamically developing being whose whole personality is involved with the processes of the social and natural world around him. At the same time, every person has his own unique identity and powers which he may mould and shape to his own advantage. In this sense, he both transcends the whole and belongs essentially to it.

Destiny and Personality: the Yoruba

The Yoruba concept of man involves a similar set of ideas. Here the theme is the relationship between destiny and personality. Like the Dogon, the Yoruba think of man as having multiple souls, each representing a significant dimension within Yoruba social experience.

The "life-breath" given by Olorun at birth contains a man's personal vitality and strength. It is nourished by food and hence its power may be increased or decreased. It may also be "trapped" by witches when it leaves the body in sleep (in dreams), causing death. Witches can also send their "breath" outside their bodies at night to do evil deeds. In some areas of Yorubaland these latter functions are assigned to a second soul called the "shadow."

More important is a third component called the *ori* or "head."[6] It is a semi-split entity having two complementary aspects. One aspect is located in the person's head and constitutes the essence of his personality or ego. The other is located in the heavens and constitutes the person's alter ego or "guardian" soul. Taken as a whole, the ori represents the partial rebirth and incarnation of a patrilineal ancestor; hence it is sometimes called the person's "guardian ancestor."

Before a person is born, the ancestor ori in heaven chooses his destiny. It is called the "predestined share" or ori's "lot." It determines a person's character, occupation, success in life, and time of death. This destiny is permanently affixed to the ori by Olorun, while the ori kneels before him. Thereafter, the ori in heaven helps a person to realize his destiny during his life time on earth.

For this to happen successfully, the ori must receive careful ritual attention through sacrifices and offerings known as "feeding the head." If well treated, the ori will assure that the best portions of a person's destiny, whether it be good or bad, actually come to pass. In this respect, the ori is said to be more important than the gods themselves, for what the ori refuses to grant, the gods cannot confer. Indeed, their task is to aid the ori in leading everyone through his destined course in life. As stated in the following Odu verse, the ori is the key to personal success and failure,

> It is *ori* that guides,
> That we wear the crown of money,
> It is the *ori* that guides,
> That we walk with the royal stick of heads.
> *Ori* is the jewellery chain, *Ori* is silver,
> He creates one and never forgets him,
> Oh, hail *Ori*.[7]

But there are limits to ori's powers. If, through error, the ori chooses a "bad" destiny, nothing can effectively change it. There are certain modifying rituals, but in the end, the individual has only his ori to blame. According to one explanation, the destinies are made in the form of human heads by the heavenly gate keeper, named Ajala. Because of his carelessness some are poorly made, but they are indistinguishable from well-made ones. If a person's ori chooses one of these, there is nothing the person or his ori can do, and the person will fail.

Even a "good" destiny is subject to the malevolent influence of the gods, witches, and sorcerers. They have the power to partially spoil a good destiny and even to kill, thus doing permanent damage. For this reason, everyone must align himself with a particular divinity who will serve as his protector. Usually this is the same divinity worshiped by his lineage group. Through this relationship, the individual gives full religious expression to the anxieties and desires of his own situation in life, and he also participates in those of his wider kinship group. In order to protect himself and his destiny, a person must constantly inquire through divination about the harmful vicissitudes of life, especially about what witches and sorcerers, the "people of this world," may do, and these may be members of his own kinship group.

Still, within the framework of predestination there is room for considerable personal freedom and initiative. As the Yoruba see it, life is a delicately balanced scale. On the one hand, it is divinely preordained and sociologically conditioned, yet it is also significantly related to controllable personal and spiritual elements, one's character and one's ori. Each person must find his own way, guided by his personality and his destiny and attuned to the numerous countervailing socioreligious forces.

Destiny and the Unconscious: the Tallensi

The Tale concept of man described by Meyer Fortes exhibits these same themes in slightly different form. The Tallensi of the Volta region of Ghana recognize a basic polarity between a man's personal destiny and his acquired social identity. Like the Yoruba and Dogon, the Tallensi see that a person's inner life is intimately related to the external social facts of his existence, but they also know that every person's life history is unique and individual. Like the Yoruba, they attribute this uniqueness to a person's prenatal or "spoken" destiny, which is chosen in heaven. This determines whether children will develop into human beings or whether they will fail and become social dropouts.[8]

The exact nature of a person's destiny does not become known until he or she begins to reach maturity and to enter into responsible social roles. In the beginning, a child's prenatal destiny and social identity are closely merged with that of its parents; it is their destiny, especially the mother's, which controls the child's early life. Thus a chronically sick child or one who dies is usually said to suffer from an evil aspect of its mother's prenatal destiny, not its own. But when the child reaches adolescence and begins to assume a certain social identity, his or her own prenatal destiny becomes stronger and exerts more influence. Death or chronic illness at this point is then usually attributed to the child's own prenatal destiny.

At this juncture in a boy's life, when his social identity begins to emerge, society steps in under the guise of the ancestors to mediate his maturing prenatal destiny. Each youth finds himself chosen by a specific group of guardian ancestors who will preserve and guide his life beyond the stage governed by his infantile and dangerous prenatal destiny. Under their guidance, the youth's destiny also changes. It becomes what Fortes calls "a good destiny," shedding its evil propensities and assuming a more positive role.

A boy's destiny ancestors reveal themselves in critical adolescent experiences—for example, during a serious illness or when the youth first kills big game. When their presence is disclosed by divination, a destiny shrine is erected. Henceforth the youth and his father make regular offerings of food and drink to the guardians, for they will determine the success or failure of the young man's life. This shift towards the ancestors also marks a crucial shift towards maturity and moral responsibility. In this way the youth moves out from under the arbitrary grip of his prenatal fate, over which he has no personal control, and acquires the freedom to assert his own personality. Hereafter, his own moral behavior (subject to ancestral guidance), not his prenatal fate, will determine a large measure of his personal success or failure.

The shifting location of a man's destiny shrine clearly expresses the phases of his growing social identity. When first constructed, the shrine is placed in his mother's quarters. Later, when the young man marries, it is moved to his wife's quarters, though it still remains within the sphere of his father's compound. Until his father dies, a son lives within his father's household and remains subject to the overriding power of his father's destiny. Indeed, the destiny of the eldest son and his father are said to be opposed, especially when the son marries and has a child. From this time onward, the eldest son impatiently awaits the time when he can assume his father's legal and social position as the compound head. Custom prescribes that he must enter the compound by another entrance in order not to encounter his father face to face—that is, destiny to destiny—and thus avoid a confrontation damaging to both. With the death of his father, the eldest son finally moves his destiny shrine outside the compound to the main entrance, where it stands together with the family's ancestor shrines, guarding the whole family group.

Women, by contrast, never emerge from the sphere of their prenatal destiny and acquire an independent social identity of their own, and they never assume authoritative social and legal roles. They continue to be governed by their own prenatal destinies and by the destinies of their fathers and husbands. Consequently, women suffer more frequently than men from the evils inherent in prenatal destinies. For them, destiny always remains an arbitrary fate, usually revealed in the illness and death of their children. In the rare instances of evil destiny among men, this is usually connected with some irremediable physical or psychological infirmity which prevents them from marrying or having children.

Such situations are not, however, entirely hopeless. There is a last resort: the exorcism of the prenatal destiny. This involves the marshaling of all the relevant social and spiritual forces—the person's kinsmen and their destiny ancestors. In the case of women who repeatedly lose their children, the exorcism is performed by their father's lineage group, supported by the guardian ancestors. Using ritual means, the woman's prenatal destiny is transferred to certain objects and thrown out of the compound onto a barren spot. But if this remedy fails and the prenatal destiny proves too strong, there is no further recourse. Society helplessly faces the social demise of one of its members.

In this respect, the notion of destructive prenatal destiny serves to explain the failure of people to fulfill the basic social roles of husband and wife, and father and mother. Its victims are socially marginal people who, for one reason or another, have failed to become socially mature. Since the notion of prenatal destiny is primarily an amoral one, it relieves the persons who suffer from it and their kinsmen of any responsibility for such basic failures in life and therefore from feelings of guilt.

As Fortes has pointed out, the Tale view of man rests upon notions of fate and responsibility which are comparable to classical Western formulations—for example, the stories of Oedipus and Job. The first is a fatalistic and amoral vision; the second is freedom-affirming and supremely moral. But whereas in Western thought these two visions of man are irreconcilably opposed (the one Greek, the other Biblical), in Tale thought they are dynamically combined as two related phases in man's socioreligious development. Men move beyond the infantile, presocial sphere of destiny (Oedipal Fate) into the realm of moral responsibility before the ancestors (Job's God). Women, too, make this move, though indirectly through the men to whom they are related. Like the Yoruba, the Tallensi project a dualistic and dynamic vision of man: he is both fated and free, innocent and responsible, Oedipus and Job. While the Yoruba see these contrasting themes as simultaneous polarities within the human condition, the Tallensi see them in a developmental relationship. Fortes observes that

> They reconcile the two main alternatives in the hazardous progress of the individual from the state of unchecked dependence, as an infant at the mother's breast, to that of constrained independence, as an adult and citizen. It is a law of nature that some people must fail in the whole or in parts of the task of becoming and remaining social persons. The predicament this gives rise to is interpreted, given moral value, and brought under control in the interests of society and of the individual, by means of the beliefs and rituals focused in the notion of Predestiny, or Oedipal Fate. Most people will succeed; but they can do so only by coming to terms with unforeseeable hazards and precarious rewards. To give meaning and absolute moral value to this experience the Tallensi invoke personified supernatural figures cast in the mould of glorified parents who intervene justly in the life of the individual and of society. The image of the Good Destiny in which these ideas are focused is, in essentials, a simple version of Job's God.[9]

The Tallensi also coordinate these ideas to their social structure. Man is free to the extent that he is mature and socially responsible; his is not free to the extent that he is immature and outside of the social order.

From another point of view, Robin Horton has suggested that the Yoruba and Tale notions of destiny can be compared to the Western idea of the unconscious.[10] Fundamental to both concepts is the notion that a successful life requires the "acceptance" of factors stemming essentially from within the self. In this respect, the African concept of personal destiny is not analogous to the Greek concept of an arbitrary, impersonal, and unalterable Fate. Rather, like the idea of the unconscious, destiny is understood to be a hidden but determinative part of the self which is both controllable and uncontrollable to the extent that it is revealed to the individual and accepted by him. As part of the personality, "chosen" before birth, destiny is only gradually disclosed to the individual in a series of traumatic situations. But once it is revealed, it can be partially modified, as can the hidden desires and conflicts imposed by the unconscious. In this way a person may better adjust to the circumstances of his society and to the exigencies of life.

DEATH AND ESCHATOLOGY

So far we have seen the way in which African concepts of man involve the notion of multiple souls, and we have seen how the ritual process repeatedly deals with the relation between the individual and community throughout the course of a person's life.

At death, new problems of social and spiritual identity arise. When a family loses one of its members, especially a senior member, a significant moral and social gap occurs. The family together with other kinsmen must close this gap and reconstitute itself through a series of ritual and social adjustments. At the same time, the soul of the deceased must also undergo a series of spiritual adjustments if he or she is to find a secure place in the afterlife and continue to remain in contact with the family left behind.

Here we touch upon one of the most fundamental features of traditional religious life: the relation between the living and the dead. This relationship, commonly though somewhat misleadingly called "ancestor worship," has powerful moral and psychological dimensions and plays a vital role in the everyday life of almost every African society.

What is of importance here is not the afterlife itself but the way in which the dead continue to be involved in *this life* among the living. There is little speculation about "last things"—that is, about the nature of the afterlife or about immortality or final judgment—for there are no "last things" towards which human life is headed. There is no vision of a culminating "end" to individual lives or to human history in general.

Unlike Western religious thought, speculation about the meaning of human existence does not project forward to a distant and transcendent future; it projects back upon itself to the present, in cyclical fashion, to the all important *now*. Thus, the afterlife and the notion of personal immortality have meaning only in concrete terms in relation to the present life of the community.

There are, however, some notable exceptions to this rule among certain West African societies. From the perspective of world religions, these eschatological systems are too important to be ignored, especially since it is widely held that eschatological thought is found only among the so-called "higher" religions. Here we shall look briefly at the eschatology of the Dogon, Yoruba, and LoDagaa.

The Dogon

Dogon eschatology consists of three major phases: death, journey to the afterlife, and the achievement of paradisal immortality.[11] On the ritual and social level, the funerary rites of the first phase separate the newly dead from the living and send the soul of the deceased on its way to the realm of the dead. This accomplishes the all-important transition from the dangerous and unstable state of death to the controllable and stable state of ancestorhood.

The process of dying begins with Amma's decision to separate the "intelligent" soul from the body. Henceforth, this soul goes to the bush to await the time of death. There it may sometimes be seen by the living as a premonition of the person's impending death. This state of "pre-death" occurs several days, sometimes several years, before the event of death itself. During this time the person still leads a normal life supported by his nyama, or life-force, and his "shadow" soul. Death, which is the sole prerogative of Amma, occurs when Amma strangles the "intelligent" soul. At this time, the "intelligent" soul rejoins the nyama which has escaped from the person's body with his expiring breath, and together they lodge in the corpse's hair. Later, the soul and the nyama enter the funeral shroud and are taken to the home of the deceased, where they reside in a specially carved wooden image.

Liberated by death and reunited with its soul, the nyama anxiously searches for another human host to support its waning life. This is a dangerous time for the family and kinsmen of the deceased, for the nyama starts to attack them in quest for a substitute body. It is a marginal time, disrupted and polluted by death, when the surviving spouse is confined to the house of the deceased and surrounded by prohibitions, lest the spouse's proximity to death contaminate the rest of the living community.

Gradually, a series of rites clears the atmosphere of pollution. At the same time the social and symbolic integrity of the family is restored and the relation between the living and the newly dead is brought under control. On the social level wives, husbands, sons, and other kinsmen reforge the temporarily broken family and lineage structures by taking up the social roles left vacant by the dead. On the spiritual level the family normalizes its relation to the deceased and begins the process of transforming the dangerous, newly dead into a venerated ancestor spirit.

Death alone does not guarantee ancestorhood nor do burial rites confer it. First it is necessary to ritually "reunite" the separated souls of the deceased. Then a pottery shrine, called the "womb of Amma," is made so that offerings can ensure the continued sustenance of the deceased. Finally, the spirit of the deceased must choose several members of the family, called "respondents," who will perform the rites. These will nourish and strengthen the soul of the deceased during its long journey "back to the Creator."

The concluding rite, called *Dama,* brings to an end the long period of mourning and spiritual transition. Because of the expense and effort involved, this ceremony is performed only after several deaths have occurred in a village. It begins with a sacrifice to the Great Mask, which is associated with the origins of death. In the beginning, it is said, people did not die. When they grew old they changed into nommo spirits and continued to live on earth in the form of serpents. One day a deceased chief in the guise of a serpent came across a group of young men who had stolen some sacred fibers. Angered by their crime, he reproached them, speaking in the Dogon language so they could understand, and this was the cause of his death. For, as a spirit he was prohibited from speaking in human terms. By speaking to the men in their language, he cut himself off from the supernatural world and made himself impure, so that he could no longer live in the spirit realm. As a spirit he was also unable to return to the human world; so he died. In this way death came into the world, the result of an infraction of a prohibition, itself provoked by the breaking of a moral rule. Frightened at the serpent's death, the young men made a great wooden serpent, called the Great Mask, as a new abode for the soul of the first dead man. Meanwhile the soul of the dead man chose a child (a "respondent") to perform the rituals which would nourish it in the afterlife, and this is what every departed soul does today.

At the beginning of the Dama a sacrifice is made to the Great Mask and to the soul of the first dead man in expiation for man's responsibility for introducing death into the world. After the sacrifice, a group of masked dancers climbs up to the flat roofs of the homes of the deceased and dances vigorously to frighten away the lingering souls of the dead. In solidarity with the living, the masked dancers defend them from the anxieties and terrors of the newly dead. By means of their frightening dance, they compel the dead to join the assembly of the ancestors in the afterworld. In addition, the masquerade also helps to restore the world order by representing in masked form all the important varieties of men, animals, and things in the universe. After the accumulated disorder caused by several deaths in the community, this dance serves to reestablish order and harmony on the cosmic and social level. As Ogotemmeli has observed, "The masked dancers are the world; and, when they dance in a public place, they are dancing the progress of the world and the world-order" which has been momentarily interrupted by the occurrence of death.[12]

Having been safely ushered out of the world of the living, the souls of the departed begin their voyage northwards to the region called Manga, the Dogon paradise. Their long and arduous journey traverses a way which is said to be the hottest and driest in the Sudan. The journey itself is a form of retribution for misdeeds done on earth. It lasts a minimum of three years, even when Amma takes an interest in helping someone who has led a good life. Often the journey lasts a number of years and requires the ritual assistance of two or three generations of devoted "respondents."

At regular intervals during the voyage, the sex soul of the deceased is "given drink" through offerings at its shrine to slake its thirst and to restore its life-force. In return, the deceased transmits some of its life-force to its living "respondents." Should the soul become forgotten over the years, it may attack its living agents by sickness to remind them of their ritual duties. Afflictions of this kind have the moral effect of strengthening the spiritual bond between the living and the dead.

Once the soul has completed its journey of purgation and reaches the place called Manga, it no longer needs ritual sustenance and can be safely forgotten. Fully redeemed, the soul remains in Manga, eternally at rest, sitting under the trees in the perpetual cool of the evening. For those who have led good lives, there is an even better paradise called Alsana.

The Yoruba

Yoruba eschatology involves a similar threefold process of separation, transformation, and incorporation. Immediately after death, the deceased is provided with a "fare-fowl" for his journey to the sky. The burial ceremony, called "Entry into a covenant with the deceased," both separates the soul of the deceased from the family and gives expression to the family's desire for its continued interest and protection. If the deceased was a family head, he will later be represented by a masked *egun-gun* dancer who will appear to the assembled members of the family and tell them what has happened in the household since his death. He will also rebuke them for their misdemeanors and assure them of his continued watchfulness. If the deceased was an important person in the town or a member of the egungun society, he will have a mask carved and named after him. Under this guise he will appear at yearly festivals together with other ancestors and entertain the townsmen with satirical mimes of local political events.

At a second burial ceremony called, "Bringing the spirit of the deceased into the house," a shrine is consecrated to the ancestor spirit in the family compound. In this way the members of the family restore their ties with the deceased and he with them. At the same time this ceremony also confirms the restructured relationships among the living, especially the social replacement of the deceased by his living heirs.

When the ori, or ancestor soul, of the deceased reaches heaven, it goes before Olorun and Obatala and receives judgment, in accordance with the belief that "All we do on earth, we shall account for kneeling in heaven." If the person's life has been good, the ori will go to the "good heaven," where there is no sorrow or suffering. Here it may choose another destiny and "turn to be a child" on earth again. Indeed, the same ori may be reborn in several people at the same time. But if the deceased has led a bad life, the ori will go to the "bad heaven" of broken potsherds, where everything is unpleasantly hot and dry, and where it will remain forever.[13]

The LoDagaa

The LoDagaa, an agricultural people of northern Ghana, also have a developed eschatology involving a notion of final judgment and rites which incorporate the deceased into the afterlife.

The final ritual phase is accomplished by ceremonies known as the Cool Funeral Beer. They bring to an end the period of transition between a person's death and the assumption of his role as an ancestor. From the moment of death, the soul of the deceased has been hovering about the treetops unable to return to its domestic hut and equally unable to depart for the land of the dead.

During the Cool Beer Ceremony a shrine is carved from a special branch cut from a tree so as to fall into the arms of the deceased's senior son. The branch is said to be his "father" and it represents the soul of the deceased "falling" into his son's possession. Funerary rites are performed over the carved image and food is placed in front of it. In this way the living descent group creates both a material symbol of the departed soul and an altar by which they may communicate with it. Only after this is done can the deceased continue to participate in the system of social relationships as a supernatural being. In this connection the anthropologist Jack Goody observes, "the set of ties of which he [the deceased] was the focus during his life now centers upon his ancestor shrine." Goody goes on to say that, "we may therefore speak of the ancestor cult as a projection of social relationships in a perfectly concrete and meaningful sense." [14]

What makes this "projection" possible is the symbolic substitution of the deceased by a physical representation. Without it there can be no transformation of the deceased into an ancestor spirit.

While this process is taking place within the community of the living, the departed soul begins its journey to the land of the ancestor spirits, known as the country of the Great God. The spirit travels west in the direction of the setting sun. There lies the River of Death, which it must cross before reaching its final destination.

If the person has died by witchcraft, the soul will meet a One-Breasted-Woman who will reveal the name of the witch. If the soul becomes angry and wishes to take revenge, she will joke with the soul and cause it to laugh. This curtailment of the soul's anger prevents its return, and spares the living its destructive wrath. Once the witch who was responsible dies, the two souls will meet on the road and continue their journey together.

When the soul reaches the river, it pays the ferryman the fare provided by the living relatives at the time of the funeral ceremonies.

If the deceased has led a good life, he will travel across the river to the land of the dead. If he has not led a good life, he will fall through the bottom of the ferry and must swim across the river, a task which takes three years. If the deceased owed anything to people who are still living, or if he unjustly denied someone something, then he must wait on the opposite bank until the people to whom he owes things have arrived, so he may pay them. If the person has been a witch, then he is forced to eat his own arm and leg before swimming across another river which has no ferry.

Once in the Land of the Dead, the newly arrived soul is subjected to a number of ordeals whose duration is determined by the gravity of his past misdeeds. First, the person must sit on the top of a tree under the burning sun. "If you had a good heart, you'll sit there for three months; if you had an evil disposition, for six months; if you were a thief, for five months; if you told lies, for four months; if you were a witch, for three years; if you were a rich man, for three years [since others must suffer for the rich to be well-off]." [15] Afterwards the soul must farm very diligently for a length of time depending upon how hard the person worked during his lifetime.

Then a form of final judgment occurs. The women and their progeny are divided into separate kinship groups. If any group contains a great number of witches, liars, or thieves, that group will receive all the bad things in the Land of the Dead, "everything that causes pain and only salt water to drink." Conversely, the good groups will receive all good things, including good food and plenty of rest. The men in these groups do not have to cultivate their food; they have only to think of what they want, and they get it. But those in the bad groups have to laboriously work the fields to get what they want.

What is involved here is the notion of collective judgment. It implies that the moral worth of an individual cannot be evaluated apart from the moral character of the kinship group to which he belongs and to which he is deeply related. This perspective is especially important in small-scale kinship-based societies, such as the LoDagaa, where personal identity is intimately bound up with descent group membership.

Finally, those who belong to the bad descent groups are forced to meditate more deeply upon the rationale behind their fate. Like Job, they ask the Great God to explain the reason for their suffering:

> "Why do you make us suffer?" . . . God replies, "Because you sinned on earth." And they ask, "Who created us?" To which God replies, "I did." And they ask, "If you created us, did we know evil when we came or did you give it [to] us?" God replied, "I gave it to you." Then the people ask God, "Why was it [that] you knew it was evil and still gave [it] to us?" God replies, "Stop. Let me think and find the answer."
>
> God thought for a thousand years and came back; they were still suffering. He said, "The things we were talking about, I want you to tell me of them again." They said, "Why did you say you would make us suffer?" He replied, "Because of the evil deeds you've done." They said, "Who made us that way?" And he replied, "I did." And they said, "Then we can't have done wrong. If you have a child and give him something bad to keep, then whatever he gets hold of as bad as that, it's your fault. So you can't make us suffer." When they had spoken in this way, God put an end to their suffering and set them to farm to get food." [16]

This sparsely eloquent dialogue expresses what for the LoDagaa is a fundamental and paradoxical moral truth: The capacity for evil comes from God, but man is responsible for the exercise of it.

ANCESTORS AND ETHICS

God, however, rarely intervenes in the moral life of men on earth; for the most part, it is the ancestors who act as the official guardians of the social and moral order. This is especially true of small scale, stateless societies whose sociopolitical rules are almost entirely governed by a descent system based on genealogical frameworks. In such societies, ancestors become the focus of religious activity. This is not because of a special "fear" of the dead or because of an especially strong "belief" in souls, but rather because of the importance of the descent system in defining moral relations. The same is true of large-scale kingdoms where dynastic ancestors define the broader national values of the political order. Wherever they are found, the ancestors constitute the basic categories of moral and legal thought. This function raises them above the transitory human level and invests them with sacred significance. Superior and powerful, beyond all human challenge, the rights and duties sanctioned by the ancestors both define and regulate basic social and political relations.

From a purely sociological perspective, the ancestors are a society's projection (in Goody's sense) of its authority system onto the supernatural sphere. Thus, ancestor rites are seen to be a function of a society's need to maintain itself, a ritualization of its rules about social relations. But from the African viewpoint, neither world is a projection upon the other; both are equally real. Society depends as much upon the ancestors as the ancestors depend upon society.

The ancestors do not, however, govern the whole of the moral order. They govern the more narrow sphere of moral obligation. They do not concern themselves with personal moral virtue or with the performance of good deeds but rather with adherence to public norms. In this sense, wicked persons may prosper, even in the eyes of the ancestors, as long as they fulfill the social duties required of them.

The LoDagaa

Among the LoDagaa, the ancestors control social relationships pertaining to the sphere of domestic productivity. They retain general rights in the land and in movable property, such as livestock and agricultural and hunting implements, which they bequeath to their descendants. As a result, a man and his descent group must return to the ancestors part of any wealth which he or they have acquired through the use of their inheritance. Every heir must periodically sacrifice a small portion of his livestock to the ancestors in return for their gift to him. He must also sacrifice other animals which he and his descent group have acquired through the fruits of their labor on the land and through the use of inherited implements, such as spears or drums.

Most offerings are therefore made because they are owed to the ancestors. Furthermore, since the descendants are continually in debt to their ancestors, offerings are made only after an ancestor indicates his desire for repayment by causing some misfortune among the living. As elsewhere, the actual process of the ancestor cult begins among the Lo-Dagaa with a particular misfortune, e.g., an illness, whose cause is diagnosed by a diviner as the revenge of an offended ancestor. This diagnosis includes not only the name of the ancestor but also the type of sacrifice to be offered to him. For example, a man named Jerry inherited his uncle's livestock. This meant that he was also entitled to any other livestock owed to his uncle at the time of his death. Some livestock was, in fact, owing to him in the form of the second bridewealth payment for his uncle's daughter. She had married a headman, called Nibe, and later bore a son. When the child became ill, Nibe consulted a diviner, who attributed the illness to the spirit of his wife's father, Jerry's uncle. The spirit was angry at Nibe because he had not yet paid the rest of the bridewealth cattle. As an ancestor, the spirit was entitled to the Bull of Childbearing. This is the prescribed sacrifice for the maternal forebears when they prove their worth by ensuring the birth of an offspring to one of their daughters; and Nibe had failed to provide it. To express her displeasure on both these counts, Nibe's wife had left his compound and moved back with her child to her father's house. The child's illness was therefore attributed to the two wrongs done by his father. Nibe was thus forced to provide the rest of the cattle, not only to appease his father-in-law's spirit but also to get his wife back. Jerry himself was not directly affected by his uncle's vengeance, but he was indirectly implicated because his descent group should have insisted upon the payment of the bridewealth to the deceased uncle's herd.[17]

This example illustrates the way in which the ancestors control social relationships. Their role is not to instill moral virtue or to promote benevolent acts but to govern the jural relations which keep the social order together.

The Tallensi

Among the Tallensi the ancestors serve a similarly regulative function by controlling the parent-child relation. This relation is based upon the norm of filial piety, and it extends to the ancestors themselves. Just as the child owes his parents, especially his father, complete service and submission, so an adult owes his ancestors the same filial service. The same obedience, economic service, and respect required by a parent on the domestic level are transformed, on the religious level, into the ritual service, sacrifice, and reverence required by the ancestors. It is they who stand behind the rules of filial piety in the parent-child relationship, and they who demand the same recognition for themselves.

The ancestors also take an active interest in human affairs. Like parents, a man's personal destiny ancestors help to determine his overall destiny and fortune in life once he has proved himself worthy of assuming social responsibility. When the human father dies, the ancestors "take charge of the house" and "dwell" on the roof of the father's room in the family compound. Tali ancestors may therefore be regarded as projections onto the supernatural sphere of the parental relationship.

As such, the morality which the ancestors enjoin upon their descendants is not a matter of doing good deeds but of adhering to specific filial duties and to broader kinship norms. The following story of Pu-eng-yii well illustrates this point. In search of greater wealth, Pu-eng-yii left his own patrilineal kin and settled among a rival lineage group. In this way he rejected his own filial status within his lineage. At the height of his prosperity abroad, Pu-eng-yii suffered a bad leg injury in a car accident. He consulted a diviner, who told him that his lineage ancestors had caused the accident. They were angry at him because he had deserted his paternal kinsmen and had repeatedly failed to join with his father's spirit in friendship with them. For this they intended to kill him. However, his destiny ancestors had intervened to save his life. The diviner told Pu-eng-yii that he must apologize to his lineage ancestors to show his filial submission. In addition, he must make a sacrifice of thanksgiving to his destiny ancestors, expressing his filial gratitude to them. He must also return to his kinsmen forthwith and give up his association with the rival lineage. This Pu-eng-yii did, believing that death would be the penalty for refusing.[18]

The Lugbara

Among the Lugbara the ancestors exercise control by regulating disputes about authority, typically between a father and his son and between a lineage head and his subordinates. If the ancestors feel neglected, they intervene on their own initiative, or they may be specifically called upon, usually by lineage elders and heads of family segments, to discipline kinsmen or relatives for insubordination or for almost any form of antisocial behavior.

Typically, the process begins with the occurrence of some kind of misfortune. The stage may already have been set by a public threat to invoke the ancestors against a disobedient person. This was the case when Olimani's son, Okavu, became sick. He had previously rebelled against his father's authority by refusing to share his earnings from migrant labor with his brother Ngoro, as Olimani had urged him to do. Ikavu wanted to save his money to use as bridewealth for his own marriage, but Olimani maintained that as the family head, he alone was entitled to decide how his son's money was used, and he wanted it to pay Ngoro's government tax. An open quarrel ensued in the course of which Olimani uttered the threat, "We shall see," which refers to invoking the ancestors' judgment. Later, when Ikavu fell sick, Olimani consulted a diviner, who confirmed that the ancestors had responded to his invocation against his son.[19]

As this example shows, what was at stake was not simply the morality of the son's behavior but the larger issue of parental authority. The maintenance of this authority is crucial to the order of the family cluster, which is the basic unit of Lugbara society.

MAN AND EVIL

The suffering and misfortune caused by the ancestors and gods are not evils. They are punishments aimed at correcting immoral behavior. Evil is a different matter; its effects are both undeserved and socially destructive.

Unlike Western religions, African thought does not conceive the source of evil to be a fallen god or spirit like Satan or the Devil. Instead, the source of evil is located in the human world among the ambitions and jealousies of men. The source of evil is thus demonic humanity: the witch or sorcerer.

The image of the witch or sorcerer is the image of an inverted or reversed human being. Witches and sorcerers act only at night, fly or walk on their hands or heads, dance naked, feast on corpses, exhibit insatiable and incestuous lusts (despite sexual impotence), murder their relatives, live in the bush with wild, even predatory, animals or excrete and vomit in people's homesteads.

This symbolic image is consistent with the sociological image of the witch or sorcerer as an antisocial person: morose, unsociable, disagreeable, arrogant, ambitious, sly, ugly, dirty, lying envious, shifty-eyed, staring. The witch or sorcerer is thus both an antisocial person and an antihuman being.[20]

Most anthropological accounts of African witchcraft and sorcery concentrate on the social function of witchcraft and sorcery accusations, the way in which they exert social control. Thus Max Marwick has stressed what has been called the "obstetric" function of witchcraft accusations among the Chewa of central Malawi. Such charges help to "dissolve relations which have become redundant"; "blast down the dilapidated parts of the social structure, and clear away the rubble in preparation for new ones"; and "maintain the virility of the indigenous social structure" by allowing "periodic redistribution of structural forces." [21]

But this is not always the case. As Mary Douglas has observed among the Lele of Zaire, "witchcraft is also an aggravator of all hostilities and fears, an obstacle to peaceful co-operation." [22] Victor Turner also notes that "If witch beliefs were solely the products of social tensions and conflicts, they would betray their origins by possessing a more markedly rational form and content." Once they are formed, Turner argues, witchcraft beliefs "feed back into the social process, generating tensions as often as 'reflecting' them." [23]

If witchcraft beliefs are not solely the products of social tension, what is their basis? As Evans-Pritchard demonstrated among the Azande, they are attempts to explain the inexplicable and to control the uncontrollable—undeserved misfortune, death, and illness.[24] But in many societies the roots of witchcraft beliefs go deeper than this. They lie in the notion that evil is a human perversion of the sacred.

Like priests and prophets, witches and sorcerers derive their power from the sacred. The difference is that they exploit it for destructive purposes. As manipulators of sacred power, Nuer witches and ghouls share important attributes with Nuer priests and prophets. They act at night, disobey relatives, break sexual and dietary taboos, dwell in the bush, and pronounce curses. But whereas Nuer priests and prophets indulge in these acts in order to obtain sacred power for the benefit of the community, witches and ghouls commit them for the opposite end in order to destroy the community.[25]

In the same way, Lugbara think of witches and sorcerers as having the inverted characteristics of their hero-ancestors and prophets. Inversion is a sign of sacred power which may be used either to destroy or to create. Hence, the Lugbara ancestors, who created the world, the Europeans who introduced new powers, and the prophets who developed new forms of authority, are all said to be evil (*onzi*). According to Middleton, " 'Evil' is only a very rough translation of this word [*onzi*]; essentially it refers to any power that comes to destroy or change authority and power relations, relations which were originally created by Divinity." However, the world of the witches is not just a different world; it is a mirror world, a complete reversal of the original sacred order. It exists only at the periphery of Lugbara society, at the center of which lie order and goodness. "In other words," Middleton observes, "orderly relations of authority, unchanging from the time they were created by Divinity and the founding ancestors, are 'good'; relations purely of force are 'evil'." [26] What distinguishes witches and sorcerers from prophets is not their "evil" power but their perverse motives and goals. Prophets, like Rembe, act from divine inspiration and use their power to renew society. Witches act from envy or jealousy (*ole*) and use their power to cause illness and to kill.

The difference between witches and sorcerers indicates another dimension of the concept of evil. Unlike sorcerers, witches inherit their power and need not use any special means, such as sacred objects, to employ it. Thus in some societies anyone may be a potential witch. Among the Dinka, Lienhardt found that witches were mainly anonymous and that witchcraft accusations were rarely made. Yet the Dinka harbored genuine witchcraft fears and suspicions which to Lienhardt appeared to be expressions of personal feelings towards others:

> . . . a man who easily thinks himself hated is one who easily hates, and . . . a man who sees others as bearing malice towards him is one who himself feels malice. This is the situation of witches. . . . The night witch is an outlaw because he embodies those appetites and passions in every man which, if ungoverned, would destroy any moral law. The night witch may thus be seen to correspond to the concealed intention, the amorality and hence the opposition to those shared moral values which make community possible, of the unique self, existing and acting as such. . . . It is understandable that he should be associated with deformed and imperfect creatures, who by their very nature cannot be full members of society.[27]

Thus Dinka witchcraft concepts represent an assessment of human nature in general. "For them," comments Mary Douglas, "hell is other people." It is the "unique individual," the utter egotist whose behavior subverts the social order. In a kinship-based society evil is self-willed individualism which exploits society for personal ends. This image is well summarized in the statement that "the witch is demonic *precisely because he is so resolutely finite, banal,* self-determined" in a world governed by sacred and social forces.[28]

NOTES

1. Mbiti, *African Religions*, p. 282.
2. Deng, *Tradition and Modernization*, p. 26.
3. *Ibid.,* p. 282.
4. Griaule and Dieterlen, "The Dogon," in *African Worlds*, ed. D. Forde.
5. Griaule and Dieterlen, *Le Renard Pale*, pp. 36-39.
6. On this important concept, see Idowu, *Olódùmarè*, chap. 13; William Bascom, "Yoruba Concepts of the Soul," in *Men and Cultures*, ed. A. F. C. Wallace (Philadelphia: University of Pennsylvania Press, 1960).
7. Samuel Oyruloye Abogunrin, "Man in Yoruba Thought" (Bachelor of Arts thesis, Department of Religious Studies and Philosophy, University of Ibadan, 1972), p. 45.

8. MEYER FORTES, *Oedipus and Job in West African Religion* (Cambridge: Cambridge University Press, 1959), pp. 26-81.

9. *Ibid.*, p. 80.

10. ROBIN HORTON, "Destiny and the Unconscious," *Africa* 31, no. 2 (1961).

11. GERMAINE DIETERLEN, *Les ames des Dogon* (Paris: Institut d'ethnologie, 1942), pp. 92-126, 140-47; Marcel Griaule, *Masques dogons* (Paris: Institut d'ethnologie, 1938), pp. 775-801.

12. MARCEL GRIAULE, *Conversations with Ogotemeli* (London: Oxford University Press for the International African Institute, 1965), p. 189. Used with permission.

13. IDOWU, *Olódùmarè*, chap. 14; PETER M. MORTON-WILLIAMS, "The Egungun Society in South-Western Yoruba Kingdoms," in *Proceedings of the Third Annual Conference of the West African Institute of Social and Economic Research* 3 (Ibadan: University College, 1956); ISAAC O. DELANO, *The Soul of Nigeria* (London: T. Werner Laurie Ltd., 1937), p. 117; ULLI BEIER, "The Egungun Cult," *Nigeria Magazine*, no. 51 (1956); SAMUEL EMILOLA AJAYI, "Egungun Festival in Oyo Division," (Bachelor of Arts thesis, Department of Religious Studies and Philosophy, University of Ibadan, 1970).

14. JACK GOODY, *Death, Property and the Ancestors* (Stanford, Calif.: Stanford University Press, 1962), p. 228.

15. *Ibid.*, pp. 372-73.

16. *Ibid.*, p. 373.

17. *Ibid.*, p. 401.

18. FORTES, *Oedipus and Job*, pp. 54-55.

19. JOHN MIDDLETON, *Lugbara Religion* (London: Oxford University Press for the International African Institute, 1960), pp. 162-63. Used with permission.

20. See LUCY MAIR, *Witchcraft* (New York: McGraw-Hill Book Company, 1969), pp. 37-47.

21. M. G. MARWICK, "The Social Context of Cewa Witch Beliefs," *Africa* 22, no. 4 (1952), 232. As quoted in MARY DOUGLAS, "Techniques of Sorcery Control in Central Africa," in *Witchcraft and Sorcery in East Africa*, ed. John Middleton and E. H. Winter (London: Routledge & Kegan Paul Ltd., 1963), p. 124.

22. "Techniques of Sorcery Control," p. 141.

23. TURNER, *Forest of Symbols*, p. 114.

24. E. E. EVANS-PRITCHARD, *Witchcraft, Oracles and Magic Among the Azande* (Oxford: The Clarendon Press, 1937), chap. 4.

25. BEIDELMAN, "Nuer Priests and Prophets," pp. 380, 401-2, 405.

26. JOHN MIDDLETON, "Witchcraft and Sorcery in Lugbara," in *Witchcraft and Sorcery in East Africa*, ed. John Middleton and E. H. Winter (London: Routledge & Kegan Paul Ltd., 1963), pp. 271-72.

27. R. G. LIENHARDT, "Some Notions of Witchcraft among the Dinka," *Africa* 21, no. 4 (1951), 317-18. As quoted in MARY DOUGLAS in Introduction to *Witchcraft: Confessions and Accusations*, ed. Mary Douglas (London: Tavistock Publications, 1971), p. xxxv.

28. EVAN M. ZUESSE, "On the Nature of the Demonic: African Witchery," *Numen*, 18, fasc. 3 (1971), 238.

6

Religion and Rebellion

The imposition of colonial rule was generally accomplished through military means and often involved protracted and brutal wars. After this period of initial violence, African response to colonial rule was largely peaceful, though it was filled with constant tension and resentment. There were, however, some scattered uprisings and resistance movements in which African resentments and aspirations became overtly expressed in militant form.

What is distinctive about most of these rebellions is their religious impulse. Many were led by religious figures and most were sustained by powerful religious symbolism.[1] The Sudanese Madhiya described in the next chapter was one of the most successful. In this instance the religious impetus was provided by Islam. Elsewhere, Christianity played a similar role, as in the Nyasaland Rising of 1915, examined below.

But it would be wrong to assume, as many scholars have, that with the coming of colonialism initiative for religious leadership passed entirely to the adherents of Islam and Christianity, leaving the traditional religions broken and passive in their wake. On the contrary, traditional religious authorities continued to assert themselves throughout the colonial period, even in the political sphere.

We have already seen how Shona, Nuer, Dinka, and Lugbara prophets drew upon indigenous religious traditions in responding to the colonial situation. The same is true of the Maji Maji and Mau Mau movements described in this chapter. Contrary to what has been assumed (often in the face of counter evidence), prophetic leadership did not result from the arrival of Arabs and Europeans and the introduction of Islamic and Christian notions of time and history. Nor were prophetically inspired resistance movements mere backward-looking, atavistic struggles against the forces of change.[2] They were forces of change in their own right and introduced new levels of organization and new symbols of unity and power. Of course, they failed to accomplish their immediate goals (all were suppressed and defeated), but they did not fail to achieve a broader purpose. In most instances, these rebellions stimulated a new historical awareness which later issued in the nationalistic consciousness of the pre-independence period.

155

THE MAJI MAJI REVOLT

The Maji Maji revolt of 1905–1907 was a mass resistance movement waged against colonial rule in southern Tanzania, then known as German East Africa. It began in the Matumbi Hills area near the coast approximately 100 miles south of Dar-es-Salaam, where a particularly oppressive cotton-growing scheme had been forced upon the local population. The revolt soon spread inland to other areas where there were other grievances against the German administration.[3]

The revolt was precipitated by a diviner named Kinjikitile. As G.C.K. Gwassa points out, Kinjikitile was not only possessed by the divination spirit Lilungu but was also "possessed by the Hongo spirit, which was itself very powerful, and it was believed that the Hongo spirit had been sent to Kinjikitile by the superior divinity, Bokero." [4] This link to the more widely known divinity Bokero enabled Kinjikitile to transcend the confines of the traditional diviner's role, and to become a prophet with an ideological appeal to people far outside his ethnic origins.

Kinjikitile's notoriety began at Ngarambe where he was taken by the spirit into a river pool and emerged unhurt and wearing dry clothes. He told the people that "All dead ancestors will come back; they are at Bokero's in Rufiji Ruhingo. No lion or leopard will eat them." He also ridiculed Europeans, calling them "red potter's clay" and "ugly fish of the sea," and proclaimed in song that "we [Africans] are all freemen, all by ourselves."

The movement began with a "whispering campaign" which secretly circulated the following message about Kinjikitile's prophecy:

> This is your year of war, for there is a man who has been possessed. He has Lilungu [divine power]. Why? Because we are oppressed by the *akidas* [Arab police captains]. We work without payment. There is an expert at Ngarambe to help us. How? There is *Jumbe* [chief] Hongo . . .[5]

In response to this message people came to Ngarambe to see for themselves. There they obtained *maji*, "sacred water," which would make them invulnerable to the white man's bullets. This began the second phase of the movement. The pilgrims arrived at Ngarambe in clan "detachments" led by their own military leaders. Kinjikitile confirmed these leaders and equipped each of them with war medicine and a large amulet. During the night of their arrival, the "detachments" practiced military drill under their leaders. The next day they departed, fortified with maji and with the message of the impending revolt.

When the rains came and impeded travel to Ngarambe, Kinjikitile sent local leaders (*Waganga*) as ambassadors to the outlying regions. They took maji with them and began to organize and train the people in military drill and discipline. In several instances, the movement developed millennial expectations, and undermined the authority of some local chiefs who were not strong enough to resist it. Kinjikitile had told his ambassadors not to begin fighting until he commanded it:

> "The Germans will leave," he said, "There will definitely be war. But for the time being go and work for him. If he orders you to cultivate cotton or to dig his road or to carry his load do as he requires. Go and remain quiet. When I am ready I will declare war." [6]

No doubt Kinjikitile realized that he needed time to build a coordinated organization. But after waiting several months, his lieutenants became impatient. Full of millennial expectation, they chafed at the delay:

> This *Mganga* said he would declare war. . . . Why then is he delaying? When will the Europeans go? After all we have already received the *dawa* [the maji] and we are brave men. Why should we wait? And yet we continue to dig and clean his roads, carry his loads, grow his cotton and carry bales to Kilwa. And always he continues lashing at us with his *kiboko* [whip] on our behind . . . And yet he was not one of us . . . he was not our ruler.[7]

In July 1905, some of the maji delegates in Kinjikitile's own area uprooted cotton, and the revolt began. Kinjikitile had inspired it, but it was taken out of his hands by local leaders. His prophecy and his sacred maji had proved too strong. The spirit of independence was too great for the people to wait until the movement was fully prepared. Kinjikitile was betrayed to the authorities, seized, and sent to the gallows.

The movement spread northwards, then to the south, and finally to the east, where it culminated in the assault of an estimated 8,000 Pogoro and Mbunga on a German garrison in August of 1905. The rebels were defeated, but the movement continued on a minor guerrilla scale in the south, and the Emergency was not lifted until 1907.

It is estimated that 75,000 Africans died in the uprising, mostly from famine as a result of the German scorched-earth policy. At Ngarambe and elsewhere people felt betrayed, and they denounced Kinjikitile:

> The swindle of Kinjikitile
> He deceived people
> To go to Ngarambe
> To drink the *maji*.

Having suffered a devastating defeat, the movement towards nationalism declined among the peoples of the south. During the years prior to independence, they saw a connection between Maji Maji and nationalism and were at first suspicious of joining the new political party TANU (Tanganyika African National Union):

> When TANU began some people cried, "This is how Maji Maji began. We failed to drive away the Europeans by war. How can we do this by a mere fifty cents? Do not believe these, they are cheats. It is another Kinjikitile."

Yet TANU's widespread popularity reminded them of Maji Maji and the spirit of freedom it kindled:

> The movement of Kinjikitile and his maji went around like TANU. . . . It is true that a source of salvation cannot hide itself from the people. . . .[8]

Though Maji Maji failed as a religious prophecy, it had awakened nationalistic aspirations. This was accomplished through the religious dimensions of Kinjikitile's movement. He utilized traditional religious ideas and institutions to mobilize action across ethnic boundaries in an area without prior political unity. He drew upon the widely known water cult of Bokero, ancestor and possession cults, and hunting and warfare magic. He universalized these symbolic forms into a national religion preached by his emissaries to diverse ethnic groups. What he lacked was a firm political base on which to carry out his religious leadership. This did not develop until much later with the rise of national political organizations.

In this connection, it is significant that President Nyerere described his national leadership as a fulfillment of the aspirations started by Maji Maji. Speaking before the United Nations Fourth Committee in 1956, Nyerere recalled the Maji Maji revolt and described its spirit of liberation:

> They [the Maji Maji] rose in a great rebellion not through fear of terrorist movement or a superstitious oath, but in a response to a natural call, a call of the spirit, ringing in the hearts of all men, and of all times, educated and uneducated, to rebel against foreign domination. . . . Its [TANU's] function is not to create the spirit of rebellion but to articulate it and show it a new technique.[9]

JOHN CHILEMBWE AND
THE NYASALAND RISING OF 1915

In contrast to the Maji Maji revolt, the Nyasaland Rising of 1915 was a brief local affair, inspired by a native Christian leader. Yet even the British protectorate governor referred to it at the time as opening "a new phase in the existence of Nyasaland," a phase which led eventually to independence and to the creation of the new state of Malawi in 1964.[10]

As the leader, high priest, and principal martyr of the revolt, John Chilembwe afterwards became Nyasaland's symbol of the new African. He also became part of pre-independence folklore, a martyred messiah who would return again in some miraculous way to deliver his people from British rule. Today, he is Malawi's foremost national hero. He is the "patriot" who returned from America to share his lot with the oppressed people of his homeland. His name has also been associated with the old Malawi empire from which modern Malawi takes its name. According to a brief history written to commemorate independence in 1964, "Another term of respect in the old Malawi empire was Chilembwe, a name that was to loom large in the later history of the country." [11] The name and example of Chilembwe thus stand at both ends of Malawi political history.

Why did Chilembwe, a successful missionary who had been educated in America, lead an uprising, and why did it fail? Thanks to a masterly biography of Chilembwe by George Shepperson and Thomas Price, some answers can be given to these questions. Consideration of them reveals a great deal about the nature of settler-colonialism and Christianity in Central Africa and the African response to it. It also sheds light on the relation between black Americans and Africans in the colonial period and their understanding of each other.

In 1892, when Chilembwe was about twenty years old, he befriended a missionary named Joseph Booth and became his first convert and household servant. Booth himself was a radical idealist who came to Nyasaland independently of any church or missionary organization to establish a self-supporting, African-led mission dedicated to the principle of "Africa for the Africans." His plan was anathema to the Scottish missionaries and settlers who dominated the area, and he immediately aroused suspicions by paying Africans higher wages and by taking them into full partnership in his project. Booth also became a much resented critic of Nyasaland's settler-land policy, taxation, and the use of punitive expeditions against the local people.

In 1895, Booth took Chilembwe along on a visit to America and introduced him to an educated and aggressive black leadership of the kind Chilembwe had never known before. He also met other Africans who were imbibing the radicalism of the black American scene. One of these was the Zulu leader John Dube, whose opinions paralleled those which Chilembwe was later to adopt when he returned to Africa: "The reason that the Christian native [in Africa] has a bad name, among the lower classes of Europeans especially, is that he does not submit to being treated like a dog." [12]

Black Americans taught Chilembwe about their heritage in America and eventually launched him on a path to a new black consciousness in colonial Africa. From American blacks Chilembwe learned of the slave revolts in the U.S. prior to the Civil War, when black men rose up, futilely but symbolically against their oppressors, and he learned of successful slave revolts in the Caribbean and Latin America. Chilembwe was also in daily contact with black separatist churches which were experiencing a new-found integrity of self-leadership and mission to the black world. In addition, Chilembwe was exposed to the growing debate between Booker T. Washington and William Edward Burghardt Du Bois about the proper means for black advancement. Washington's conservative program of gradual social advancement through hard work in blue collar jobs resembled the industrial education program of the Nyasaland missionaries. In contrast to this was Du Bois' militant demand for the acquisition of rights through political activism.

After two years of training at the newly founded Virginia Theological Seminary and College, Chilembwe was forced to leave America because of an asthmatic condition and return to Africa. He did so as a missionary on behalf of the Foreign Mission Board of the black National Baptist Convention. In the eyes of the American Negro Baptist Church, Chilembwe's missionary venture would show white America that the black man could succeed in a cause which the white man believed was uniquely his own: spreading the Gospel of Christian righteousness to the world. It would be a protest against black Americans' loss of rights at home. This point was emphasized in the first report of Chilembwe's mission to the national Baptist Convention:

> We serve notice on the world to-day that there will be no more begging for our own . . . there will be no more courting of favours, there will be no more divorcing ourselves from this soil, there will be a standing until either Shiloh or our rights as American citizens come. Nothing but the gospel of Jesus Christ ruling in every heart, in black and white alike, will bring these rights. . . .[13]

When Chilembwe returned home to throw in his lot with his countrymen's colonial servitude, he arrived, clothed in full clerical respectability more than a decade before the neighboring Scottish missions would ordain their first African ministers. For his countrymen, Chilembwe was the example of the new African, educated on a par with most Europeans, and therefore equal to them.

During the period of 1900–1914, Chilembwe erected a sizable mission establishment which he called the Providence Industrial Mission, modeled upon Booth's idea of a self-sustaining church group. In the beginning he had the help of three black American Baptist missionaries, all of whom were resented by the colonials, who feared they might incite Africans against British rule. Indeed, they might well have done so, for these American blacks, like Chilembwe himself, were dedicated to the goal of African leadership. One of them, the Rev. Landon N. Cheek, wrote home the following observations to an American newspaper:

> The negroes are looked upon with suspicion. These brethren here need a
> start in civilization, and that at most is a few ploughs and farming
> implements. The plough and the mule are unknown. While the native
> bends down with a hoe-handle about one and one-half feet in length and
> digs in the earth, making his hills for corn and beans, we cannot expect
> him to dream of heaven and a higher ideal. When the village hut-life
> is broken up and the Government will run schools with some of the
> taxation money used for standing armies and Imperialism, we can hope for
> a great change. Will we really hope for this change from any other race
> [but the Negro]? Can we expect the foreigners in Africa to plead for
> higher wages and more education while they still sell barter goods to
> natives and get the majority of them for seventy-five cents per month? Is
> there no power to save? Who will make a move for justice and mercy? [14]

As Chilembwe built up his mission, he hardly appeared to be following a radical course. All his energies went towards Booker T. Washington's goals of education, cleanliness, good clothes, the learning of manual skills (sewing, masonry, agriculture), reading, and writing. In time, he also built an impressive brick church rivaling the Scottish mission headquarters in Blantyre. These things were the pride of his mission converts, and Chilembwe occasionally invited Europeans to see what he had accomplished. But he received little recognition. Constantly short of funds, Chilembwe tirelessly trained his converts as best he could, giving them outward skills and inner pride, so that they, or some of them, could slowly move up to higher socioeconomic positions. Indeed, Chilembwe had attracted to his church the few African entrepreneurs in Nyasaland, who served as examples for the rest of his followers.

Throughout this period, Nyasaland's socioeconomic problems were growing. The land question—which had always been a primary problem in East and Central Africa, where European settlers were given African land—was further exacerbated in 1912, when the government imposed a hut-tax on the population. As Africans saw it, they were forced to pay rent on their own land for a government they did not want. Half of this tax could be rebated by a month's work on a settler's land. Africans saw this to be simply a way of providing white settlers with slave labor. In 1914 Chilembwe secretly advocated the non-payment of this tax. In the same period, a local famine was severely aggravated by the introduction of European cash crops which Africans sold off without saving enough for themselves. The colonial government also used Africans to fight European battles on African soil. In 1900 Nyasaland Africans were conscripted for the British Ashanti wars in West Africa. Later, at the outbreak of the First World War, Africans were conscripted for defense against the neighboring territory of German East Africa.

There were also stirrings of independence in the religious sphere as several educated Africans formed their own separatist churches in Nyasaland. These churches sprang from the American Watch Tower and Adventist missions. As World War I approached, the separatist preachers raised millennial hopes about the abolishment of the present order in Nyasaland. When the predicted millennium did not occur, many of Chilembwe's followers who were influenced by these beliefs may have looked to him for a more militant solution. In addition to their resentment against the subservience in which Africans were held, there was the growing frustration induced by European education. This affected only a few, but it was deeply felt by the emerging class of African leaders (school teachers, government clerks, small business men, church preachers), of whom Chilembwe was the most outstanding example. After the Rising was over, the missionaries would have to answer to the settlers' charge that "to educate natives very highly and then not find suitable employment for them is a mistake." [15] Chilembwe's rebellion had been planned and led by mission-trained Africans who felt they did not deserve the permanent contempt colonial society showed them. They had become marginal men, educated and skilled beyond their peasant origins but denied any meaningful political or economic role in colonial society.

Adding to these internal tensions were other events outside Nyasaland which helped to increase the strain. There were the Maji Maji rebellions in neighboring German East Africa in 1905–1907 and the Zulu rebellions in British Natal in South Africa. Some of Chilembwe's acquaintances had traveled to these areas and had seen the similarities between conditions in Nyasaland and those which led to these revolts. Chilembwe himself would not have been unaffected by the news of these uprisings. But it was the outbreak of World War I which tipped the scales of his relation to the colonial government. It drew the British forces in Nyasaland to the northern German border, away from the south, where the government and Chilembwe were located. It also resulted in high casualty rates among the African troops on both sides.

In late November, when the fighting was still going on, Chilembwe wrote a denunciatory letter to the *Nyasaland Times*. The issue in which it was printed was immediately suppressed. In this letter Chilembwe expressed a feeling of deep frustration. He wrote with biting sarcasm and implied an ultimatum:

> . . . We have unreservedly stepped to the firing line in every conflict and played a patriot's part with the Spirit of true gallantry. But in time of peace the Government failed to help the underdog. In the time of peace everything for Europeans only. And instead of honour we suffer humiliation with names contemptible. But in time of war it has been found that we are needed to share hardships and shed our blood in equality.
>
> . . . It is too late now to talk of what might or might not have been. Whatsoever be the reasons why we are invited to join in the war, the fact remains, we are invited to die for Nyasaland. We leave all for the consideration of the Government, we hope in the Mercy of Almighty God, that someday things will turn out well and that Government will recognize our indispensability, and that justice will prevail.
>
> John Chilembwe
In behalf of his countrymen.[18]

Instead of immediately arresting Chilembwe, the government made plans to deport him at some later date. Almost certainly Chilembwe knew of this. In the meantime, he felt the suppression of his letter to be the last straw. If his legitimate protest could not be heard, he would try other more desperate means. He is said to have begun "strong" (i.e. militant) teaching to his followers. He told them to be ready for impending "trouble." He read them Acts 20:29-32, in which Paul speaks his farewell to the Ephesians before going to Jerusalem to vindicate himself before hostile authorities. "After my departing shall grievous wolves enter among you, not sparing the flock . . . ; now brethren I commend you to God . . .".[17] With these words of Paul, Chilembwe prepared his followers for his departure and for the uncertainties of the future. According to various accounts, Chilembwe repeatedly emphasized "It is better for me to die than to live."

It is unclear whether Chilembwe planned to take over the country, as some of his followers and the government later believed, or whether he intended his revolt to be simply a form of protest. He did, however, draw up an extensive plan of attack and spend three to four months preparing for it. His own followers would lead the main attack in the south against the government and the settlers. In the north, some of the Ngoni were to attack and march south to link up with him. In the southeast, other tribal chiefs were to take over a small government center.

But nothing succeeded as planned. One of Chilembwe's forces did manage to kill the hated foreman of one of the major estates along with two other settlers, but another group failed in their attempt to obtain the necessary arms from a trading store near Blantyre. Chilembwe probably realized that even with the colonial army still in the north, his plan was too shaky and did not have the broad popular support it needed. Hence, he may have revised his original aims and settled for a symbolic gesture.

This is essentially the conclusion reached by Shepperson and Price in their biography. They argue that Chilembwe was somewhat confusedly aiming at two different goals simultaneously, at a political revolution and, if that failed, at a gesture of protest. These two aims perhaps represent different phases in Chilembwe's thought. Knowing that he would fail, he may have opted for the latter goal and sent forth his men "to strike a blow and die," though they still attempted to follow the larger plan of action.

But the ambiguous and circumstantial nature of the evidence has led other scholars to different interpretations. Robert Rotberg has stressed the protest theme and the "personal quest for martyrdom and psychological redemption," thus agreeing with Franz Fanon's therapeutic theory of violence.[18] Given Chilembwe's deeply distressed and frustrated situation, this interpretation has some psychological validity. But it does not accord with the extensive scope and planning involved in the Rising. It also draws heavily upon George Simeon Mwasa's account of the Rising, which, though based upon the testimony of a leading participant, takes some liberties with Chilembwe's words and puts contrived speeches in his mouth.[19] A more religious interpretation is suggested by Jane and Ian Linden, who object to the political interpretation of Shepperson and Price and to the psychological view of Rotberg. They argue that Chilembwe and his lieutenants acted primarily on the basis of millennial beliefs, hoping to actively assist in bringing about an expected Final War and a new age.[20] This, too, would explain why Chilembwe and his followers rebelled in the face of almost certain defeat and why they proceeded in a rather disorganized way. It would also explain why members of other Christian sects did not join in: either they did not possess millennial convictions, like the Scottish and Catholic converts, or, if they did, like the Watchtower and Adventist converts, they conceived their role to be a passive one, waiting upon God's own direct intervention. But even granting some millennialist influence, Chilembwe himself does not appear to have acted from specifically millennialist motives. This, however, is not to say that Chilembwe acted primarily for political reasons. On the contrary, it seems clear that he acted out of a Christian commitment to God's righteousness. As he wrote in his letter on behalf of his countrymen: ". . . we hope in the Mercy of Almighty God . . . that justice will prevail." In the final analysis, this seems to be the point that Chilembwe and his followers most fervently wished to make.

THE MAU MAU UPRISING

Like the Maji Maji rebellion, the Mau Mau uprising in Kenya during 1952–1956 helped to shape the political processes leading towards national independence, which was achieved in 1963. In the eyes of the colonial government, however, the Mau Mau movement was nothing more than a "subversive movement based on the lethal mixture of pseudo-religion, nationalism and the evil forms of black magic" aimed at turning Kenya into a land of magic and murder.[21] But far from being a "nativistic" cult, looking in no sense to the future, the Mau Mau movement helped to create a new national consciousness and to set the stage for the politics of independence.[22]

Fundamental to understanding the rise of Mau Mau and the political consciousness it created are the traditional religious rites and symbols which articulated and sustained its aims in the Kikuyu lands. Mau Mau ideology was, to be sure, aimed at the secular goal of political freedom, but this goal was framed largely in terms of traditional Kikuyu moral and religious values. Moreover, while the aim of Mau Mau was the organization of militant rebellion, this, too, was significantly implemented and maintained by traditional symbolic and ritual means. Here I shall focus on two symbolic components which played a fundamental role in the early phases of the uprising: the land and the ritual oaths.

The Importance of the Land

The political purpose of the Kenya African Union (KAU), the major independence party, was the liberation of Kenya from British rule. Its slogan was the nationalist cry of *Uhuru*, "Freedom," for all Kenya's people. Translated into traditional terms, Uhuru meant the re-acquisition of the land from the colonial government and from the European settlers. For land, especially among the Kikuyu who dominated the KAU, symbolized political autonomy and identity. President Kenyatta himself has described the traditional meaning of land in Kikuyu society:

> [Land tenure is] the most important factor in the social, political, religious, and economic life of the tribe. As agriculturalists, the Gikuyu people

depend entirely on the land. It supplies them with the material needs of
life, through which spiritual and mental contentment is achieved.
Communion with the ancestral spirits is perpetuated through contact with
the soil in which the ancestors of the tribe lie buried. The Gikuyu
consider the earth as the "mother" of the tribe, for the reason that the
mother bears her burden for about eight or nine moons while the child
is in her womb, and then for a short period of suckling. But it is the
soil that feeds the child through lifetime; and again after death it is the
soil that nurses the spirits of the dead for eternity. Thus the earth is the
most sacred thing above all that dwell in or on it. Among the Gikuyu the
soil is especially honoured, and an everlasting oath is to swear by the
earth (*koirugo*).[23]

As this statement implies, land serves the symbolic function of
representing the living social and historical identity of the people who
live on it. By virtue of their ownership of the land, the members of a
descent group participate not only in the historical past and future of
their own lineage, but also in the past and future of the Kikuyu nation
as a whole. For all Kikuyu are descendents of the original ancestors
Gikuyu and Mumbi, to whom the land was first given by the Kikuyu
supreme god, Ngai or Mogai, who dwells on Mt. Kenya. Kenyatta records
this tradition:

According to tribal legend, we are told that in the beginning of things,
when mankind started to populate the earth, the man Gikuyu, the
founder of the tribe, was called by Mogai (the Divider of the Universe),
and was given as his share the land with ravines, the rivers, the forests,
the game and all the gifts that the Lord of Nature (Mogai) bestowed on
mankind. At the same time Mogai made a big mountain which he called
Kere-Nyaga (Mount Kenya), as his resting place when on inspection tour,
and as a sign of his wonders. He then took the man Gikuyu to the top
of the mountain of mystery, and showed him the beauty of the country
that Mogai had given him. . . . After the Mogai had shown the Gikuyu
the panorama of the wonderful land he had been given, he commanded
him to descend and establish his homestead on a selected place which he
named Mokorwe wa Gathanga. Before they parted, Mogai told Gikuyu
that, whenever he was in need, he should make a sacrifice and raise his
hands towards Kere-Nyaga (the mountain of mystery), and the Lord of
Nature will come to his assistance.[24]

Kikuyu ownership of the land was therefore given the highest
sanction. Local and national rights to the land were established in the
ancestral times by the supreme god himself. Moreover, the Kikuyu
were also given a prophetic promise. Ngai would come to their assistance
in time of national need.

Prior to the arrival of the British in Kikuyuland, Ngai took a
famous Kikuyu diviner named Cege wa Kibiru to an unknown land

and showed him what would happen in the near future. Strangers with oddly colored skins would come carrying sticks which spat fire. They would build an iron snake which belched flames as it traveled to and fro across Kikuyuland between Lake Victoria and the sea. Unable to persuade Ngai to avert these dangers, Kibiru came back and told the Kikuyu his prophecy. He also told them not to resist, for their spears were no match for European guns. Above all he warned them not to part with their lands. Other seers gave similar warnings.[25]

What these accounts indicate is that under the pressure of momentous social change, the Kikuyu diviners developed a truly prophetic sensitivity. With this attitude, the Kikuyu prepared for their historic confrontation with the colonial government over the issue of their land and freedom.

It is understandable then, that Kenyan nationalism framed its prophetic ideology in terms of the peoples' alienation from their tribal land. Recovery of the land was the major symbolic thrust of the KAU flag, and the flag became a prophetic statement both of KAU's national goals and of the means to achieve them. This is how Kenyatta explained the three colors of the flag to a crowd of over 30,000 people at a rally in 1952:

> Black is to show that this is for black people. Red is to show that the
> blood of an African is the same colour as the blood of a European, and
> green is to show that when we were given this country by God it was
> green, fertile and good but now you see the green is below the red and is
> suppressed.[26]

Since government police were recording Kenyatta's every word, he could not fully explain the color symbolism. But his meaning was clearly grasped. According to one Kikuyu who was present at Kenyatta's speech, "What he said must mean that our fertile lands (green) could only be regained by blood (red) of the African (black). That was it! The black was separated from the green by red; the African could only get his land through blood."

The political songs sung at the nationalist rallies also expressed the issue of freedom in terms of the mythical and prophetic traditions about the land. One song began with the words,

> Gikuyu and Mumbi, what do you think?
> You were robbed of your land, you didn't sell it.

The chorus of another song proclaimed:

> God blessed this land of ours, we Kikuyu
> And said we should never abandon it.[27]

Since in traditional terms nationalism meant the recovery of the God-given land, the Kikuyu believed their cause had the highest moral and religious sanction. The concepts of land, God, and Kikuyu political identity were thus symbolically fused together in the prophetic ideology of the nationalist movement.

This can be seen in one of the symbolic procedures of the oath-taking rites of the Mau Mau, the fighting wing of the KAU. "Naked, I stood before Mt. Kenya, holding high a dampened ball of soil (dampened by milk, animal fat and blood—the most important dairy products) in my right hand and the other ball against my navel with the left hand," repeating the vows of the oath in the name of Ngai and in the memory of Gikuyu and Mumbi.[28]

The earth mixed with cattle products symbolizes the basis of Kikuyu life and identity. Remembering the mythical injunction to call upon Ngai in times of need, the resistance fighters faced Mt. Kenya, where he dwelt, and held aloft with the right hand the symbol of their identity, which they pledged to reclaim. In the left hand they held the same symbol against the sacred root of their own personal center.

Oath-Taking Rites

Of course, symbolism alone was not sufficient to recruit, organize, and launch a militant struggle against the colonial government. For this the Kikuyu needed an effective instrument to forge a militant and revolutionary force. This instrument was the Oath of Unity, later supplemented by the more militant Warrior or Platoon Oath.

To most Europeans, the oath-taking rituals seemed to be a "nativistic" return to the savage and barbarous past, at best a pathetic and desperate attempt to unite the people by appealing to the superstitions of their tribal heritage. This was an uninformed and prejudicial judgment. The important question to consider is why such oaths were used by the Mau Mau and why they were effective. The oaths were first of all ceremonial and symbolic, but they were also very much more. Referring to the general Oath of Unity, one member of the resistance put it this way: "Though the oath clung on Kikuyu traditions and superstitions, yet the unity and obedience achieved by it was so great that it could be our only weapon to fight against the white community." [29] The question is, how could a ritual oath serve as a "weapon" for political liberation?

The answer is not difficult to grasp. The effectiveness of the oath lay in its traditional symbolic and social force. Initiation and oath-taking rituals were two primary instruments for creating and sustaining social and moral solidarity in traditional Kikuyu culture, and they continued to be used by the Kikuyu and other related societies (Embu and Meru) under the colonial regime. The Mau Mau oathing rites were rites of passage involving personal vows of loyalty to the resistance backed by powerful mystical sanctions, and ultimately by Ngai himself.

The oathing rites included four main features of the traditional male initiation rites: the ceremonial archway, wrist bands, lustral blessings, and collective vows. The archway was made from bound banana and maize stalks and sugar cane stems. In the traditional rites, this arch served as a medium through which the ancestor spirits were appeased. No one but the initiates could pass under the arch without suffering supernatural harm. The band of goat's skin was placed on the right wrist of those taking the oath. This was obtained from goats provided by the initiates and sacrificed during the rites. Towards the end of the oathing rite, the initiates were sprayed with a special mixture of beer and honey from the mouth of the officiant as a form of blessing. The climax of the Mau Mau initiation was the swearing of vows of duty and loyalty. These, too, were part of the traditional initiation pattern:

1. If I am called upon at any time of the day or night to assist in the work of this association, I will respond without hesitation; And if I fail to do so, may this oath kill me.
2. If I am required to raise subscriptions for this organization, I will do so: And if I do not obey, may this oath kill me.
3. I shall never decline to help a member of this organization who is in need of assistance; And if I refuse such aid, may this oath kill me.
4. I will never reveal the existence or secrets of the association to Government or to any person who is not himself a member; And if I violate this trust, may this oath kill me.[30]

In the Mau Mau ceremony, the vows took the form of ordeals. They played an important role both in the traditional Kikuyu legal system and in the operation of the Kikuyu council. In both instances, the oath involved the performance of certain otherwise forbidden procedures which could kill the person swearing the oath if he later broke his vows and thus had sworn falsely. These ordeals were traditionally used in cases of the most serious criminal offenses—murder, sorcery, and theft. They were also used to ensure that the elders of the tribal councils would conduct their proceedings and govern their territories along proper lines. It is in the latter sense that the Mau Mau used these mystically sanctioned oaths to enforce strict adherence and loyalty to the clandestine group. The supernatural sanctions of the traditional oath thus provided the symbolic instrument for Mau Mau unity, helping to create and sustain moral solidarity among the rebels under the most adverse conditions.

In addition, the oaths provided the occasion for teaching the members of the resistance about the goals of the movement, which always formed a significant part of the ritual. One Mau Mau leader, Waruhiu Itote (general "China"), has emphasized this point.

> Oath-giving ceremonies were . . . more than ritual initiations. We also used them for the opportunity they gave to educate new recruits about the history of their country, about our objectives, about military tactics and so on. As an important experience in their lives, the oathing ceremony was an excellent time to impress upon our young men the reasons for our struggle.[31]

The total effect of the oathing ceremonies was to give the person taking the oath the experience of being reborn into a new society and ultimately into a new age in which his frustrated aspirations would finally become realized. The following account expresses this feeling:

> My emotions during the ceremony had been a mixture of fear and elation. Afterwards [while hiding outside] in the maize I felt exalted with a new spirit of power and strength. All my previous life seemed empty and meaningless. Even my education, of which I was so proud, appeared trivial beside this splendid and terrible force that had been given me. I had been born again and I sensed once more the opportunity and adventure that I had had on the first day my mother started teaching me to read and write. The other three [companions] in the maize were all silent and were clearly undergoing the same spiritual rebirth as myself.[32]

Many, however, were forced to take the oath against their will, for it was sometimes used as a recruiting technique. Those who were coerced still felt its power and sought traditional means of removing it. Hence the government devised oath "cleansing" ceremonies administered by traditional Kikuyu diviners. However, for the majority the oath expressed deep feelings of commitment and provided a means of sanctifying them. As Itote put it,

> Participating in the ritual ceremony gave people a chance to attach their feelings and devotion to a sacred part of their own society; they did not have to take an oath to know that they were suffering and that they wanted to do something to help themselves, but rather many people took the oath just to show how *deeply* they felt these things.[33]

In addition to this general Oath of Unity, there was a Warrior or Platoon Oath which was administered only to young men of "warrior" age who constituted the actual fighting wing of the resistance. Since this oath has been claimed by some writers to have been "bestial" and "depraved," even by Kikuyu standards, it is worth considering briefly.

It was a powerful oath precisely because it broke conventional Kikuyu standards. Besides using one of the most powerful oathing instruments, the thorax of a goat, the oath also involved the imitation of an act of sodomy with the carcass of a slaughtered male goat. This was typical of certain traditional oaths which employed similar sexual acts and symbolism. These were intentional violations of acknowledged taboos. The more highly tabooed such acts were, the stronger and more binding the oath became. In other words, the oath was powerful because it was so vile and repulsive to the Kikuyu. Therein lay its effectiveness, especially upon uneducated peasants for whom the traditional world view was very much alive.

In 1952–53 at the height of the movement most Kikuyu had taken the Oath of Unity. An estimated 15,000 fighters had also taken the Warrior Oath and had found their way into the Abedare and Mt. Kenya forests. But conflicts of leadership and lack of communication and supplies kept the guerrillas from being an effective fighting force. Against them the British deployed over 10,000 soldiers and 40,000 police and reserve guard. Kikuyuland itself was sealed off and all Kikuyu were moved into specially constructed and fortified villages. In addition 30,000 Kikuyu were rounded up and removed to detention camps. Denied any basis of support, the forest fighters were defeated as a military threat by the end of 1954. The Emergency was lifted in 1956.

Although the movement created considerable social and economic upheaval, its principal effect was to form the prelude to political independence and to provide legends for the future. Today, twenty years after the Emergency, the Mau Mau episode has become part of Kenya's national myth-history. At first, President Kenyatta was forced to diminish the significance of the movement for the sake of national unity and European relations. As a predominantly Kikuyu movement, the experience had created intense antagonisms with Kenya's other ethnic groups which did not support it, and it created major leadership conflicts. Immediately after independence Kenyatta tried to offset these divisions by proclaiming that "we all fought for Uhuru." The possibility of renewed hostilities also threatened to scare away much needed European investment in the new nation. However, in 1971 Kenyatta began a deliberate policy of reviving the memory of the Mau Mau experience. Historical sites connected with the Mau Mau events were named and marked. Major streets in cities and towns were renamed for dead Mau Mau leaders, who were now called "freedom fighters." Living Mau Mau fighters were also given frequent recognition in the newspapers and at public festivals. At present this process is continuing, and it is a sign of Kenya's growing unity. Although the movement was mainly Kikuyu in terms of its symbols and membership, it was basically a nationalistic struggle with which many Kenyans now wish to identify as they create their own version of modern Kenyan history.[34]

NOTES

1. For accounts of several such movements, see ROBERT I. ROTBERG, *Rebellion in Black Africa* (London: Oxford University Press, 1971).

2. T. O. RANGER and I. N. KIMAMBO, eds., *The Historical Study of African Religion,* pp. 18-19; T. O. RANGER, "Connexions between 'Primary Resistance' Movements and Modern Mass Nationalism in East and Central Africa, Part I," *Journal of African History* 9, no. 3 (1968).

3. JOHN ILIFFE, "The Organization of the Maji Maji Rebellion," *Journal of African History* 8, no. 3 (1967).

4. G. C. K. GWASSA, "Kinjikitile and the Ideology of Maji Maji," in *The Historical Study of African Religion,* ed. T. O. Ranger and I. N. Kimambo (Berkeley: University of California Press, 1972), p. 205.

5. GWASSA, "Kinjikitile," p. 212.

6. GWASSA, "Kinjikitile," p. 212; cf. G. C. K. GWASSA and JOHN ILIFFE, eds., *Records of the Maji Maji Rising, Part I,* Historical Association of Tanzania, Paper no. 4 (Nairobi: East African Publishing House, 1968), pp. 9-10. Used with permission.

7. GWASSA, "Kinjikitile," p. 214; cf. GWASSA and ILIFFE, *Records,* p. 12.

8. GWASSA and ILIFFE, *Records,* pp. 28-29.

9. *Ibid.,* p. 29.

10. Cited in GEORGE SHEPPERSON and THOMAS PRICE, *Independent African* (Edinburgh: The University Press, 1958), p. 396.

11. Cited in GEORGE SHEPPERSON, *Myth and Reality in Malawi* (Evanston, Ill.: Northwestern University Press, 1966), p. 16.

12. Cited in SHEPPERSON and PRICE, *Independent African,* p. 92.

13. Ibid., p. 123.

14. *Ibid.,* pp. 137-38.

15. *Ibid.,* p. 363.

16. *Ibid.,* pp 234-35.

17. Cited in G. SHEPPERSON, "The Place of John Chilembwe in Malawi Historiography," in *The Early History of Malawi,* ed. B. Pachai (London: Longman Group Ltd., 1972), p. 418.

18. R. I. ROTBERG, "Chilembwe's Revolt Reconsidered," in *Rebellion in Black Africa,* ed. Robert I. Rotberg (London: Oxford University Press, 1971). See FRANTZ FANON, *The Wretched of the Earth,* tr. Constance Farrington (New York: Grove Press, Inc., 1965).

19. Published as *Strike a Blow and Die,* ed. Robert I. Rotberg (Cambridge: Harvard University Press, 1967).

20. JANE and IAN LINDEN, "John Chilembwe and the New Jerusalem," *Journal of African History* 12, no. 4 (1971).

21. Cited in A. M. MACPHEE, *Kenya* (New York: Frederick A. Praeger, Inc., 1968), p. 108.

22. See C. G. ROSBERG, JR., and J. NOTTINGHAM, *The Myth of the "Mau Mau": Nationalism in Kenya* (New York: Frederick A. Praeger, Inc., 1966), p. xvii.

23. JOMO KENYATTA, *Facing Mt. Kenya* (New York: Vintage Books, Random House, Inc., 1962), p. 22; cf. JOHN MIDDLETON and GREET KERSHAW, *Kikuyu and Kamba of Kenya,* Ethnographic Survey of Africa, East Central Africa, Part V, rev. ed. (London: International African Institute, 1965), p. 48.

24. *Facing Mt. Kenya,* p. 5.

25. KENYATTA, *Facing Mt. Kenya,* p. 43; cf. GODFREY MURIUKI, *A History of the Kikuyu 1500-1900* (Nairobi: Oxford University Press, 1974), pp. 137-38.

26. DONALD L. BARNETT and KARARI NJAMA, *Mau Mau From Within* (New York: Monthly Review Press, 1966), pp. 75, 76. Copyright © by Donald L. Barnett. Reprinted by permission of Monthly Review Press.

27. *Ibid.,* pp. 75-76.

28. *Ibid.,* p. 131.

29. *Ibid.,* p. 121.

30. *Ibid.,* pp. 58-59.

31. WARUHIU ITOTE, *"Mau Mau" General* (Nairobi: East African Publishing House, 1967), p. 283.

32. JOSIAH MWANGI KARIUKI, *"Mau Mau" Detainee* (London: Oxford University Press, 1963), p. 27.

33. *"Mau Mau" General,* p. 283.

34. See ROBERT BUIJTENHUIJS, *Mau Mau: Twenty Years After—The Myth and the Survivors* (The Hague: Mouton, 1973).

7

African Islam

In the eleventh and twelfth centuries Islam spread from north Africa across the Sahara via the trade routes into the western and eastern Sudan. Further east, it moved up the Nile into the eastern Sudan and down the sea lanes of the Red Sea and Indian Ocean into the East African coast. Carried by traders and itinerant scholars, Islam first penetrated these regions not as a proselytizing religion seeking converts but as the religion of a foreign merchant class bent primarily on trade. In this initial phase, Islam was seldom adopted as a comprehensive system of belief requiring total conversion. It was only partially assimilated alongside traditional African religious and social patterns.

The first to adopt the new religion in the western and central Sudan were the ruling classes of the great empires of Ghana, Mali, Songhay, and Kanem-Bornu, and the rulers of the central Habe states. For these classes, Islam presented many religious and social advantages. It offered potent Arabic charms and techniques of divination, new ideas of civil law and government, heightened social prestige, and strong mercantile support for the ruling elite. In the eastern Sudan, Islam spread more pervasively among clan-based confederacies and among the pastoralist peoples of the Eastern Horn. It provided these societies with new sources of religious and political unity and with an impetus for territorial expansion. Only along the eastern coast was Islam initially confined to the foreign peoples (Persians, Arabs, and Indians) who originally brought it there.

In the eighteenth and nineteenth centuries a number of local Muslim reformers arose in the western and central Sudan with the desire to purge Islam of its predominantly African features. This led to a *jihad,* or Holy War, and to the establishment of the Islamic ideal of a theocratic state in several areas. These regional movements of religious nationalism were sometimes tinged with millennial expectations. In the eastern Sudan a reformer rose up against the northern Egyptian government and declared himself to be the messianic Mahdi. In part, the reformers were inspired by the mystical teachings and puritanical practices of the Sufi religious orders which carried great influence in many regions.

Yet there was much in Islam which was compatible with traditional African religious and social customs, and much was retained in Islamized form. The real agents of this synthesis were the local Muslim clerics, called *malams* or *marabouts.* They were the prayer leaders, jurists,

175

teachers, and ritual specialists, and they created the eventual assimilation between Islamic law and African tradition.

The history of Islam south of the Sahara is therefore a history of several phases and types of religion. It is a history of developing ortho-doxy and of developing synthesis in which Islam both strengthened and blended with local communal and ritual values and permanently widened the African religious and social world. The result was not a confused syncretism, but a variety of new religious and cultural syntheses which bear the unique character of sub-Saharan Islam.[1]

REFORMATION AND MESSIANISM
IN THE SUDAN

The Shehu Usuman dan Fodio.

By the eighteenth century the large Hausa-speaking population liv-ing in the vast savannah lands of what is now northern Nigeria were organized into seven kingdoms known as the Habe states. The chiefs of these states were nominal Muslims who did little more than extend patronage to local Muslim traders and scholars and observe a few Muslim rites and festivals, while allowing their Hausa subjects to remain largely unconverted. Settled among the Hausa were small numbers of Fulani cattle-herding clans which were more thoroughly Islamized than their Hausa neighbors. Most of the Fulani clans lived a semi-sedentary pastoral-ist life scattered in small communities among the agricultural Hausa. But one clan, the Toronkawa, was unique in devoting itself entirely to seden-tary scholarly pursuits, and was noted for its Islamic piety and learning. Into this clan the Muslim reformer, the Shehu Usuman dan Fodio, was born, and he was nurtured on its high Islamic ideals. Like his kinsmen, the young Shehu received his learning at the feet of local teachers who were his relatives, and later from several renowned masters. Under their guidance he steeped himself in the study of the Koran, Arabic religious poetry, Islamic Law, and the teachings and deeds of Muhammad (*hadith*). At this time, the study of hadith was particularly important, for there was a growing debate among Fulani and Hausa about the place of Islam in Sudanese society. The hadith told what the early Muslim community was like under the authority of the Prophet, and this provided the norm whereby all other Muslim communities could judge the orthodoxy of their existence. As the basis of Islamic political theory, the hadith also provided the scholars with grounds for examining their own sociopolitical situation.

According to Mervyn Hiskett's perceptive biography, the young Shehu was most influenced by the study of Islamic mysticism (Sufism) taught by the Qadiriyya Order to which he belonged. As a young man the Shehu led an austere and ascetic life, often going out into the desert alone to pray and meditate. From the beginning he seemed to be modeling his life upon that of the Prophet to whom he felt personally drawn. In one of his early poems he expressed a deep longing to visit the Prophet's tomb at Medina and thus to achieve spiritual communion with him:

> There is no other good than following Muhammad,
> He is the most generous, his favours cover all mankind, nay,
> All God's creation is beneath Muhammad.
> Were I to visit Tayba [Medina], I would achieve the height of my ambition,
> Sprinkling myself with the dust of Muhammad's sandal.[2]

In later life the Shehu's mystical devotions were rewarded by visions. These heightened his sense of chosenness as the reformer of Islam:

> And I was able to see the near like the far, and hear the far like the near, and smell the scent of him who worshipped God, sweeter than any sweetness; and the stink of the sinner, more foul than any stench. And I could recognize what was lawful to eat by taste, before I swallowed it; and likewise what was unlawful to eat. . . . That was the favor of God that He gives to whom He will.

The Shehu was not the first to talk about reforming Sudanese Islam, but he was the first to preach it actively. In 1798 he embarked upon missionary journeys into the countryside, preaching mainly to Fulani Muslims, but also to Hausa nobility and peasants. He exhorted them towards more orthodox faith, "calling people to religion" so his brother wrote, while "destroying customs contrary to Muslim law." In this early phase, many "repented and travelled to him in groups when he returned to his country, listening to his preaching, and God caused them to accept."

Against the local spirit cults, the Shehu preached the all-embracing transcendence and immanence of Allah;

> All created things had a beginning and He who gave that beginning was God. . . . He is not like created things. He has no body and no semblance of a body. He has neither direction nor place. He is now even as He was before creation. He has no need or room for a helper. He is one by Himself with all His qualities and all His works. He is powerful with His own power. He wills by His own will. He knows by His own knowledge. He is living by His own life. He hears; He sees; He speaks. . . .

In contrast to the more mundane orientation of African religiosity, the Shehu taught the cultivation of inner piety as the way to salvation in the next world:

> You know the qualities of the soul are of two kinds. One kind are those of destruction; the other are those of salvation. The qualities of destruction are: self-conceit; vanity; jealousy; envy; covetousness; ostentation; vainglory; seeking wealth if it is for display; evil desire and evil thinking against Muslims. These are the qualities of destruction. They are in origin of evil character, and it is the duty of every Muslim to keep away from them, and cultivate the qualities of salvation, which also are ten in number. He shall make repentence to God; and purify his heart with good works; and be patient; and flee from worldliness; and trust God; and leave his affairs to God; and be obedient to God's commands; and desist from all wickedness; and fear God; and think reverently of God.

Although the Shehu stressed the mercy of God, his underlying message concerned the judgment to come. He vividly described the sensuous rewards of the Islamic Paradise, "there shall be brought to them goblets of flowing drink that is white and sweet. . . . there shall be women for them, pleasant to look upon." And he portrayed the fiery damnations of Hell, "He who doeth not what God has commanded and keeps not far from what God has forbidden, in truth he shall fall into the Fire. . . . Those who commit idolatry shall have clothes of fire made for them, and hot water shall be poured over their hands."

What was "forbidden" and "idolatrous" included a wide range of traditional Hausa ritual and social custom. Despite their nominal adherence to Islam, the Hausa continued to practice spirit possession and animal sacrifice. They also ate pork and let their women appear in public unveiled, and they engaged in prohibited degrees of marriage, practiced matrilineal inheritance, and danced to drums—all of which were anathema to the Fulani purists. But the Shehu was willing to distinguish between misguided believers, who mixed African tradition with Islam out of ignorance, and deliberate perverters of the faith, whom he considered infidels subject to damnation. Those whom the Shehu especially singled out were untrained Hausa "scholars" who compromised the Law to accommodate their wealthy Habe patrons. It was they, the Shehu said, who "follow avarice in everything incumbent upon them. And who have no knowledge and who do not ask for it. And each of them delights in his own interpretations." Still, it was difficult to draw the line between sinners and infidels, and the Shehu's followers generally did not. In their minds all who mixed Islam with African practices were infidels, and this equation served as the primary justification for the later Fulani jihad against the Hausa.

The political side of the Shehu's preaching was aimed at the tyranny of the Habe government. He complained about such practices as the arbitrary confiscation of peasants' cattle and livestock, the custom of Habe chiefs' taking their subjects' daughters, widespread bribery and judicial corruption, and the selling into slavery of fellow Muslims. These charges probably reflected popular grievances among the Hausa peasants and among the Fulani pastoralists, who resented control by the Habe lords. Chafing against restrictions upon water sources and grazing lands, the Fulani had already raised several small rebellions against local Habe chiefs at the time of the Shehu's preaching.

After several years of the Shehu's preaching, armed conflict erupted. The half-Muslim Habe chiefs could not conform to the Shehu's reforms without at the same time losing the support of the Hausa population, whose religion and traditions they sought to uphold. The Shehu's party also realized that Islam could not be fully reformed while it remained subject to non-Islamic African law. The only solution was to create an Islamic state governed by an Islamic leader.

Following the example of the Prophet, the Shehu led his followers on a religious *hijra,* or flight, out of his own country, in imitation of Muhammad's hijra from Mecca to Medina in the face of religious persecution. Previously, the Shehu had seen a vision of both the Prophet and Sheikh 'Abd al-Quadir al-Jilani, the twelfth-century founder of the Sufi Qadiriyya order, in which the Sheikh al-Jilani had presented him with the "Sword of Truth" to accomplish his reform. For ten years the Shehu had wielded the "Sword" through preaching. Now, fortified by another vision from al-Jilani, he prepared to unleash the "Sword" in a jihad against his enemies, as Muhammad had done against the unbelievers in Mecca. The Shehu's jihad began in 1804 and lasted until 1812. The result was the Fulani conquest of most of the Habe rulers and the establishment of an Islamic state centered in the Sokoto Caliphate, which governed most of the present territory of northern Nigeria.

In the course of the jihad, the Shehu came to perceive himself not only as the leader of a local campaign but also as a participant in a wider historical process. He saw himself as the last of the expected "Renewers of the Faith" who would usher in the Mahdi. The Mahdi was the Messiah of popular Muslim belief, who would restore the unity of Islam before the Day of Judgment and the end of the world. In the upheaval of the times, some believed the Shehu himself to be the Mahdi. But he denied it, saying only that "I am the one who comes to give good tidings about the Mahdi."

After the Shehu's death in 1817, his son Muhammad Bello succeeded to the Caliphate of Sokoto and consolidated the Hausa states into a Fulani empire which lasted until British occupation in 1907. Today, many of Sokoto's Islamic institutions still remain, especially its written law and court system. An even greater legacy lies in the area of religion and culture. Before the jihad, Islamic religion and learning were confined to a small Arabic-speaking elite; afterwards, Islam spread widely in both Arabic and vernacular form, permanently changing the nature of Hausa society and civilization. Thus it has been said of the Shehu that "He found Islam in the central Sudan corrupt and persecuted; he left it purified and supreme. He found the Fulani landless and insecure; he left them a ruling aristocracy." [3]

The Mahdi Muhammad Ahmad

The Shehu and his followers were not the only Islamic community looking forward to the arrival of the messianic Mahdi. In 1881 a Muslim leader named Muhammad Ahmad appeared in the eastern Sudan and declared himself to be the awaited Mahdi. In a brief period, his army of followers overthrew Egyptian rule in the southern Sudan and established an Islamic state which lasted until 1899. Western scholars have generally dismissed the Mahdi's revolt as a reactionary struggle against the advancing forces of modern civilization, a throwback to tribal times. It is now evident that the Sudanic Mahdia is better seen in the broader context of Islamic religious nationalist movements, such as the Shehu's, as attempts to carry forward the process of Islamization on the fringes of the Muslim world. [4]

Like the Shehu, the Mahdi was trained in a puritanical Sufi order (called the *Sammaniya*), and he was given to visionary experiences. One of these visions, which he later wrote down, convinced him of his prophetic mission:

> An angel descended from Heaven bearing in his hand a green crown. He saluted the Prophet [Muhammad] and addressed him as follows—'Your Lord salutes you and sends you His blessings, and He informs you that this is His crown of victory, and He orders you to give it to him [Muhammad Ahmad] with your own hands.' Thereupon the Prophet presented it to the Mahdi, saying 'There is no victory save from God.'
> . . . 'God has guarded you by His angels and prophets. No nation shall be able to face you in battle, whether of the human race or of the race of genii [demons].' [5]

As further proof of his Mahdiship, Muhammad Ahmad pointed to a mole on his right cheek and to the mysterious "banner" of light that his followers saw above them in battle, both of which were traditional signs of the promised Mahdi. Muhammad Ahmad also modeled his rebellion on the example of the Prophet. He led his followers on a hijra to the Nuba hills of Kordofan, where he "discovered" the mythical Mt. Masat on which the expected Mahdi was supposed to appear. He named his followers the Ansar, or "Helpers," the title by which the Prophet called his supporters at Medina; and he led them on a jihad which culminated in the conquest of Khartoum and in the founding of a Mahdist state.

The Mahdi's message was both religious and political. He called for the reform of the community of Islam and for its liberation from northern Egyptian rule. Although the Egyptians were Muslims, the Mahdi regarded them as backsliders in the Faith, no better than the Ottoman Turks whose rule preceded them. Under the Egyptians, Arab emigrants moved into the southern Sudan to administer and exploit the region. Slave armies, used to suppress the profitable slave trade, devastated areas of resistance. Government favoritism set tribes and religious sects against each other. Urban centers developed, inequitable taxation increased, and local tribal structures began to break down. Corrupt and ineffectual administration set in, and the whole region became ripe for rebellion. The Mahdi needed only a few startling military victories to make him the focus of a massive revolt.

But the Mahdi, like the Shehu, was primarily a religious leader who left the generalship of his armies to other men. He preached primarily about the vanities of the world and the renewal of faith in God:

> Ye faithful worshippers of God, look on the things of this life with a piercing eye. Be sure of the nothingness of it, turn your hearts to things above, to the way of everlasting life. Devote yourselves to God, and abstain from worldly pleasures and enjoyments. God Himself, in the Holy Koran, has said, "This life is but amusement. The life to come is the true life." Consider this, O man of reason. . . . Prepare always for your own salvation, repent, and ask God's forgiveness for having ever indulged in the trifles and enjoyments of this world. . . . Each man is responsible for his own soul, be not therefore negligent. . . . This world is for the infidels. . . . Forsake it, therefore, and choose that which God wishes. . . .

The key to the Mahdi's message was the recognition of his Mahdiship. To deny him was to deny Islam itself, as the Mahdi warned in a report of one of his visions:

> The Prophet [Muhammad] then repeated several times that if any man doubts my message, he sins against God and His Apostle. And should anyone oppose me, destruction will come upon him, and he will lose all hope in this world and in the world to come.[6]

At this culminating point in history the Mahdi was the only channel to God, and all who recognized him took an oath of allegiance to the Mahdi himself. This oath well summarizes the religious and moral bonds within the Mahdia and the political protest that gave rise to the movement:

> We have sworn allegiance to God and His Apostle, and we have sworn allegiance to you, in asserting the unity of God, that we will not associate

anyone with Him, we will not steal, we will not commit adultery, we will not bring false accusations and we will not disobey you in what is lawful. We have sworn allegiance to you in renouncing this world and abandoning it, and being content with what is with God, desiring what is with God and the World to come, and we will not flee from the *jihad*.[7]

Allegiance to the movement also meant adherence to a new moral code drawn up by the Mahdi which governed personal dress, prayers, public ceremonies, the conduct of women, and smoking and drinking. In addition, the Mahdi promulgated a new administrative code which defined the duties of chiefs and subjects and the procedures of justice.

Although the Mahdi claimed to be the expected messiah who would rule the world before the final day of judgment, the emphasis of his preaching fell on his mission of reform rather than on his millennial role as the prophet of the End. He saw himself primarily as a leader who would bring into being a new religious and political community, stretching ultimately beyond the Sudan to Cairo, Mecca, and Theran. The idea of the future millennium was thus secondary to that of the creation of a renewed Islamic community in this world.

Like the Shehu, the Mahdi used Islam as a way of galvanizing local communities into a wider polity. But behind this nationalistic thrust was a more fundamental religious vision. It was the vision of a new man, a man like the reformers, who was both African and Muslim. For the reformers, the major features of this new man were his religious intensity and his universal moral outlook. He was to live under a universal Law, not merely the local law of his own society, and this Law would bring him into a wider moral community which transcended all social and cultural divisions. At the same time, he was to apply this Law to every dimension of his personal life, so that it became the new measure of himself before God. For both reformers, local variations in ritual and custom did not matter as long as they did not compromise the Law and the personal commitment to God. Widespread acceptance of this vision was the main accomplishment of the reformist movements, and it permanently changed the religious character of the societies which adopted it. African Muslims would remain African, but in joining Islam they linked themselves to a wider historical community under one Law and to a personal faith in one God.

TEACHING AND PRACTICE

Essential to the community of Islam are its teachers and scholars. Without them the religious vision of the reformers would never have taken hold and Islam would never have succeeded in making a fruitful synthesis with African culture. By teaching the Koran the scholars maintain a basic level of literacy which is essential to the Faith, and by studying Islamic Law they shape and preserve the conformity between local practice and the general precepts of the Prophet's religion. As an educated elite, the scholars maintain links with the wider Islamic world. In this way they unite their often dispersed minority communities to the larger centers of Islamic orthodoxy in North Africa and the Near East. In the absence of any official priesthood, the scholars also perform the rituals of the Faith. They officiate at naming ceremonies, marriages, funerals, and public festivals, guiding the ceremonial life of the people in the path of Islamic Law and tradition.

As a group the scholars vary widely in training and competence and in the services they perform. Usually two grades are recognized. Those belonging to the lower grade possess only a rudimentary knowledge of the Koran, consisting of a few memorized chapters and prayers. These scholars become diviners and charm-sellers whose skill depends mainly upon the ritual manipulation of written verses of the Koran. Higher-grade scholars study long and deeply in Koranic exegesis and in Islamic Law and theology. At the conclusion of ten to fifteen years of study they receive a certificate, called an *isnad*. This records the chain of scholarly tradition in which they have been taught and authorizes them to wear the turban as the sign of their profession.[8]

Most Muslim boys attend elementary Koran schools from the ages of six to fourteen years. Here they learn portions of the Koran, certain prayers, and elementary reading and writing in Arabic. The pupils pay no fees, apart from a gift their parents make to the teacher at the end of their studies, for teaching is not done for profit but for the glory of the Faith.

A few students continue to a higher level of study which begins when they attach themselves to more learned teachers. In Kano, Nigeria, such teachers usually hold their schools in the entrance huts of their compounds. Seated on a raised couch of piled carpets and surrounded by a library of Arabic texts, the Kano teachers instruct groups of about thirty students. In front of the teacher lies the paraphernalia of his profession, a shallow tray of sand in which he draws letters, numbers, and diagrams, a wood-burning brazier, and a gourd spittoon. The method of instruction is uniform. The teacher reads aloud an Arabic text, then repeats a standard commentary in Hausa or Fulfulde (the language of the Fulani), while his students listen and make notes and occasionally ask questions. In this way the advanced students receive rigorous training in classical Arabic and in Islamic law and theology. The curriculum consists, first of all, of memorizing the whole of the Koran in addition to the rules of exegesis and the standard commentaries. Through the study of

Arabic prose texts and panegyric poetry, the scholars also learn about the life and mission of Muhammad, including the revelation of the Koran, the battles he fought, the miracles he performed, and his establishment of Islam in Mecca. All of this is told and studied in a manner of reverence and worship. At the core of their studies lie Islamic legal theory *(fiqh)*, which covers civil, criminal, and religious law, and the hadith, the record of the sayings and acts of the Prophet. Thus the students become adept at applying the Shari'a, the code of legal and social regulations, and at guiding their people in the way of the Prophet. They also study astronomy, which determines the farming cycle and the dates of religious festivals. Many also learn some form of Sufi teaching and mystical practice.[9]

But the scholarly elite is only a tiny minority among the mass of unlearned and less orthodox believers. Despite the success of the reformist movements, it would be misleading to speak of the process of Islamization as a process of "conversion" from African belief to orthodox Islamic religion. A gradual blending took place between African and Islamic elements, making a new configuration which assumed different forms in different areas. None of these forms can be called orthodox if what is meant is strict conformity to Islam as practiced in North Africa or the Near East. For the large proportion of African Muslims, the "five pillars" of the Faith—profession of the One God, reciting the five daily prayers, observing the Fast (Ramahdan), giving alms, making the pilgrimage to Mecca—remain an unattained ideal. In actual practice, being a Muslim means attending Koran school, going to the Friday prayers, keeping the fast of Ramahdan, participating in public festivals, and observing some of the rules governing naming and funeral ceremonies, marriage, inheritance, and the conduct of women.

In the northern Nigerian territory of Nupe, S. F. Nadel observed that the five basic duties of Islam are reduced to two: the saying of the daily prayers and the keeping of the Fast. The declaration of faith in the One God is largely ignored, for the Nupe regard "Allah" as but another name for their own remote supreme deity Soko; hence Allah's uniqueness seems of no special importance. The giving of alms on ceremonial occasions is a common though not obligatory practice, while pilgrimage to Mecca is such a remote possibility for most people that it is hardly regarded as one of the duties of the Faith. Yet, as Nadel points out, Islam does set the basic tone of Nupe life. Formalized Arabic prayers at home and in the mosques are utterly distinct from the informalism of traditional African religious language, even though the Nupe supplement them with their own vernacular prayers to Soko concerning more immediate events such as harvest and rain. Daily prayers and weekly mosque services also set a routine of personal piety which is fundamentally different from traditional group ceremonials held on infrequent festival occasions or in times of specific need. However, the Nupe celebrate only three of the seven orthodox Muslim festivals—the Muslim New Year (Muharram), the feast which closes Ramahdan (Id al-Fitr), and the feast commemorating the month of pilgrimage (Id el Kibir)—thus conforming the Muslim ritual calendar to the traditional level of frequency. Moreover, although the Islamic calendar is the occasion for these ceremonies, their meaning is more locally defined. In keeping with traditional Nupe town festivals, the Id ceremonies are focused on the Emir at the capital and on his representatives at the villages. They emphasize the solidarity of Nupe towns through "display of kingship" and "confirmation of political allegiance." The New Year festival also follows the traditional pattern and stresses the symbolic reversal of the social order through rites of youthful sexual license.[10]

Entirely traditional rites may also persist in Islamic form, as for example, in the *bori* spirit possession cult among the Muslim Hausa. Prior to the Shehu's jihad, the bori were the clan deities of the Hausa. As the guardians of the family compounds and personal welfare, they were the chief agents in the cause and cure of illness, and sacrifices were constantly made to them. Many people were specially initiated into the bori possession cult as the "sons" and "daughters" of the bori, and these initiates performed colorful public possession dances, exhibiting the personality and behavior of the spirits. After the Fulani jihad, the bori cult was officially banned and displaced to the periphery of Muslim Hausa society. It became a women's cult, reflecting the changed circumstances of Hausa women under Muslim law. Traditionally, Hausa women had enjoyed a higher status than they now do as Muslims. Some held political offices and owned farms, and many employed themselves in the market place. Divorce was also easily obtainable. Under Islam, Hausa women lost these rights. Excluded from public life, they became confined to the home as legal minors and economic dependents in a Muslim society dominated by men. Through the bori cult, Muslim women are able to assert a measure of social independence against their husbands, for husbands generally defer to wives possessed by the bori spirits, and try to meet their demands for clothes, jewelry, and money, lest they suffer reprisal and public embarrassment. A woman may also escape a difficult marriage by taking refuge in the bori cult house to await a legal hearing against her husband. Meanwhile, she may partake in the community's activities of public bori dancing and prostitution. The bori spirits themselves exhibit a wide range of Islamic and Hausa social roles involving status, political power, and display in public life, all of which are normally denied to women. Some spirits are kings or chiefs or warriors, others are Islamic scholars and judges, some are farmers and hunters, others are animals of the bush; all are powerful agents of illness and demand appropriate recognition and payment. For instance, one Muslim spirit, Mallam Alkali, is a learned judge, whose medium sits on a mat, counting heads and "hearing" cases; he prescribes medicines and charms to supplicants and asks them to offer sacrifices and give away food and alms. The women who manifest these spirits thus vicariously participate in a world of power and status which is otherwise forbidden them.[11]

Although Muslim scholars condemn the bori cult as unlawful, they nevertheless admit to the reality of the spirits and to the effectiveness of their power. As elsewhere, the scholars regard these traditional spirits as local forms of Arabic *jinn* spirits which are recognized in the Koran. According to the Koran, some of the jinn were converted by Muhammad's preaching; others are destined for Hell because they rejected the Prophet. This distinction between Muslim and non-Muslim bori has been adopted by the Hausa; there are "good" Muslim spirits which live in the towns and cities and "black" or "evil" non-Muslim spirits which live in the rural areas. The continuing vitality of these spirits also stems from their relation to more immediate and personal areas of experience, such as illness, which are largely excluded or ignored in the orthodox worship of Allah and his Prophet. "To this extent," I. M. Lewis has observed, "all these peripheral cults [of traditional gods], whether condemned or condoned, may be seen as an attempt to bridge the gap between the moral intensity of traditional personal and social interaction and aspirations—with their customary mystical overtones—and the lofty and fatalistic concepts of Muslim eschatology." [12]

Although Islam is a universal religion focused on a transcendent God, it has been fairly tolerant of elements of traditional religion which deal with the microcosmic level of experience. As Robin Horton points out, "[Islam] has never itself renounced a concern with the explanation prediction, and control of space-time events" characteristic of traditional African religions. Thus Islam permits the practice of divination and ancestor worship performed in the name of Allah; for example, the Somali cult of the clan ancestors has become a cult of Muslim clan saints. At the same time, Horton suggests that in the context of modern social and cultural change Islam has played a unique "catalytic" role in orienting African thought more towards certain universal concepts which were already present in the traditional religions, such as the idea of a supreme god and the notion of destiny and judgment. Far from being abandoned, much of traditional religion has thus been remolded along Islamic lines, while much of Islam has been molded along African lines. The result is a new system which is maximally open at both the transcendent and the ritual levels. As Horton has put it, Islam "has accepted that those who come to the mosque form a continuum rather than a band of total converts; and it does not nag excessively at those who lie towards the pagan end of the continuum." [13]

THE BROTHERHOODS

Like the reformist movements the formation of Islamic religious brotherhoods is a concrete instance of this catalytic process. At once Islamic and African, they constitute a new social and religious response to times of acute historical change.

The Mourides of Senegal

The Mouride brotherhood originated in western Senegal following the French conquest of the Wolof states in 1866.[14] In the aftermath of national defeat and political collapse, increasing numbers of Wolof, most notably the defeated warriors and dispossessed slaves, attached themselves to the new leadership of a saintly Muslim cleric, named Amabu Bamba, and became his disciples (or *mourides*). This transition to religious leadership was not an escape from the harsh realities of colonial rule but a means of reconstituting the old social order on a new foundation. In this sense, it was a new and more subtle form of resistance to the colonial situation.

The shift to religious leadership was actually facilitated by the last ruler of the Wolof, the Damel Lat Dior, who met with Amabu Bamba on the eve of the Damel's last battle with the French and begged him for a farewell blessing. According to Mouride tradition, the Damel died in battle wearing a robe Amabu Bamba had given him. The transition was a natural one because Islam had already established itself as an anti-colonial religion during the early years of French expansion when warrior clerics led much of the most effective local resistance. In the later colonial period the role of the clerics increased as they replaced discredited chiefs, who became servants of the colonial government, as leaders of the people.

Amabu Bamba is little remembered, apart from his two primary teachings concerning salvation and work. He taught the Orthodox Sufi doctrine about the need to submit to a religious guide, a sheikh, whose intercession could guarantee his disciples salvation. "Whosoever he may be," promised Amabu Bamba, "he who becomes my disciple shall be saved in this world and the next." The authority to make such a promise was dramatically confirmed by Amabu Bamba's great *baraka,* or spiritual power, which his followers saw manifested among themselves in moments of extreme religious ecstasy. Such occurrences have been vividly described by a French official:

> The mere sight of Amabu Bamba at prayer or giving his blessing with a stream of saliva on the prostrate faithful plunges some into hysterical

outbursts which everyone wants to share. They roll at the feet of the saint, they kiss his sandals and the hem of his robe, they hold out their hands to him. With compunction he lets fall a stream of saliva on the open palms, which close up, clasp together and then spasmodically rub the face and body. Then there are shudderings, fainting fits, epileptic convulsions, followed by contortions and extraordinary leaps, all this accompanied by a horrible yelling. Madness finally takes hold of everyone.

After Amabu Bamba's death in 1927 his baraka was transmitted to his successors, the Khalif Generals, and also to his sheikhs, thereby maintaining the channel of grace through Amabu Bamba to Muhammad and to God. Hence, to be attached to a sheikh is to be attached to a chain of salvation: the sheikh is a link with Amabu Bamba, who is the intermediary with the Prophet and through the Prophet with God. The primary act of membership in the brotherhood is therefore the rite of submission of the disciple to his sheikh. The disciple, called a *talibe,* prostrates himself and declares: "I submit my body and my soul to you. I will do everything you order me, and abstain from anything you forbid me." In return the sheikh pronounces his blessing and spits into the hands of the disciple who rubs them on his face, transferring to himself some of the baraka derived ultimately from the Founder himself. Of course the disciple must also adhere to the "five pillars" of the faith, but he recognizes that without his personal allegiance to a sheikh, salvation would be impossible.

Amabu Bamba's second main teaching dealt with the need for work. From the beginning he founded his community on the premise that "work is a part of religion." This doctrine instilled in his followers a kind of "work ethic" which has made the Mourides the most distinctive and successful brotherhood in Senegal. Above all, Amabu Bamba emphasized the value of work in the service of a sheikh as conducive to salvation:

> He who works in his own interest, his toil shall be entirely wasted. He must work in the service of one whose good pleasure can protect [the disciple] from that which he fears in this world and in the next.

In the beginning, most of Amabu Bamba's new followers came seeking not religious instruction but a new leader to replace those whom the French had deposed. They came to serve him in the widest sense and to build a new society. For this purpose the followers developed the working *dara,* a farming group of young men acting in the service of a sheikh. In the early years, the dara was the chief instrument of Mouride expansion and colonization, enabling the followers to collectively seize new lands and to overcome the hazards of settlement in uncultivated areas. Today the dara is no longer a pioneering instrument but an institution for routine agricultural production of peanuts, Senegal's leading export. Only a small minority of the brotherhood now engage themselves in work on the daras. Most prefer to render service to their sheikhs in the form of cash payments derived from work on their own lands. Those who join a dara, usually for a period of eight or more years, experience a time of material hardship and voluntary servitude. But at the end of their service (usually at age twenty-five) they can look forward to a life of close association with their sheikhs, often involving a grant of land, and to public recognition of a special religious achievement, for they are assured of ultimate entry into paradise.

Even for those not attached to the daras, work has a theological value, especially work of the soil. It keeps the disciples away from temptation; hence it is the "only labor free of sin." When a portion of one's labor is remitted to a sheikh, either through periodic service on his fields (called the "Wednesday field") or through the cash proceeds from work, it serves as an offering to God and thus is accorded a special grace. In this sense, all work is sanctified as the "Key to Paradise" and the "ladder to attain God." But it is an investment not only in the afterlife, but also in this life. Monetary gifts and service in labor to one's sheikh are a way of insuring his continued obligations of assistance and protection through the legal, economic, and social powers he can exercise on the disciple's behalf. In this way the Mouride brotherhood fuses the characteristically African concern with communal solidarity and salvation in this life with the more transcendent Islamic ideas of universal moral judgment and future salvation.

The Hausa Tijaniyya

Another instance of Islam's ability to provide a new basis for community is the establishment of the Tijaniyya brotherhood among the Hausa immigrants in the city of Ibadan, Nigeria.[15] Like the Wolof, the Hausa organized themselves into a religious brotherhood in the face of changing political circumstances. With the passing of British colonial rule and the development of ethnically-based political parties, the Hausa traders of Ibadan found themselves unable to preserve their cultural autonomy in this predominantly Yoruba city. In the space of two years (1951–1952) the Hausa overwhelmingly joined the Tijaniyya brotherhood, thereby redefining their former ethnic polity in terms of a religious ideology and a ritual power structure. This transition introduced a major change in the politics of the Hausa quarter of the city. The deteriorating leadership of the chief of the quarter was replaced by that of a group of Tijani clerics. As in the Mouride brotherhood, the authority of the Tijani clerics is based on the concept of salvation by submission to a religious guide. When men join the order, at about age twenty, they become bound to a ritual master whose guidance also extends to daily social matters. No man will undertake any business or social enterprise without asking the advice of his master. Important men patronize the masters, who in turn lend support to their undertakings. In this way the Hausa quarter holds itself together as a minority culture within the competing social and economic forces around them.

The basis of this newly structured identity lies in the intensified ritual life of the community. In addition to the usual five daily prayers, the Tijani members also perform two other forms of prayer, the *wirds* and *wazifa*. The wazifa is held in the evening and requires the men to gather before their masters, filling almost every yard and verandah of the quarter. These ritual groups have spawned smaller sub-groups for personal prayer, eating, religious study, and social activity. On Fridays, the Hausa attend the Central Mosque of the quarter, and keep themselves apart from the Yoruba-controlled Central Mosque of Ibadan. As Abner Cohen has emphasized, the key symbol which dominates both the private and public prayers of the Tijani is Allah.[16] The wirds and wazifa involve hundreds of repetitions of Allah's name in petitions for His forgiveness and affirmations of His uniqueness. In the Friday two-hour *dhikr* ritual, the name "Allah" is recited over a thousand times. It is a Tijaniyya doctrine that intercession through prayer is a means of receiving Allah's special baraka mediated by the ritual masters. By linking themselves directly to Allah and by constantly renewing this link through ritual, the Hausa ground their community in a transcendent source. They also bind themselves to the larger Hausa community in the north by following northern ritual authority, not the authority of the local Muslim Yoruba. Islam has thus answered local social needs with a more universal religious orientation.

What is characteristically "African" in sub-Saharan Islam is therefore a question of local cultural form. Many pre-Islamic spirits, ancestors, public ceremonies, systems of divination, techniques of witchcraft and healing, prophetic leadership, and special cult groups continue to exist. Nature deities and possession spirits have become Muslim jinns or devils; ancestors have become Muslim saints, angels, or jinns; witchcraft, oracles, and divination have become *sihr*, or mystical techniques. Islam has not replaced them; it has put them on a broader religious footing. It has linked them to new, more universal archetypes—Allah, the Prophet, the Law—to new forms of ritual—personal prayer, fasting, Islamic festivals— and to new forms of leadership and community—the sheikhs and their brotherhoods. The effect has been to unify and reinforce much traditional religion and social structure around a wider religious focus, while at the same time deepening the sense of personal moral commitment to a universal God. On this level, traditional concepts of supreme divinity have generally identified with Allah. This, again, is not a replacement, but a reinforcement of a traditional religious concept, expanding it along wider theological and historical lines.

NOTES

1. A brief and informative survey of sub-Saharan Islam has been written by J. SPENCER TRIMINGHAM, *The Influence of Islam upon Africa* (London: Longmans, Green & Co. Ltd., 1968).
2. As quoted in MERVYN HISKETT, *The Sword of Truth: The Life and Times of the Shehu Usuman dan Fodio* (New York: Oxford University Press, 1973), p. 33. Subsequent quotations and references to the Shehu are taken from this source, pp. 64-65, 42-43, 50-51, 122, 129.
3. H. A. S. JOHNSTON, *The Fulani Empire of Sokoto* (London: Oxford University Press, 1967), p. 111.
4. See L. CARL BROWN, "The Sudanese Mahdiya," in *Rebellion in Black Africa,* ed. Robert I. Rotberg (London: Oxford University Press, 1971), and P. M. HOLT, *The Mahdist State in the Sudan 1881-1898* (Oxford: The Clarendon Press, 1970).
5. F. R. WINGATE, *Mahdism and the Egyptian Sudan* (1891; 2nd ed., London: Frank Cass & Co. Ltd., 1968), pp. 47-48. Used by permission.
6. *Ibid.,* pp. 43-44.
7. HOLT, *The Mahdist State,* p. 117.
8. IVOR WILKS, "The Transmission of Islamic Learning in the Western Sudan," in *Literacy in Traditional Societies,* ed. Jack Goody (Cambridge University Press, 1968).
9. HISKETT, *The Sword of Truth,* pp. 34-36.
10. S. F. NADEL, *Nupe Religion* (London: Routledge & Kegan Paul Ltd., 1954), chap. 8; see also *A Black Byzantium* (London: Oxford University Press for the International African Institute, 1942).
11. MICHAEL ONWUEJEOGWU, "The Cult of the Bori Spirits among the Hausa," in *Man in Africa,* ed. Mary Douglas and Phyllis M. Kaberry (London: Tavistock Publications, 1969). See also I. M. LEWIS, *Ecstatic Religion,* pp. 82, 95-96.
12. I. M. LEWIS, Introduction to *Islam in Tropical Africa,* ed. I. M. Lewis (London: Oxford University Press for the International African Institute, 1966), p. 66.
13. ROBIN HORTON, "African Conversion," *Africa* 41, no. 2 (1971), 105. Used with permission of the International African Institute.
14. See a recent study by DONAL B. CRUISE O'BRIEN, *The Mourides of Senegal* (Oxford: Clarendon Press, 1971), whose account I have used. Quotations and references are taken from pages 51, 53, 85, and 89.
15. ABNER COHEN, *Custom and Politics in Urban Africa* (Berkeley: University of California Press, 1969).
16. *Ibid.,* pp. 176-180.

8

Independent Christianity

Christianity entered North Africa in the first century A.D. In the fourth century it spread into Ethiopia and in the sixth century up the Nile into Nubia. Despite this initial penetration, Christianity did not take root beyond a few major cities, nor did it cross the Sahara into tropical Africa. With the Islamic invasion of North Africa in the seventh and eighth centuries, Christianity everywhere fell to Muslim conquest, surviving only in the small mountain kingdom of Ethiopia.

In the fifteenth century Portuguese maritime expansion brought Christianity to the western and eastern shores of sub-Sahara Africa. The most successful missionary venture occurred in the Congo in the sixteenth century under the leadership of the converted monarch, King Alfonso Mvemba Nzunga. But this was a short-lived experiment which lasted only fifty years, ending with the collapse of the kingdom. Elsewhere, Christianity failed to establish itself primarily because of its ties to inept colonial regimes.

Not until the late nineteenth century, when colonialism was firmly advancing, did Christianity begin to make any progress. Consequently, the establishment of Christianity went hand in hand with the process of acculturation to the colonialist order. Christian missionaries may have believed they were merely converting Africans to the Gospel of Christ, but in fact they were converting them to a whole range of Western values—including literacy, medicine, clerical and industrial education, town life, wage earning, and social mobility—as well as instilling in them a distaste for traditional African values.

As a result many African Christians adopted a new identity based upon the colonial-Christian order. They became the new African leaders who were admitted to the junior ranks of the missionary and government hierarchies. However, many within the churches became frustrated with their subordinate positions, especially in light of their supposed equality as Christians, and began to develop leanings towards independence. By contrast with this group, the majority of African Christians remained only partially converted. Still attached to much of their traditional culture, they were not always inclined to pursue their new faith within the bounds of missionary orthodoxy.

Under these circumstances, it was not long before African Christians asserted their independence. Some broke away from the mission establish-

ment and founded churches of their own. For the most part these seces-
sionist churches retained orthodox forms of doctrine, worship, and polity.
Their distinguishing mark was their spiritual independence from mission
support and control. Bishop Sundkler has called them "Ethiopian," following the early use of this word by independent churches in South
Africa, and stressing the scriptural origin (Acts 8:27) and ancient African
heritage of this term.

Other churches were founded through the work of prophet-healers
and the movements to which they gave rise. These churches developed
among the less acculturated Christians and attracted a large proportion
of converts straight from the traditional religions. Unlike the Ethiopian
churches, these prophet-led sects represent a radical indigenization of
Christianity in Africa. Often called "Zionist," "Prayer," "Spiritual,"
or "Prophet" churches, these sects have created a thorough synthesis of
Christian and African ritual forms. They emphasize revelation from the
Holy Spirit through prophets and a practical, this-worldly notion of
salvation in which healing is prominent. They stress communal solidarity
in terms of the Old Testament ideal of a prophet-led community based
in a Holy City. Some have developed millennial expectations and look
upon their founders as messiahs sent by God to redeem Africa. In general,
the prophet-healing churches have attempted to make Christianity relevant to everyday life, especially through the use of practical ritual techniques, which are lacking in the colonial churches. The rapid expansion
of the independent churches, which now number over 6,000, has presented a serious challenge to the established churches which are still
seeking ways of Africanizing Christianity.[1] So far the most creative inno-
vations have occurred within Independent Christianity, especially within
the burgeoning prophet-healing churches. Three of the most well-known
churches will be examined in this chapter.

THE CHURCH OF JESUS CHRIST ON EARTH
THROUGH THE PROPHET SIMON KIMBANGU

Like most religious prophets, Simon Kimbangu has been seen from
different perspectives. He has been called a nationalist revolutionary, an
African messiah, a Christian prophet. Today, the leadership of his church
in Zaire, "The Church of Jesus Christ on Earth through the Prophet
Simon Kimbangu," firmly denies the first two interpretations and affirms
only the last. But Kimbangu has been understood in each of these ways at
different times by different groups, and each of these perceptions has contributed to his significance as a national figure in Zaire's recent political
and religious history.

As a young man, Simon Kimbangu was educated at a Baptist mission near his home village of Nkamba. He became a catechist in the Baptist Missionary Society, but his lack of further training prevented him from advancing to the higher positions of teacher, deacon, or pastor. In 1918 a serious flu epidemic took thousands of lives, and many other Kongo died as the result of forced labor on a government railroad project. At this time Kimbangu heard a voice telling him: "I am Christ, my servants are unfaithful. I have chosen you to witness to your brethren and to convert them." [2] At first, Kimbangu resisted the call, believing that others could do the work better. When the voice persisted, Kimbangu fled from the mission and went to Kinshasa in hopes of escaping the repeated calls. In Kinshasa he worked as a laborer, but he was forced to return home and take up farming because he was not paid his wages for three months. In 1921 the Holy Spirit took him against his will to a sick woman's house in a nearby village and told him to heal her. He laid his hands on her in the name of Jesus Christ and she became well. Later, he performed other acts of healing, one of which was a dramatic raising of a child from the dead. Rumors of his miraculous healing powers spread, and soon people began to flock to Nkamba in search of healing. It was not long before the village of Nkamba came to be known as "Jerusalem."

Kimbangu performed his work in a special enclosure in front of his house. The services began outside the enclosure with singing, followed by prayer, Bible-reading, and a sermon. In the course of his sermon, Kimbangu would start to tremble in the manner of the traditional diviner-healers, and become possessed by the Spirit. He would enter the enclosure and await those who sought help, surrounded by a chorus singing hymns which helped to sustain his trance state. One of the early Songs of Fellowship refers to this possession phenomenon and to the healing powers of the Spirit:

Many troubles on Earth,
Sickness all the time we see,
Tears forever flowing,
O Spirit, come, come down
O come and help us.[3]

Kimbangu bade the people enter where he stood shaking and holding his prophet's staff. "Come, come, come so that I may help thee." Each came forward and told him of an illness. Kimbangu put his hands on the patient's head and raised his eyes toward Heaven, saying, "In the name of Jesus I will cure you, be whole again." Those who were not seriously ill left by a side door and went to a sacred pool, called Bethesda, where they bathed. Those with more serious illnesses went to another room, where Kimbangu asked if they were Christians. If they were, he advised them to "Hold fast to Jesus Christ." If not, he told them to "Change your mind, believe in Jesus Christ, and He will save you." [4] Thus comforted and encouraged, the patients departed for home.

From the very beginning Kimbangu presented himself as a messenger or prophet *(ngunza)* of God, and he healed in the name of Jesus Christ. He did not claim to be a messiah, only a servant of God and Christ to the Kongo. He exhorted people to become Christians, to practice monogamy, and to renounce the spirit cult associated with charms called *minkisi*. So emphatic was Kimbangu's denunciation of the minkisi that many people cast them away in heaps by the roadside, a phenomenon which centuries of missionary work had failed to accomplish. As an orthodox Christian, Kimbangu firmly opposed separation from the mission churches. He also upheld the payment of government taxes, refusing to become a leader of resistance to the government.

But his work created such a sudden, large scale sensation that the colonial government immediately took notice. Thousands of Kongo had temporarily left their jobs to undertake pilgrimages to the new "Jerusalem." Hospitals in the vicinity fell vacant as patients went to seek Kimbangu's spiritual help, and Catholic missions began to lose some of their converts. Complaints were made about the health problems of the crowded multitudes (estimated at one time to be 10,000) descending upon Nkamba-Jerusalem, where the sick and dying and even the dead were brought to be healed and raised.

When a government administrator visited Nkamba, he found the village thronged with people in a high state of excitement.

> A weird group of people came to meet him, howling and gesticulating. Two young men and two girls surrounded the chief personage who wore red trousers and a white shirt, and carried a staff in his hand. This was Kimbangu himself.[5]

Kimbangu took this occasion to read aloud the story of David and Goliath. When the administrator tried to speak, the prophet turned away to address the Holy Spirit. "We have found the God of the blacks," cried Kimbangu's followers.

Elsewhere radical leaders urged the people in Kimbangu's name not to pay taxes, and some began to collect money for the establishment of a national Church. Rumors spread about abandoning work on the government railway, and new prophets claiming authority from Kimbangu arose everywhere. In a few weeks it was evident that Kimbangu had sparked a nationalist movement which he neither had intended nor could control.

A warrant was issued for Kimbangu's arrest only two months after the miracles had begun. He was seized but escaped, and rumors immediately elaborated the event into a miracle. Revolutionary ideas became overt and some "prophets" proclaimed the Second Coming of Christ. At this time, it is likely that the idea of Kimbangu as an African Messiah developed. He was said to be the "ruler of Africa" who would reclaim the lost "throne of the Bakongo." The following hymn, written at the time, expresses this point of view:

> The Country, yes, the country will change. In truth
> The apostles of this idea will rise up
> On the day appointed by the Savior.
> Let each person abandon the garment of mourning
> And take up the white garment of joy!
> Out of hope, the blacks will rise up!
> This is the last tax we shall pay! [6]

After a number of political arrests had been made, Kimbangu decided to follow Christ's example and return to "Jerusalem" in order to give himself up to the authorities. But before he could do so, he was betrayed by a local chief and arrested. Before his trial, Kimbangu was doused with cold water and scourged with a whip to prevent him from being seized by the Spirit in court. The brief trial was brought to an end when one of the apostles challenged the judge and asked him why Africans were indicted for having "their God, their prophet, their Bible, when the whites have theirs?" The indignant judge closed the hearing.

Kimbangu was sentenced to death and eleven of his followers were given life imprisonment. The legal charges against Kimbangu reveal the government's perception of the movement:

> Whereas . . . [Kimbangu] has persevered in his work of persuading the people that a new God was going to come, that this God was more powerful than the State itself. . . . Whereas . . . the sect is hidden under the veil of a new religion, but intends to demolish the present regime. . . . Whereas . . . whites are the object of profound hatred by the adepts of Kimbangu, this hatred has infiltrated and spread with alarming rapidity among the indigenous population; the doctrine of Kimbangu is the cause of a serious defect: the absence of a great number of workers from their jobs. Whereas . . . the [government's efforts] at persuasion have been interpreted by the ignorant, the prophets, and the adepts as the weakness and impotence of the State against spiritual, magical, and ecstatic power . . . [hence] the march of events could fatally lead to a great revolt, . . . [thus] the severity in applying the law can be understood.[7]

Later, Kimbangu's sentence was commuted to life imprisonment by King Albert of Belgium against strong opposition from the Belgian missionaries and traders. The prophet was sent away to prison in Elizabethville, where he spent the rest of his life, mostly in solitary confinement. He died in 1951.

Many believed that Kimbangu was killed after his trial, and this only made the movement grow with renewed vigor. In the eyes of his followers, Kimbangu was a messianic martyr chosen by God to sacrifice himself for the Gospel and for his people. In him they saw the repetition of Christian salvation history. Using the Biblical paradigm of Christ's passion and resurrection, they gave redemptive meaning to Kimbangu's acts and to the movement in general:

> He whom God sent as a Savior to the blacks was *betrayed* to the Authorities, who sent him to Elizabethville, where he was imprisoned and enslaved for many years. Finally, the authorities decided to put him to death by force of arms. But no sooner did they make him stand up and fire at him, than he *appeared* in our country. He came to Kinzwana and to Kituenge, where he made himself known to P.M., to Dembo, Kwanga, and Kinhoni. It was then that he himself appointed the *apostles* and ordered them to create places of prayer.[8]

Eventually, the government banned the movement, which had come to be known as Ngunzism (from *ngunza,* "prophet"), and attempted to stamp it out by a policy of mass deportation. The movement went underground, new leaders arose, and sects spread through the Belgian and French Congos and Portuguese Angola. Some expected Kimbangu to return miraculously and lead a revolution:

> Mfumu Simon Kimbangu is the sacred sceptre of dominion, which the Lord God has given to the black race that it may have dominion through it. He is the ruler's rod of the blacks.
> Mfumu Simon Kimbangu is the shining lamp over the way that the Lord has given to the black race so that the blacks, when they come to the valley of the shadow of death, may be able to take this lamp in their hand, and thus the night shall be no more in their eyes.[9]

In 1959, on the eve of national independence, the movement was granted official recognition. Kimbangu's youngest son and successor, Joseph Diangienda, and his two brothers set about unifying the various Ngunzist groups into a single church, "the Church of Jesus Christ on Earth through the Prophet Simon Kimbangu," based at Nkamba-Jerusalem, the Holy City of the new Church. The Church officially renounced any involvement in politics, though its size (estimates range as high as a million members) and prestige gave it immense influence in the immediate Independence period.

Today the Church professes to be thoroughly Christian and has recently become a member of the World Council of Churches. Yet it retains its original prophetic theology. It is believed that what happened in the Congo in 1921 is "the same" as what happened in the salvation history of Israel. When Kimbangu's body was returned to Nkamba-Jerusalem in an "Ark," the Church's newspaper explained the event in the following terms:

> The works of God are neither old nor new. Whatever things of God were in ancient time, the same are found in the present age and shall be in the age which is to come.[10]

The New Jerusalem at Nkamba stands in direct order of succession to the previous Jerusalems known under the names of Salem, City of David, and City of God. Each of these names is associated with different ages or "generations" in which God sent his prophets (Abraham, David, and Jesus), first to the Jews, then to the Gentiles, and now to the Kongo.

Kimbangu himself has been likened to the Ark of Israel. Like the Ark, Kimbangu saved and inspired the Ngunza movement during its "forty years" of oppression and exile (1921–1960) under the Belgian government. Now an "Ark" containing Kimbangu's body lies at the center of Nkamba-Jerusalem.

Kimbangu was sent to lead the people to God "because the missionaries did not obey the voice of the Lord Jesus." Like Jesus, Kimbangu "raised the dead, caused the paralyzed to stand up-right, gave sight to the blind, cleansed lepers, and healed all the sick in the name of the Lord Jesus. But he chased away those who practised witchcraft."

When this happened, the jealous "hills of Satan" were also revealed.

> What kind of hills were these? The prophets of Satan, missionaries, the Belgian government. . . . Why were these hills so jealous? They knew that Jesus had given his power to the people of Africa, and that the city of the Lord God had hidden, Jerusalem, had descended here in Africa.[11]

The teaching of the Kimbanguist Church is clear: As God acted in ages past by raising prophets and messiahs to save each "generation," so he has acted anew among the Kongo and raised up a messianic prophet to establish a new Jerusalem for the salvation of Africans.

NAZARETH CHURCH

In South Africa, the theme of salvation history has been even more fully developed in the Nazareth Church founded by the Zulu prophet-messiah, Isaiah Shembe. While the Kimbanguists look upon the raising of an African prophet and the founding of an African Jerusalem as the beginning of salvation in Africa, Shembe's Nazarites take this perspective one step further and look upon it as the fulfillment of salvation history in African society. In Shembe's theology, the futuristic, other-worldly salvation of Christian eschatology is brought down to the present, here-and-now, salvational dimension of traditional African ritual systems. The partially realized "Jerusalem" of the Kimbanguists has become fully realized at Shembe's "High Place" (*Ekuphakameni*), which is "Heaven on Earth." Christianity has been fully encapsulated into African ritual forms. At the same time, the universalizing aspects of Christianity have served as a catalyst, enabling a small-scale society to reorient and re-vitalize itself in terms of a larger, more macrocosmic religious and moral ideology, while still retaining its traditional identity.

As a young man, Isaiah Shembe experienced a series of revelations in which Jehovah told him to abstain from sex, abandon his wives, and leave his home village. These revelations occurred during thunder-storms, a traditional Zulu mode of revelation. Shembe's last and decisive call occurred during a storm when lightning struck and killed his best ox and burned Shembe on the thigh. Refusing treatment from a tradi-tional healer, Shembe declared, "Jehovah has revealed to me that I must not be healed by medicine, only through his Word." [12] Thereafter, Shembe became an itinerant healer. He traveled by foot and oxcart throughout the Natal area as a migrant laborer. Inspired by the Spirit, he preached, healed, and cast out spirits, in the manner of the tradi-tional diviner-seer, and administered holy water for healing and purifica-tion. He never attended a European school, but learned how to read the Bible and took instruction as a catechist in a separatist African Methodist Church. Later, he left this church because he wished to be baptized according to the Biblical example of immersion, and joined an African Baptist Church in which he was ordained a minister. He broke away from this church convinced that the Old Testament Sabbath, not the Christian Sunday, was the proper day of worship, and he founded the *iBandla lama-Nazaretha,* or the Nazareth Baptist Church.

For Shembe, the Sabbath commandment was the essential law. This symbolized the basically Israelite orientation of his Church and distin-guished it from other forms of Christianity. Shembe also adhered to certain other aspects of Old Testament law and ritual. He removed his shoes when preaching, left his hair uncut, admonished his congregation to refrain from eating pork, and prayed in the name of the Old Testa-ment Jehovah. He also instituted a feast of Tabernacles (in July), "dancing before the Lord" (in Zulu fashion), and circumcision (an an-cient Zulu custom), permitted polygamy (since it was not explicitly pro-hibited in the Old Testament), and claimed that all Old Testament references to Nazarites referred to his Church. In 1911 he received an-other revelation from Jehovah, this time to found a religious center on top of Mt. Nhlangakazi in Natal. With the destruction of the Zulu empire still within living memory and the last vestiges of Zulu territorial authority being swept away, the Land Act of 1913 spurred on Shembe and other independent church leaders to purchase land. Shembe built his headquarters on a hill near the sacred mountain. He called the hill Ekuphakameni, or "High Place." Thereafter, Shembe continued to use most of his Church's funds to buy farms for his people throughout the Zulu area of Natal.

At this time, eighty-five percent of the population were still non-Christian, and from this group Shembe built up a substantial following, mostly of poor peasants who retained much of their traditional orientation. Everywhere Shembe went he was recognized as a charismatic leader partly because his behavior and physical appearance resembled that of a traditional Zulu diviner. Thin, nervous, and high-strung, he often created an immediate visual and spiritual impact. One pastor recalls his first meeting with Shembe: "When I looked at him, I was surprised. They had spoken of him as being a pastor, yet he is not a pastor, but the Lord." When Shembe told the man that the girl whom he had brought to be healed would recover, the pastor recalls, "His countenance filled me with awe, he was like Jesus." Another member of Shembe's Church remembers meeting Shembe for the first time as a boy: "When I saw his face, there came a flashing of lightning from his face, and I fell down. And I asked mother, Who is this man? And mother answered me, Jesus. All this makes me say that he is with God." [13] Shembe also impressed people with his clairvoyant ability. He did not need to ask about their sicknesses, but was able to tell them what was wrong and how they could be cured.

Shembe emphasized that his prophetic calling came from Jehovah, and he regarded his lack of education as a definite asset. Once he told some European missionaries:

> If you had taught him [Shembe] in your schools, you would have had
> a chance of boasting over him. But God, in order to reveal His wisdom,
> sent this Shembe, who is a child, that he may speak as a wise and
> educated man.[14]

Shembe did not intend his work to be divisive or anti-European. When asked by Catholic priests to become a Catholic, he replied, "I was a Roman Catholic already before you were born." He also used to say, "I am of all colours (i.e., spiritually of all races)," and he called everybody my son, my daughter, my father, or my mother. In this spirit, Shembe opposed any form of anti-white or anti-government activity. "The whites have brought us the Word of God," he said, "to fight against them is to fight against God." [15]

Like other Independent Churches in South Africa, Shembe's movement has been said to be an escape from the political reality of white rule into the solace of ritualism, and to be an outlet for frustrated leadership talents. Bishop Sundkler has also seen in Shembe a revival of the royal Zulu king, who epitomized national identity and values. To a large extent these interpretations are true. But at the same time, Shembe created a broader theology which reached beyond the past and offered a new cultural synthesis oriented towards the present and the future. This theology is now a growing and developing tradition, and since Shembe's death in 1935 it has been extended and partially modified by his son and successor, Johannes Galilee Shembe.

The Church's theology is expressed primarily in its hymns, which were composed by Shembe and his son. G. C. Oosthuizen's study of the Church's hymnbook reveals the main lines of this implict theology, especially its notions of God, Messiah, kingship, and eschatology.

Shembe's conception of God was derived more from the Old Testament than from Zulu religion. Zulu names for God are less frequently used in the hymnbook than the Old Testament name Jehova (Jehovah), associated with the Sinai revelation in thunder and lightning and the giving of the Law. This name was most prominent in Shembe's vocabulary because it was Jehova that gave the Sabbath law, which distinguishes the Nazarites from the other Christian Churches. Jehova revealed himself to Africa because his law had been rejected by his enemies:

> The enemies of Jehova rise up against thee,
> Wake up, wake up Ye Africans.[16]

Jehova was the new symbol of African faith, and Shembe was his manifestation among the Zulu, as Christ was among the Jews. Christ had returned to Heaven, and now Shembe had come to the Africans. The Zulu did not have a cult of the supreme god *uNkulunkulu*, for he was too far away. At this crucial juncture in history, the Zulu sought a more direct relation to divinity and this they found in Jehova as represented by Shembe. "Jehova alone is *Inkosi* [king] with power," and he dwells at the Nazarite headquarters at Ekuphakameni, where Heaven has come down to Earth:

> All generations of heaven
> They will rejoice through you at Ekuphakameni
> When they enter through the gates
> may they come to praise *Jehova*.[17]

The name of Jesus is rarely mentioned in the Church's hymns and prayers and this omission is conspicuous. It appears that Shembe

I took the place of Christ, though Shembe II now upholds the centrality of Christ in the Church's life. However, in the liturgy of the Church, Shembe, not Christ, is still the central figure. The Holy Spirit which Jesus sent to his Church has now come to the Zulu. Shembe is the Promised One, the Holy Spirit come to earth:

He has arrived who is followed by nations
He has arrived, we have heard him.
Spread (the news) ye men
Spread (the news) all ye nations.
It was said we shall not be left alone
He has come we have heard him.
Follow him all ye people
He has arrived, we have heard him.[18]

The few references to the life of Jesus in the hymnbook are interpreted as being repeated and reenacted through Shembe. Jehova is working out his Law, only now it is in Africa through Shembe:

They came, the wise men
arriving from the East,
Saying: Where is He,
Who is the King of the Jews
Chorus: So it is also today
On the hill-tops of Ohlange.

According to Sundkler, this hymn means that "What happened once through Jesus, among the Jews for their salvation is now being reenacted through Shembe, among the Zulus and for their own salvation." [19] Shembe was the Christ of the Zulus. The way of Jesus was replaced by the way of Shembe; it is the way of the old Law—symbolized by the Sabbath—not the way of the worshipers of Jesus who break the Law. They worship the Sunday God, not Jehova, who has acted *anew* in Africa.

Shembe bears many titles, the most prominent being *Nkosi*, chief or king. This title is also applied to Jehova, and in this way Jehova and Shembe are virtually identified as one and the same. In using the title Nkosi, Shembe took upon himself the image of the national ruler.

Come ye Zulus
We have seen our *iNkosi*
We come from the world that is to come
We have seen our *iNkosi*.[20]

When Shembe died, he was buried like a king in a mausoleum at Ekuphakameni. Shembe took his place in the "world to come"—that is, in the afterlife—as Jehova's agent, just as in the past the royal ancestors

became the intermediaries between the Zulu and the supreme god
uNkulunkulu.

The reason for Shembe's success lies in several different dimensions
of his work and in the conditions of his times. His healing was effective;
his theology adapted Christianity to traditional Zulu forms; and his
message of salvation was relevant to the religious and social needs of
an oppressed Zulu people.

At Ekuphakameni, the High Place, the promised kingdom was
effectively made present "here-and-now." In Zulu religion, there was
no vision of a future salvation. For Shembe and his people, the saving
effects of sacred power were experienced in the present. Through the
establishment of the High Place as an archetype of Heaven, salvation
could be realized.

Situated eighteen miles north of Durban, Mt. Nhlangakazi can
accommodate thousands of people during the July festival, when the
Nazarites congregate from all over Zululand and the Natal. The holy
village, Ekuphakameni, is surrounded by an enclosure in which there
are several gates. These are the Gates of Heaven, guarded by the "angels,"
the ancestors, who keep out sinners while the saints march in:

> We stand all before you
> gates of Ekuphakameni.
>
> All the generations in heaven
> will rejoice by thee, Kuphakama
> when they enter by the gates
> they come to praise, Jehova.

All nations are called to enter, but especially the Zulu:

> Become enlarged you Kuphakama
> the new city
> the Zulu nation became dejected in the country.[21]

The history of Judah will be repeated in the Natal. Ekuphakameni
is the New Jerusalem:

> Let them investigate into the writings.
> It is so then today
> At the hillocks of Uhlanga.

The holy village is also Eden:

> When I come near
> to the garden of Eden
> I will rejoice completely
> I am now going to Ekuphakameni.[22]

At the center lies a place called *paradisi* (paradise) where all the
pilgrims congregate for the holy communion service before the climax

of the July ceremonies. Here the Nazarites drink from the springs at the Tree of Life and become strengthened, and see their God-messiah face to face. Here healing is given and paradise regained.

The ceremonies performed at the High Place involve preaching, giving of testimonies, traditional dancing, and healing. Sundkler describes a healing session for 250 barren women at the July festival, performed by Johannes Shembe:

> The Servant stands before the mass of women, stretches out his right hand over the crowd from one side to the other, moving his long nervous fingers while he prays: "Lord, I pray, give them life in their wombs and in their spirits, so that they may bear children."
>
> He unwinds his father's long black veil, which is thought to transmit hidden powers of life. . . . He walks along the rows of seated women and flicks first one, then the other with that veil, giving it a rapid jerk, as if cracking a whip.
>
> The effect is astounding. Almost everybody starts, as though receiving a powerful electric shock. One woman, wearing a top knot, who has been hiccoughing more and more loudly, is struck by the veil and starts to cry with a terrible loud, shrill voice, and continues crying long after the prophet has left her. Next to her is sitting another woman who also begins to cry. She throws herself to the ground. The prophet touches her, placing his finger tips on her shoulders . . . . she accuses herself of having murdered her children, her *indiki*-demon has told her so: "I ate my children," she cries in her terrifying voice. . . . She continues to cry, but the prophet moves on. And then, with a most pathetic effect, the crying of this desperate woman changes suddenly into a lullaby of four notes which are continually repeated,
>
> . . . .
>
> Sometimes the prophet shouts, as he hits out with his veil: "Get out, demons! Depart immediately!" And as he moves along, the din of cackling, hiccoughing, crying, shrieking, singing, weeping, grows into a tremendous volume of sound. Bitter is their need—and here is their great hope, perhaps their last chance. Can this veil, can this man, can God give life? [23]

This scene was recorded over twenty years ago when Johannes Shembe was still under the shadow of his father and drew upon his power. Today, Shembe II emphasizes the limits of his power:

> It is true . . . I sometimes lay hands on the afflicted ones. . . . My father never laid on hands. He simply pointed his fingers and would say, "You diseased part—you had blood in the head . . . you come forward and come out." And then we would see the blood come out. I do not have that power!

Shembe II acknowledges only the power of prayer, though most of his congregation regard him as the "Lord God of the Hill."

> I believe I have only the power of God and Christ. To be helped these
> sufferers must make up their minds that they will be helped. I can help
> them to make up their minds but I can be of no help to them if they
> do not! [24]

Throughout the year, a steady stream of supplicants comes to the
Hill with a variety of ills and requests. In most cases, Shembe does not
pray or perform rites of healing. It is sufficient for people to relate their
problems and hear Shembe's advice. The advice is usually practical like
that of a traditional chief ministering to his people. "It is a therapy,"
observes James Fernandez, "which consists of quietly maintaining an
atmosphere of chiefly presence and power while carefully listening to
complaints. It is accompanied by the implicit promise to include each
afflicted person in the Prophet's prayers." Fernandez, who witnessed a
number of such interviews, suggests that "The powerful psychological
situation of the public audience and the implicit promise of prayer would
seem . . . to have considerable psychological consequence regardless of
any further techniques." [25]

Twice a year thousands of Nazarites make pilgrimages to the Hill
for the July and New Year's festivals. These pilgrimages are a significant
feature of the Nazarite church and they make its theology a living reality.
As Victor Turner has shown, the pilgrimage process is a rite of passage.[26]
People move away from the secular habits of life in towns and villages
and become temporary "nomads," stripped of worldly involvements.
They embark upon a journey, often difficult and expensive, to reach a
common goal, in this case the sacred center at Mount Nhlangakazi. Following in their Prophet's footsteps, they leave the world behind in order
to come closer to nature and to God, and thereby to be renewed and
transformed. Johannes Shembe emphasizes this pilgrimage process in
one of his New Year's sermons:

> You have left all your properties, your wife and children, your welfare
> and good houses, and you have come to Nhlangakazi, where the rain runs
> through the poor huts, because there are no solid houses on this mountain;
> and you spread your sleeping mat on the bare ground, because here there
> are no soft beds; and you have only a little food, because most of the
> money went on traveling expenses from Zululand and Swaziland, from
> Durban and Johannesburg.

Shembe prays that the Nazarites will strip themselves of the burden
of history as they have stripped themselves of the world, and that they
will reorient themselves to the Christian life:

> Have mercy upon us! Our fathers have done many evil and harsh things:
> they have killed and burned human beings. These evil things God must
> take out of us, because they still cleave to us.

And he asks the Nazarites to "bid farewell to the sins of the old year. Start a new life!"

> Put an end to the quarrels in which you live! And do not only love those people whom you like, but especially those who make it difficult for you to love them.

As the Nazarites draw together at Nhlangakazi, Shembe II bids them to become open to the universal dimensions of their faith, to shed their local identity and sectarian beliefs:

> Do not forget to offer prayer and intercession: pray for the government, for your magistrate and for your Bantu Affairs Commissioner, for the Prime Minister of the Republic of South Africa, for the police . . . Pray for the pastors, I mean for them all, not only for your parish and pastor, but also for the other ones . . .[27]

At the sacred Center, the structures of society and history are surpassed as the Nazarites strive to experience the oneness of man in unity with God. This is a liminal, initiatory experience. It changes the participant's inner condition and stands as a moral paradigm for behavior in the secular world. Situated behind closely guarded gates, the Hill exists as a world of its own, an alternative to the dissolute life of the cities and townships. It provides a spiritual atmosphere to which the Nazarites may periodically return for spiritual renewal. At the center of the Hill lies Shembe II, whose daily efforts are expended in its service. Although Shembe II is not the prophet that his father was, he is the custodian of the world his father created.

CHURCH OF THE LORD (ALADURA)

Independent Christianity has developed in many directions other than the "messianic" ones represented by the churches of Shembe and Kimbangu. The character of both these churches has in fact diminished in the course of time as leadership has passed to the second generation. Healing and prophecy, however, remain central features of most Independent churches. The *aladura* (praying) churches of western Nigeria are important examples of this form of Christianity. One of the most prominent is the Church of the Lord (Aladura), whose history and theology have been well described by Dr. Harold Turner in his two-volume study, *African Independent Church*.

As the Yoruba term *aladura* implies, prayer is the focal point of the Church of the Lord's doctrines and practices. Prayer was the primary emphasis of the Church's founder, Josiah Oshitelu, and it became the foundation of his teaching.

Oshitelu was educated in Anglican mission schools in the early 1920s. He served for six years as a teacher-catechist in the Church Missionary Society in his home town of Ogere in the Ijebeu-Yoruba area north of Lagos. In 1925 he experienced a series of terrifying visions which he believed were caused by witches. Greatly troubled, he was granted a year's leave to find a cure. He tried traditional remedies, but they only made his condition worse, so he sought the advice of a Christian elder named Shomoye. Shomoye told Oshitelu that he was not bewitched but being called and "tested" by God for an important mission. He advised Oshitelu to throw away his traditional charms and medicines and to put his faith in God. He told him that the evil powers could be overcome by using certain psalms, and by assiduous use of prayer and fasting. Oshitelu followed this advice, which proved marvelously effective. He dreamed his tormentors were reduced to harmless animals, and later he heard heavenly voices assuring him that an important task lay ahead. As a result, Oshitelu transformed his own cure into a new gospel: faith in God and prayer and fasting are the solution for the evils of this world.

From the beginning, Oshitelu wrote down his revelations, which numbered into the thousands. As the early revelations show, Oshitelu felt himself from the outset to be a great prophet, possessed of special powers and of knowledge of God's secret names. Like Elijah and John the Baptist, he was chosen by God and by Christ for an almost messianic mission:

> I will build new Jerusalem in you. You are the one whom Jesus Christ has sent like the last Elijah to repair the Lord's road and make his way straight.
>   I will give you the key to power like Moses, and will bless you like Job . . . I am the God of Kah . . . the God of Jah.[28]

These visions came replete with a new holy script (resembling Arabic), new religious symbols, taboos against eating pork and other "unclean things," mysterious "holy names" of God or "seal words" (Kadujah, Taroja), and information on the "blunders" of other churches. Oshitelu began talking about his visions and his devotional techniques, and was dismissed from the Church Missionary Society for "erroneous beliefs and teachings." For two years he fasted and prayed, serving as an apprentice to his counselor, Shomoye, who established his own aladura church. Finally Oshitelu received orders to found his own church and the promise that he would spread God's fame "from Syria to America."

About this time a severe outbreak of the plague was ravaging the

Ijebu area, followed by serious economic depression and famine. This sudden upheaval, especially in the urban areas, was the occasion for the Aladura revival movement in which Oshitelu briefly took part. The Aladura message paralleled Oshitelu's own gospel: the present trials are God's judgment; only faith in God, the power of prayer, and the abandonment of paganism can overcome them. Oshitelu wrote down a ten-point outline of his own preaching at this time, of which Turner provides the following summary:

> The first three points address Christians, Muslims, and pagans; the Christians have strayed and disobeyed God, the Muslims have shunned his precepts, and the pagans have been idolaters. The next three predict the imminence of judgment through locusts, famine, and war—all as part of the "Gospel of Joy"!—for "the world is old and broken," but it will "be changed immediately," for the kingdom of God is at hand. The last four points of this gospel condemn "native doctors" and promise divine healing, the curing of all woes and ailments, through the "water of life" which is given to all who believe in God. The message may be summed up as an offer of blessings in all one's troubles through faith in God alone, with judgment for those who fail to respond.[29]

The early 1920s was a period in which Yoruba Christians were experiencing a severe ideological crisis. After several decades of missionary activity, the traditional religions were on the wane and Christianity was steadily growing; but the bubonic plague had caused widespread distress, and the new cash economy of the towns and cities was in a state of collapse. Oshitelu and the other Aladura preachers explained these catastrophic events as the signs of the breakdown of the pagan world and of the "immediate" coming of the Christian age. J. D. Y. Peel has characterized the situation in the following way:

> Christianity was widely conceived of instrumentally, that is, was believed to be efficacious in attaining this-worldly goals, though Christians were in the habit of taking every other possible insurance and protection that they considered effective. When therefore, at a time of heavy religious change, the Yoruba were inflicted with a series of natural disasters— influenza, plagues, famines, and depression following the rapid growth of a monetary economy—these demanded a religious interpretation. Their unusually severe nature meant that the traditional religion, already fast declining, was inadequate to explain or relieve them, and Christianity (which had every sign of permanence and was generally associated with what the young and ambitious felt desirable) was so used. The God whom the Christians preached had sent the disasters as a punishment, but the Christian religion provided a way out.[30]

The logic seemed compelling: God, not the orisha, was the cause of the world's present ills; therefore Christianity, not the orisha cult, was the solution. What was needed was a clean break with the pagan past and a total commitment to Christianity—in other words, a religious reformation. Most people who responded to the revival were already nominal Christians, but as Peel indicates, on the practical everyday level they still partook of pagan religion and even of Islam without coming to terms with the underlying contradiction:

> Jolted by the events of the 1920s and 1930s the Aladuras . . . proposed a radical reordering of this moral and logical confusion, this welter of rationales. They insisted that there was one principle of action alone, to rely solely on God, especially for healing, the focus of so much religious concern. The intellectual revolution was made acceptable to a wide range of people by the events of the revivals. The hard doctrine of divine healing was vindicated and supported by the emotions of the revival.[31]

Hence, in Peel's view, the Aladura movement to which Oshitelu initially belonged presented a new rationalization, a new ordering of the world, the proof of which could be seen and felt in the new preaching and in rites of the revival movement.

Yet, despite this change in religious allegiance (from the orisha to God), the Yoruba world view remained essentially unchanged. This is what gave Aladura Christianity its this-worldly and integrated character. In a real sense, the religious rules and goals remained the same; only the content was changed. God and the Holy Spirit became the new orisha and Christianity became the new cult system. In keeping with the traditional world view, Oshitelu and his fellow preachers conceived of suffering, disease, and morality as integrated together in an undifferentiated theological outlook whose focus was still the quality of life in-this-world. For the Aladuras and Oshitelu in particular, conversion to Christianity was a religious revolution, but it was not a total intellectual revolution. It occurred within a larger and more archaic cosmology. This molded Christianity into a prophet-healing cult based on the power of Christian prayer and ritual.

Although Oshitelu was expelled from the movement after only six months for his unorthodox witch-finding techniques and for his use of secret names of God in healing, he secured some able assistants and established footholds in a few major towns and cities. On this slender basis, the Church of the Lord gradually expanded across western Nigeria and into the northern and eastern regions. In 1962, the Church of the Lord had established approximately seventy-two branches and an equal number of ministers throughout Nigeria. Through ardent missionary efforts, the Church also founded a large number of congregations outside Nigeria in Ghana, Liberia, and Sierra Leone, and even a small branch in London. Oshitelu died in 1966. He was succeeded by his able lieutenant Emmanuel Adejobi, who currently heads the Church.

As already mentioned, belief in the power of prayer is a prominent feature of the Church of the Lord. The Church provides a great range of prayer booklets and techniques, and each member is exhorted to pray every three hours, day and night. Although most members do not follow this rule, those who are especially devout or are in distress try to approximate it. Prayers at midnight and at 3 A.M. are deemed particularly effective; and there is a special "mercy ground" at the church where members may come at any hour for this purpose. This is called "struggling in prayer." In Turner's view, it is a "special form of the wider concept of strenuous endeavour, and emphasizes the earnestness, frequency, and importunity of prayer." [32] The underlying idea, as explained by Emmanuel Adejobi, is that "If we are tired of praying then we shall resort to human means of protection," namely, paganism. But "God will never be tired to hear and to render your request to you." [33] Adoration, confession, intercession regularly occur; petitions and thanksgivings form the main content. As in the orisha cults, Turner has observed that "most petitions concern the avoidance of evils and dangers, healing or the gift of children, and promotion, business prosperity, or examination success." [34] The following portion of a prayer prepared by a prophet for a student illustrates the character and tone of these private petitions:

> Make me holy for my blessing. Send me this moment Divine Helpers, Divine Intelligence, Divine Intermediaries and gracious look of Jesus Christ my Saviour. . . . My examinations will come up (mention time and place) . . . I call unto Thee for success . . . grant that I may study the right text and passage and subject. . . . Jesus Christ let me feel Thy influence. . . . Thy breath, and Thy assistance. Send to me most powerful angels, that these may fight out for me all dangers and evil besettings, that I may not be frightened, careless, nervous, and obsessed. . . .[35]

Such prayers usually end with the formula, "if God so wills." This closely resembles the traditional expression, "May Olodumare accept it," which concludes the prayers to the orisha. It expresses the same, almost fatalistic note of resignation before a God of Destiny who predetermines one's fortune.

Petitions are also made in the form of special psalms and the recitation of Holy Names. This accords with the traditional idea that ritual language and sacred praise names have an intrinsic power of their own. The following is one of many which appear in Oshitelu's *The Book of Prayer with Uses and Power of Psalms:*

For Pslam vii:

> If enemies rise against thee, recite this Psalm, standing facing the East in midnight with the Holy Name—ELL ELLIJJONI. You will be naked. And the enemy will be defeated at will.[36]

Next to prayer, fasting is the most practiced spiritual technique in the Church. Its purpose is to purify the individual so that this ritual state will support his prayers and make them more effective.

Fasting also helps to induce revelations in the form of dreams, visions, and voices. These are the work of the Holy Spirit which, according to Bishop Ovebanjo, is "the inner person and inner voice" dwelling in every man. The importance of personal revelation in the Church suggests that it is a carry-over from the traditional sphere, a modified form of divination.

General "prophecies" are often given during worship services or in private homes. According to Turner, "much of this is indistinguishable from general pastoral advice or spiritual exhortation, cast in the form that gives extra divine sanction and secures closer attention." For example:

> And the voice said unto me . . . your house needs rededicating to free it from bad dreams . . . call upon the Lord in prayer for seven days from 3 A.M. till 5:30 A.M. . . . many should have faith in the holy water, but don't use it carelessly, . . . pray for Ghana, there'll be war . . . there must be no smoking or drinking and beware of adultery . . . many who have lapsed will return . . . And the voice passed.[37]

People ask their minister for special revelations (called "divine inquiries") concerning personal problems. Prophecies may also be obtained regarding significant events within the Church, e.g., the marriage of a minister, the appointment of main church officers, the building of a church. In addition, annual prophecies are announced to the public concerning the course of the new year and the welfare of the people and their chiefs.

Another direct importation from the traditional sphere is spirit possession. This is a common occurrence in the Church of the Lord, especially during public worship when, at the climax of the service, members of the congregation come forward to dance, sing, and testify to God's saving power. These acts are used to induce possession. Adejobi explains: "Why do you need to sing, dance, clap and engage in all sorts of lively entertainments before the Holy Spirit could descend? Because sweet songs, drums, and the like are relished goods of the Holy Spirit. The Spirit would therefore descend on hearing them." [38]

The whole purpose of prophecy-divination in the Church of the Lord is to save men from the evils of this world. And illness is the primary concern. Despite the widespread introduction of Western medicine into West Africa, medical services are still in very short supply and the treatment given is often far from adequate. Consequently, many Africans are not entirely convinced of the effectiveness of Western medicine. There is also a tendency in the Aladura Churches to reject all Western medicine, because the African word for medicine is a generic term that does not distinguish between pagan medicines, which the Churches condemn, and Western medicines. There is also a tendency to reject all "medicine" as the "work of man."

As Turner points out, the healing techniques of the Church of the Lord conform to traditional methods. Only the content has been changed. In keeping with the traditional approach, the healing procedures of the Church treat the "moral" man by using spiritual and symbolic means. The Church's healing service consists of prayers for the intervention of Christ and the Holy Spirit, confessions of moral wrongs, expulsion of evil (i.e., pagan) spirits, priestly blessings (including laying on of hands or application of the ministerial rod of office), and the administration of holy water.

Part of the confession reads as follows:

Confess, confess, confess! We've broken his commandments and given chances for all dreadful diseases to attack us. Our sin of having other gods. Trusting power of men. Calling his name in vain. Breaking Sabbath. Dishonouring father and mother. . . . Our ghostly enemy uses all these to bring on us all deadly diseases.

Then follow private confessions and prayers:

Adoration, praise for the life of Christ, "our doctor in our midst," petitions that the healing presence of Christ, and of "the Holy Dove and Pigeon," "might rest on our heads, examine us from top to toe and heal every bit of sickness in us." [39]

After the singing of hymns, prayers, dancing, Spirit possession, and a sermon, people are called forward to be healed. In each case, Turner observes, the "demons" of asthma and palpitations, stomach gas and fever, earache, influenza, "weakness," and "pains," are exorcised: "Come out! Come out! In the name of Jesus you cruel demon loose your hold in the name of Jesus." Sometimes holy water is directly applied to the afflicted part of the body. The service concludes with the consecration of holy water, which the people take home.

A final feature of the Church of the Lord is the annual festival of Mount Taborar. In Nigeria the festival takes place on August 22nd at Oshitelu's home town of Ogere, where an elevated site, called Mt. Taborar, has been constructed. Outside Nigeria, the festival is held at other Mt. Taborars in Freetown, Sierre Leone and in Monrovia, Liberia, and at several elevated places in Ghana. Like the annual festivals of Shembe's Church, the Mt. Taborar ceremony is primarily a pilgrimage festival. Members of the Church of the Lord come from all over the country, clad in white gowns, carrying special banners on behalf of each of the Church's congregations. Many come bearing offerings in fulfillment of vows made during the previous year. The festival is also open to non-members, and each year advertisements over the radio and in the press attract thousands of pagans, Muslims, and members of other Christian churches. All who come to Mt. Taborar, the "Holy Mountain of Power," receive forgiveness of sins and spiritual cleansing. At the end a spokesman reads aloud a general prophecy concerning the country and its rulers and their welfare during the coming year.[40]

Sociologically, the festival unites people of all religions and all social classes, including traditional rulers and local politicians. This fits into the general pattern of religious toleration and eclecticism in Nigeria and the traditional pattern of annual orisha festivals shared by all. In a fundamental sense, the festival expresses an accommodation between the Church of the Lord and the larger social structure in which it lives. Theologically, the festival proclaims that God has acted in Nigeria through an African prophet whose message is available to all. For members of the Church, the festival demonstrates that the whole world is now under God's direction. In whatever geographical and sociological position a member of the Church finds himself, he knows that God and his Spirit are constantly available to him.

As Robin Horton has pointed out, this emphasis upon the universality of God is not solely the result of Christian influence. It represents, in part, a natural development within traditional religion in response to the effects of modern social change. It is the result of the widening of the spatiohistorical field of experience from the traditional microcosmos to the more modern macrocosmos. As the macrocosmic dimension came more to the fore under the impact of external influence, so did the traditional concept of the supreme god, which, as we have seen, is fundamentally linked to the macrocosmic pole of experience and to the experience of personal and cultural crisis:

> If thousands of people find themselves outside the microcosms, and if even those left inside see the boundaries weakening if not actually dissolving, they can only interpret these changes by assuming that the lesser spirits (underpinners of the microcosms) are in retreat, and that the supreme being (underpinner of the macrocosm) is taking over direct control of the everyday world. Hence they come to regard the lesser spirits as irrelevant or downright evil. Hence, too, they develop a far more elaborate theory of the supreme being and his ways of working in the world, and a battery of new ritual techniques for approaching him and directing his influence.
>
> As more and more people become involved in social life beyond the confines of their various microcosms, they begin to evolve a moral code for the governance of this wider life. Since the supreme being is already defined as the arbiter of everything that transcends the boundaries of the microcosms, he is seen as underpinning this universalistic moral code.[41]

Such a process, Horton suggests, "reduces Christianity and Islam to the role of catalysts—i.e., stimulators and accelerators of changes which were 'in the air' anyway; triggers for reactions in which they do not always appear as the end products." This explains why "the actual story of Islam and Christianity in Africa . . . is one of the highly conditional and selective acceptance . . . [and why] the beliefs and practices of the so-called world religions are only accepted where they happen to coincide with responses of the traditional cosmology to other, non-missionary, factors of the modern situation." If we look at the process in this way, we can understand why Christianity made only minor advances in the beginning and why it became more successful as the colonial experience exerted a wider impact upon the traditional microcosmos. It also explains why Africans rejected the other-worldliness of modern Western Christianity while readily accepting the concept of supreme being and a universalistic morality. At the same time, it makes clear that "the typical traditional cosmology, under the catalytic influence of Islam and Christianity, has made a vigorous response to the challenge posed by the weakening of the microcosmic boundaries." [42]

Although Horton's theory tends to explain African "conversion" to Christianity largely in socioeconomic terms, it emphasizes what we have already seen: namely, that the prophet-healing churches have transformed Christianity according to preexisting symbols, rituals, and types of community.

Thus we have come full circle. The examination of African Independent Christianity has brought us back to the enduring themes of African traditional religions. Christian history has become an archetypal myth, Christian ritual a practical and expressive medium, and the Christian Church a new basis of communal solidarity.

NOTES

1. The vast amount of literature on African Independent Christianity is well served by an excellent bibliography, R. C. MITCHELL and H. W. TURNER, *A Bibliography of Modern African Religious Movements* (Evanston: Northwestern University Press, 1966). This listing is regularly brought up to date in the *Journal of Religion in Africa* (See vol. 1, fasc. 3, 1968, and vol. 3, fasc. 3, 1970). Two valuable survey articles have been written by JAMES FERNANDEZ, "African Religious Movements—Types and Dynamics," *Journal of Modern African Studies* 2, no. 4 (1964), and H. W. TURNER, "A Typology for African Religious Movements," *Journal of Religion in Africa* 1, fasc. 1 (1969). A major comparative study has been written by DAVID B. BARRETT, *Schism and Renewal in Africa: An Analysis of Six*

Thousand Contemporary Religious Movements (Nairobi: Oxford University Press, 1968).

2. MARIE-LOUISE MARTIN, *Prophetic Christianity in the Congo* (Johannesburg: The Christian Institute of Southern Africa, n.d.), p. 4.

3. EFRAIM ANDERSON, *Messianic Popular Movements in the Lower Congo* (Uppsala, Sweden: Almquist and Wiksell, 1958), p. 45.

4. *Ibid.,* p. 54.

5. *Ibid.,* p. 62.

6. *Ibid.,* p. 65.

7. MARTIAL SINDA, *Le Messianism Congolais* (Paris: Payot, 1972), p. 73. [Passage quoted in text translated from the French by the author.]

8. GEORGES BALANDIER, *Sociologie Actuelle de l'Afrique Noire* (Paris: Presses Universitaires de France, 1955), pp. 432-433. [Passage quoted in text translated from the French by the author.]

9. ANDERSON, *Popular Movements,* p. 195.

10. Cited in WYATT MacGAFFEY, "*The Beloved City:* Commentary on a Kimbanguist Text," *Journal of Religion in Africa* 2, fasc. 2 (1969), 141.

11. *Ibid.,* p. 139.

12. B. G. M. SUNDKLER, *Bantu Prophets in South Africa,* 2nd ed. (London: Oxford University Press for the International Africa Institute, 1961), p. 110. Used with permission.

13. *Ibid.,* p. 329.

14. *Ibid.,* p. 125.

15. H.-J. BECKEN, "The Nazareth Baptist Church of Shembe," in *Our Approach to the Independent Church Movement in South Africa* (Mapumulo, Natal: Missiological Institute, Lutheran Theological College, 1965), p. 3.

16. GERHARDUS C. OOSTHUIZEN, *The Theology of A South African Messiah* (Leiden, Netherlands: E. J. Brill, 1967), p. 30.

17. *Ibid.,* p. 31.

18. *Ibid.,* pp. 48-49.

19. SUNDKLER, *Bantu Prophets,* pp. 283-84.

20. OOSTHUIZEN, *Theology,* p. 40.

21. *Ibid.,* pp. 135, 139.

22. *Ibid.,* pp. 141-42.

23. SUNDKLER, *Bantu Prophets,* pp. 229-30.

24. JAMES W. FERNANDEZ, "The Precincts of the Prophet: A Day with Johannes Galilee Shembe," *Journal of Religion in Africa* 5, fasc. 1 (1972), 42.

25. *Ibid.,* pp. 53; 48, n. 11.

26. VICTOR TURNER, "The Center Out There: Pilgrim's Goal," *History of Religions* 12, no. 3 (1973).

27. H.-J. BECKEN, "On the Holy Mountain: A Visit to the New Year's Festival of the Nazaretha Church on Mount Nhlangakazi, 14 January, 1967," *Journal of Religion in Africa* 1, fasc. 2 (1967), 143, 144, 145, 146.

28. HAROLD TURNER, *History of an African Independent Church,* 2 vols. (Oxford: The Clarendon Press, 1967), I. 40. © Oxford University Press 1967. By permission of the Oxford University Press, Oxford.

29. *Independent Church,* I, 46.
30. PEEL, *Aladura: A Religious Movement Among the Yoruba,* p. 292.
31. *Ibid.,* p. 295.
32. *Independent Church,* II, 70.
33. *Ibid.,* II, 70.
34. *Ibid.,* II, 71.
35. *Ibid.,* II, 71.
36. *Ibid.,* II, 74.
37. *Ibid.,* II, 129-30.
38. *Ibid.,* II, 127.
39. *Ibid.,* II, 145.
40. *Ibid.,* II, 221-30.
41. HORTON, "African Conversion," p. 102.
42. *Ibid.,* pp. 104, 106.

Bibliography

BOOKS AND PERIODICALS

Approaches to the Study of African Religions and Other Traditional Religions

DANQUAH, J. B., *Akan Doctrine of God* (2nd ed.). London: Frank Cass and Co. Ltd., 1968.

DOUGLAS, MARY, "Magic and Miracle," and "Primitive Worlds," in *Purity and Danger*. London: Routledge and Kegan Paul, Ltd., 1966.

———, *Natural Symbols*. New York: Vintage Books, 1973.

ELIADE, MIRCEA, *Cosmos and History*. New York: Harper & Row, Publishers, 1959.

EVANS-PRITCHARD, E. E., *Theories of Primitive Religion*. Oxford: The Clarendon Press, 1965.

GEERTZ, CLIFFORD, "Religion as a Cultural System," in *Anthropological Approaches to the Study of Religion,* ed. Michael Banton. London: Tavistock Publications, 1966.

HORTON, ROBIN, "African Traditional Thought and Western Science," *Africa* 37, Nos. 1 and 2 (1967).

———, "Ritual Man in Africa," *Africa* 34, No. 2 (1964).

HORTON, ROBIN, and RUTH FINNEGAN, eds., *Modes of Thought: Essays on Thinking in Western and Non-Western Societies*. London: Faber & Faber, 1973.

IDOWU, E. BOLAJI, *African Traditional Religion: A Definition*. London: SCM Press, Ltd., 1973.

KING, NOEL, *Religions of Africa*. New York: Harper & Row, Publishers, 1970.

LEACH, EDMOND R., "Ritual" in *International Encyclopedia of the Social Sciences* (1968), 13.

LÉVI-STRAUSS, CLAUDE, "The Structural Study of Myth" and "The Effectiveness of Symbols" in *Structural Anthropology*. New York: Basic Books, Inc., 1963.

LIENHARDT, GODFREY, "Theology, Primitive," in *International Encyclopedia of the Social Sciences* (1968), 15.

MBITI, JOHN S., *African Religions and Philosophy.* New York: Doubleday & Company, Inc., 1970.

MORTON-WILLIAMS, PETER M., "An Outline of the Cosmology and Cult Organization of the Oyo Yoruba," *Africa* 34, No. 3 (1964).

NEEDHAM, RODNEY, *Belief, Language, and Experience.* Chicago: University of Chicago Press, 1972.

PARRINDER, GEOFFREY, *Religion in Africa.* Harmondsworth, England: Penguin Books Ltd., 1969.

————, *West African Religion* (2nd ed.). New York: Barnes and Noble, Inc., 1970.

P'BITEK, OKOT, *African Religions in Western Scholarship.* Nairobi: East African Publishing House, 1970.

RADCLIFFE-BROWN, A. R., "Religion and Society," in *Structure and Function in Primitive Society.* New York: The Free Press, 1965.

RANGER, T. O., and I. N. KIMAMBO, *The Historical Study of African Religion.* Berkeley: University of California Press, 1972.

SCHMIDT, WILHELM, *The Origin and Growth of Religion.* London: Methuen & Co. Ltd., 1931.

TAYLOR, JOHN, *The Primal Vision.* London: SCM Press, 1963.

TEMPLES, PLACIDE, *Bantu Philosophy.* Paris: Présence Africaine, 1959.

WILSON, MONICA, *Religion and the Transformation of Society: A Study of Social Change in Africa.* Cambridge: Cambridge University Press, 1971.

WINCH, PETER, "Understanding a Primitive Society," *American Philosophical Quarterly* 1, No. 4 (1964).

Myth and Cosmology

ABRAHAMSSON, HANS, *The Origin of Death: Studies in African Mythology.* Uppsala, Sweden: Almqvist, 1951.

BEIDELMAN, T. O., "Kaguru Symbolic Classification," in *Right and Left,* ed. Rodney Needham. Chicago: University of Chicago Press, 1973.

BEIER, ULLI, "Before Oduduwa," *Odu,* No. 3 (1956).

————, *Origin of Life and Death.* London: William Heinemann Ltd., 1966.

BIEBUYCK, DANIEL, and KAHOMBO MATEENE, eds. and trans., *The Mwindo Epic.* Berkeley: University of California Press, 1971.

BIOBAKU, S., "The Use and Interpretation of Yoruba Myths," *Odu,* No. 1 (1955).

DIETERLEN, G., "The Mande Creation Myth," *Africa* 27, No. 2 (1957).

FINNEGAN, RUTH, *Oral Literature in Africa.* Oxford: The Clarendon Press, 1972.

FORDE, DARYLL, ed., *African Worlds.* London: Oxford University Press, 1954.

GOODY, JOHN R., *The Myth of Barge.* Oxford: The Clarendon Press, 1972.

GRIAULE, MARCEL, *Conversations With Ogotemmêli.* London: Oxford University Press, 1965.

HERSKOVITS, MELVILLE and FRANCES S., *Dahomean Narrative.* Evanston, Ill.: Northwestern University Press, 1958.

LEACH, EDMOND, *The Structural Study of Myth and Totemism.* London: Tavistock Publications, 1967.

LIENHARDT, R. G., *Divinity and Experience*. Oxford: The Clarendon Press, 1961.

LLOYD, PETER, "Yoruba Myths: A Sociological Interpretation," *Odu*, No. 2 (1956).

LONG, CHARLES H., *Alpha: Myths of Creation*. New York: George Braziller, Inc., 1963.

MIDDLETON, JOHN, *Lugbara Religion*. London: Oxford University Press, 1960.

————, ed., *Myth and Cosmos*. New York: The Natural History Press, 1967.

————, "Some Categories of Dual Classification," in *Right and Left*, ed. Rodney Needham.

NEEDHAM, RODNEY, "Right and Left in Nyoro Symbolic Classification," in *Right and Left*, ed. Rodney Needham. Chicago: University of Chicago Press, 1973.

PARRINDER, GEOFFERY, *African Mythology*. London: Paul A. Hamlyn, 1967.

SHORTER, AYLWARD, "Religious Values in Kimbu Historical Charters," *Africa* 34, No. 3 (1969).

TEN RAA, ERIC, "The Genealogical Method in the Analysis of Myth, and a Structural Method," in *Right and Left*, ed. Rodney Needham.

VANSINA, JAN, *Oral Tradition*. London: Routledge and Kegan Paul Ltd., 1965.

WERNER, ALICE, *Myths and Legends of the Bantu*. London: Frank Cass, (1925) 1968.

Concept of Time

BEIDELMAN, T., "Kaguru Time Reckoning," *Southwest Journal of Anthropology* 19 (Spring, 1963).

BOHANAN, L., "A Genealogical Charter," *Africa* 22 (1952).

BOHANAN, P., "Concepts of Time among the Tiv of Nigeria," in *Myth and Cosmos*, ed. John Middleton.

D'AZEVEDO, W., "Uses of the Past in Gola Discourse," *Journal of African History* 3, No. 1 (1962).

EVANS-PRITCHARD, E. E., *The Nuer*, ch. 3. Oxford: The Clarendon Press, 1940.

LEACH, E., "Two Essays Concerning the Symbolic Representation of Time," in *Reader in Comparative Religion*, ed. William A. Lessa and Evon Z. Vogt (3rd ed.). New York: Harper & Row, Publishers, 1972.

MBITI, JOHN S., *African Religions and Philosophy*, ch. 3.

MIDDLETON, JOHN, *Lugbara Religion*, ch. 5, pt. 1.

RIGBY, PETER, "Gogo Rituals of Purification," in *Dialectic in Practical Religion*, ed. E. R. Leach. Cambridge: Cambridge University Press, 1968.

RYDER, A., "Traditions and History," in *Africa Discovers Her Past*, ed. J. D. Fage. London: Oxford University Press, 1970.

TURNER, VICTOR W., *The Ritual Process*, ch. 3. Chicago: Aldine Publishing Co., 1969.

WILKS, I., "African Historiographical Traditions, Old and New," in *Africa Discovers Her Past*, ed J. D. Fage.

Concept of Man

BASCOM, W., "Yoruba Concepts of the Soul," in *Men and Cultures,* ed. Anthony F. C. Wallace. Philadelphia: University of Pennsylvania Press, 1960.

BUSIA, K., "The Ashanti of the Gold Coast," in *African Worlds,* ed. Daryll Forde.

DENG, FRANCIS MADING, *The Dinka of the Sudan.* New York: Holt, Rinehart and Winston, 1972.

EVANS-PRITCHARD, E. E., *Nuer Religion,* ch. 6. Oxford: The Clarendon Press, 1956.

FORTES, MEYER, *Oedipus and Job in West African Religion.* Cambridge: Cambridge University Press, 1959.

GRIAULE, MARCEL, "The Idea of Person Among the Dogon," in *Cultures and Societies of Africa,* ed. Simon and Phoebe Ottenberg. New York: Random House, Inc., 1960.

IDOWU, E. BOLAJI,*Olódùmarè: God in Yoruba Belief,* chs. 13 and 14. London: Longmans, Green and Co., Ltd., 1962.

LIENHARDT, GODFREY, "The Situation of Death: An Aspect of Anuak Philosophy," *Anthropological Quarterly* 25, No. 2 (1963).

MEYEROWITZ, EVA L., "Concept of the Soul Among the Akan of the Gold Coast," *Africa* 21, No. 1 (1951).

PARRINDER, G., *West African Psychology.* London: Lutterworth Press, 1951.

Supreme Beings

CLARKE, E., "The Sociological Significance of Ancestor Worship in Ashante," *Africa* 3, No. 4 (1930).

DANEEL, M., *The God of the Matopo Hills.* The Hague: Mouton, 1970.

DANQUAH, J. B., *Akan Doctrine of God.*

ELIADE, M., *Patterns in Comparative Religion,* ch. 2 "Sky Gods." Cleveland: The World Publishing Company, 1963.

EVANS-PRITCHARD, E. E., *Nuer Religion,* chs. 1, 2, and 4.

FORDE, D., ed., *African Worlds.*

IDOWU, E., *Olódùmarè: God in Yoruba Belief.*

LIENHARDT, R. G., *Divinity and Experience,* chs. 1 and 2.

LONG, C., "The West African High God: History and Religious Experience," *History of Religions* 3, No. 2 (1964).

MBITI, JOHN S., *Concepts of God in Africa.* New York: Frederick A. Praeger, Inc., 1970.

PARRINDER, G., "Monotheism and Pantheism in Africa," *Journal of Religion in Africa* 3, fasc. 2 (1970).

PETTAZZONI, RAFFAELE, "The Formation of Monotheism," in *Essays on the History of Religions.* Leiden: Brill, 1954.

————, "The Supreme Being: Phenomenological Structure and Historical Development," in *History of Religions,* ed. Joseph M. Kitagawa and Mircea Eliade. Chicago: University of Chicago Press, 1959.

RATTRAY, R. S., *Ashanti,* chs. 13 and 14. Oxford: The Clarendon Press, 1923.

SCHMIDT, WILHELM, *The Origin and Growth of Religion.*

SMITH, EDWIN W., ed., *African Ideas of God* (3rd ed.). London: Edinburgh House Press, 1966.

Spirit Mediumship and Possession

BEATTIE, J. H. M., "Ritual and Social Change," *Man,* n.s., 1 (1966).

BEATTIE, J. H. M., and JOHN MIDDLETON, eds., *Spirit Mediumship and Society in Africa.* New York: Africana Publishing Corporation, 1969.

FIELD, MARGARET J., *Search for Security.* London: Faber and Faber Ltd., 1960.

GLEASON, JUDITH, *Orisha: The Gods of Yorubaland.* New York: Atheneum Publishers, 1971.

LEWIS, I. M., *Ecstatic Religion.* Harmondsworth, England: Penguin Books Ltd., 1971.

PRINCE, RAYMOND, "Indigenous Yoruba Psychiatry," in *Magic, Faith and Healing,* ed. A. Kiev. New York: The Free Press, 1964.

———, "Possession and Social Cybernetics," in *Trance and Possession States.* Montreal: R. M. Bucke Memorial Society, 1968.

RIGBY, PETER, and FRED LULE, "Divination and Healing in Peri-Urban Kampala," *Nkanga,* No. 7. Kampala: Makerere Institute of Social Research, 1973.

WALKER, SHEILA S., *Ceremonial Spirit Possession in Africa and Afro-America.* Leiden: Brill, 1972.

ZARETSKY, IRVING I., *Bibliography of Spirit Possession and Mediumship in Africa.* Berkeley: Department of Anthropology, University of California, 1966.

Rites of Passage

BEATTIE, J. H. M., "Initiation Into the Chwezi Spirit Possession Cult," *African Studies* 16 (1967).

ELIADE, MIRCEA, *Rites and Symbols of Initiation.* New York: Harper & Row, Publishers, 1965.

LAFONTAINE, J. S., "Ritualization of Women's Life-Crises in Bugisu," in *The Interpretation of Ritual.* London: Tavistock Publications, 1972.

RICHARDS, AUDREY I., *Chisungu: A Girl's Initiation Ceremony.* London: Faber and Faber Ltd., 1961.

RIGBY, PETER, "Gogo Rituals of Purification," in *Dialectic in Practical Religion,* ed. E. R. Leach. Cambridge: Cambridge University Press, 1968.

TURNER, VICTOR W., *Drums of Affliction,* chs. 7 and 8. London: Oxford University Press, 1968.

———, *Forest of Symbols,* chs. 4 and 7.

———, *The Ritual Process,* chs. 1 and 2.

Ritual Sacrifice

ARINZE, FRANCIS A., *Sacrifice in Ibo Religion.* Ibadan: Ibadan University Press, 1970.

EVANS-PRITCHARD, E. E., *Nuer Religion,* chs. 8, 10 and 11.

GRIAULE, M., *Conversations with Ogotemmeli,* "Sacrifice."

HUBERT, H., and M. MAUSS, *Sacrifice: Its Nature and Function.* London: Cohen and West, 1964.

LIENHARDT, R. G., *Divinity and Experience,* chs. 6 and 7.

MIDDLETON, J., *Lugbara Religion,* ch. 3.

RIGBY, PETER, "The Symbolic Role of Cattle in Gogo Ritual," in *Translation of Culture,* ed. T. O. Beidelman. London: Tavistock Publications, 1971.

Divination

BASCOM, WILLIAM, *Ifa Divination: Communication Between Gods and Men in West Africa.*

BEATTIE, J. H. M., "Divination in Bunyoro," *Ethnology* 3 (1964).

GLEASON, JUDITH, *A Recitation of Ifa, Oracle of the Yoruba.* New York: Grossman Publishers, 1973.

PARK, GEORGE K., "Divination and its Social Context," *Journal of the Royal Anthropological Institute* 93, No. 2 (1963).

Priests and Prophets

BEIDELMAN, T. O., "Nuer Priests and Prophets: Charisma, Authority, and Power Among the Nuer," in *The Translation of Culture.*

BERNARDI, B., *The Mugwe: The Failing Prophet.* London: Oxford University Press, 1959.

BURRIDGE, KENNELM, *New Heaven, New Earth.* New York: Schocken Books, Inc., 1969.

EVANS-PRITCHARD, E. E., *Nuer Religion,* ch. 12.

LIENHARDT, R. GODFREY, *Divinity and Experience,* chs. 5 and 8.

MIDDLETON, JOHN, *Lugbara Religion,* ch. 5.

TURNER, VICTOR, "Muchona the Hornet, Interpreter of Religion," in V. Turner, *Forest of Symbols,* ch. 6. Ithaca: Cornell University Press, 1967.

Sacred Kingship

BEATTIE, J. H. M., *The Nyoro State.* Oxford: The Clarendon Press, 1971.

———, "Rituals of Nyoro Kingship," *Africa* 29, No. 2 (1959).

BEIDELMAN, T. O., "Swazi Royal Ritual," *Africa* 36, No. 4 (1966).

BUSIA, K. A., *The Position of the Chief in the Modern Political System of Ashanti.* London: Oxford University Press, 1951.

CHARSLEY, S. R., *The Princes of Nyakyusa.* Nairobi: East African Publishing House, 1969.

COLLINS, J. O., *Problems in African History,* part 1, "Africa and Egypt." Englewood Cliffs, N.J.: Prentice-Hall, Inc., 1968.

EVANS-PRITCHARD, E. E., "The Divine Kingship of the Shilluk of the Nilotic Sudan" (The Frazer Lecture, 1948), in *Social Anthropology and Other Essays.* New York: The Free Press of Glencoe, 1962.

FALLERS, L. A., *The King's Men.* London: Oxford University Press, 1964.

FEIERMAN, STEVEN, *The Shambaa Kingdom.* Madison: University of Wisconsin Press, 1974.

GLUCKMAN, MAX, "Rituals of Rebellion in South-East Africa," in *Order and Rebellion.* New York: The Free Press of Glencoe, 1960.

HENIGE, DAVID P., *The Chronology of Oral Tradition.* Oxford: The Clarendon Press, 1974.

HERSKOVITS, MELVILLE and FRANCES S. HERSKOVITS, *Dahomey: An Ancient West African Kingdom* (2 vols). New York: J. J. Augustin, 1938.

IRSTAM, TOR, *The King of Ganda: Studies in the Institutions of Sacral Kingship in Africa.* Lund: Ohlsson, 1944.

KAGWA, APOLO, *The Kings of Buganda.* Nairobi: East African Publishing House, 1971.

KARUGIRE, SAMWIRI R., *A History of the Kingdom of Nkore in Western Uganda to 1896.* Oxford: The Clarendon Press, 1971.

KIWANUKA, SEMAKULA, *A History of Buganda to 1900.* London: Longmans, Green & Co. Ltd., 1971.

KUPER, HILDA, *An African Aristocracy.* London: Oxford University Press, 1947.

———, "A Royal Ritual in Changing Political Context," *Cahiers d' Etudes Africaine* 12, No. 42 (1972).

LIENHARDT, R. G., "The Shilluk of the Upper Nile," in *African Worlds,* ed. Daryll Forde.

LLOYD, PETER, "The Political Structure of African Kingdoms," in *Political Systems and the Distribution of Power,* ed. Michael Banton. London: Tavistock Publications, 1965.

———, "Sacred Kingship and Government Among the Yoruba," *Africa* 30, No. 3 (1960).

MAIR, LUCY, *Primitive Government.* Harmondsworth, England: Penguin Books, Ltd., 1964.

MORTON-WILLIAMS, PETER M., "The Yoruba Kingdom of Oyo," in *West African Kingdoms of the Nineteenth Century,* ed. Daryll Forde and P. M. Kaberry. London: Oxford University Press, 1967.

NYAKATURA, J. W., *Anatomy of an African Kingdom: A History of Bunyoro-Kitara.* New York: Doubleday & Company, Inc., 1973.

OJO, AFOLABI G. J., *Yoruba Palaces.* London: University of London Press, 1966.

RAY, B., "Royal Shrines and Ceremonies of Buganda," *Uganda Journal* 36 (1972).

ROSCOE, JOHN, *The Buganda*. Cambridge: Cambridge University Press, 1911.

SARPONG, PETER, *Sacred Stools of the Akan*. Kumasi: Ghana Publishing Corporation, 1971.

SMITH, R. S., *Kingdoms of the Yoruba*. London: Methuen & Co. Ltd., 1969.

VANSINA, JAN, "A Comparison of African Kingdoms," *Africa* 32, 1962.

———, *Kingdoms of the Savanah*. Madison: University of Wisconsin Press, 1966.

———, *The Tio Kingdom of the Middle Congo, 1808–1892*. London: Oxford University Press, 1973.

YOUNG, MICHAEL, "The Divine Kingship of the Jukun: A Re-evaluation of Some Theories," *Africa* 36, No. 2 (1966).

Ancestor Cult

FORTES, MEYER, *Oedipus and Job in West African Religion*. Cambridge: Cambridge University Press, 1959.

———, "Some Reflections on Ancestor Worship in Africa," in *African Systems of Thought*, ed. M. Fortes and G. Dieterlen. London: Oxford University Press, 1965.

———, *The Web of Kinship Among the Tallensi*. London: Oxford University Press, 1949.

GOODY, JACK, *Death, Property, and the Ancestors*. Stanford, Calif.: Stanford University Press, 1962.

HERSKOVITS, MELVILLE, *Dahomey: An Ancient West African Kingdom*.

JUNOD, HENRI, *The Life of a South African Tribe*, II. London: D. Nutt, 1913.

MIDDLETON, JOHN, *Lugbara Religion*.

RATTRAY, R. S., *Ashanti*.

TURNER, VICTOR, *Drums of Affliction*.

Witchcraft

DOUGLAS, MARY, ed., *Witchcraft: Accusations and Confessions*. London: Tavistock Publications, 1971.

EVANS-PRITCHARD, E. E., *Witchcraft, Oracles, and Magic Among the Azande*. Oxford: The Clarendon Press, 1937.

MAIR, LUCY, *Witchcraft*. New York: McGraw-Hill Book Company, 1969.

MIDDLETON, JOHN, and E. H. WINTER, *Witchcraft and Sorcery in East Africa*. London: Routledge and Kegan Paul Ltd., 1963.

TURNER, VICTOR, "Witchcraft and Sorcery: Taxonomy versus Dynamics," in *Forest of Symbols*, ch. 5.

ZUESSE, E., "On the Nature of the Demonic: African Witchery," *Numen* 18, fasc. 3 (1971).

Religion and Rebellion

BALANDIER, GEORGES, *Sociology of Black Africa*. London: Andre Duetsch, 1970.

BARNETT, DONALD L., and KARARI NJAME, *Mau Mau From Within*. New York: Monthly Review Press, 1966.

GWASSA, G. C. K., "Kinjikitile and the Ideology of Maji Maji," in *The Historical Study of African Religion,* ed. T. O. Ranger and I. N. Kimambo.

GWASSA, G. C. K. and ILIFFE, J., *Records of the Maji Maji Rising,* Part I. Nairobi: East African Publishing House, 1968.

ILIFFE, J. "The Organization of the Maji Maji Rebellion," *Journal of African History,* 8 No. 3 (1967).

RANGER, TERENCE O., "Connexions Between 'Primary Resistance' Movements and Modern Mass Nationalism in East and Central Africa," *Journal of African History* 9 (1968).

————, *Revolt in Southern Rhodesia, 1896–97*. London: William Heinemann Ltd., 1967.

ROTBERG, ROBERT I., ed., *Rebellion in Black Africa*. London: Oxford University Press, 1971.

SHEPPERSON, GEORGE and THOMAS PRICE, *Independent African*. Edinburgh: The University Press, 1958.

Islam in Africa

BRAVMAN, RENÉ A., *Islam and Tribal Art in West Africa*. Cambridge: Cambridge University Press, 1974.

BROWN, L. CARL, "The Sudanese Mahdyia," in *Rebellion in Black Africa,* ed. Robert I. Rotberg.

COHEN, ABNER, *Custom and Politics in Urban Africa*. Berkeley: University of California Press, 1969.

CRUISE O'BRIEN, DONAL B., *The Mourides of Senegal*. Oxford: The Clarendon Press, 1971.

FISHER, H., *Ahmadiyyah, A Study in Contemporary Islam on the West African Coast*. London: Oxford University Press, 1963.

GREENBERG, JOSEPH, *The Influence of Islam on a Sudanese Religion*. New York: J. J. Augustin Publisher, 1946.

HISKETT, MERVYN, *The Sword of Truth, The Life and Times of the Shehu Usuman dan Fodio*. New York: Oxford University Press, 1973.

HOLT, P. M., *The Mahdist State in the Sudan 1881–1898*. Oxford: The Clarendon Press, 1970.

KABA, LANSINÉ, *The Wahhabiyya: Islamic Reform and Politics in French West Africa*. Evanston, Ill.: Northwestern University Press, 1974.

KING, NOEL, *Christian and Muslim in Africa*. New York: Harper & Row, Publishers, 1971.

KING, NOEL, ABDU KASOZI, and ARYE ODED, *Islam and the Confluence of Religions in Uganda 1840–1966*. Tallahassee: American Academy of Religion, 1973.

KRITZECK, JAMES, and WILLIAM H. LEWIS, eds., *Islam in Africa*. New York: Van Nostrand-Reinhold Co., 1969.

LEVITZION, NEHEMIA, *Muslims and Chiefs in West Africa*. Oxford: The Clarendon Press, 1968.

LEWIS, I. M., ed., *Islam in Tropical Africa*. London: Oxford University Press, 1966.

NADEL, S. F., *Nupe Religion*. London: Routledge and Kegan Paul Ltd., 1954.

ONWUEJEOGWU, M., "The Cult of the *Bori* Spirits Among the Hausa," in *Man in Africa*, ed. Mary Douglas and Phillis M. Kaberry. London: Tavistock Publications, 1969.

PADEN, JOHN N., *Religion and Political Culture in Kano*. Berkeley: University of California Press, 1973.

SMITH, M. F., *Baba of Karo, A Woman of the Muslim Hausa*. London: Faber and Faber Ltd., 1954.

TREMEARNE, A. J. N., *The Ban of the Bori*. London: Heath, Cranton and Ouseley, Ltd., 1914.

TRIMINGHAM, J. SPENCER, *The Influence of Islam on Africa*. London: Longmans, Green & Co. Ltd., 1968.

————, *Islam in East Africa*. Oxford: The Clarendon Press, 1961.

————, *Islam in West Africa*. Oxford: The Clarendon Press, 1959.

WILLIS, J. R., *"Jihad Fi Sabil Allah*—Its Doctrinal Basis in Islam and Some Aspects of Its Evolution in Nineteenth Century West Africa," *Journal of African History* 8, No. 3 (1967).

WILKS, I., "The Transmission of Islamic Learning in the Western Sudan," in *Literacy in Traditional Societies*, ed. Jack Goody. Cambridge: Cambridge University Press, 1968.

ZEIN, ABDUL HAMID M. EL, *The Sacred Meadows: A Structural Analysis of Religious Symbolism in an East African Town*. Evanston, Ill.: Northwestern University Press, 1974.

Independent Christianity

ANDERSON, EFRAIM, *Messianic Popular Movements in the Lower Congo*. Uppsala, Sweden: Almqvist and Wiksell, 1958.

BAETA, C. G., *Prophetism in Ghana*. London: SCM Press, 1962.

BALANDIER, GEORGES, *Ambiguous Africa*, ch. 7. New York: Pantheon Books, Inc., 1966.

————, *The Sociology of Black Africa*. London: Andre Deutsch Ltd., 1970.

BARRETT, DAVID B., *Schism and Renewal in Africa*. Nairobi: Oxford University Press, 1968.

DANEEL, M. L., *Old and New in Southern Shone Independent Churches*. The Hague: Mouton, 1971.

————, *Zionism and Faith Healing in Rhodesia*. The Hague: Mouton, 1970.

FABIAN, J., *Jamaa: A Charismatic Movement in Katanga*. Evanston, Ill.: Northwestern University Press, 1971.

FERNANDEZ, JAMES, "African Religious Movements—Types and Dynamics," *Journal of Modern African Studies* 2, No. 4 (1964).

HALIBURTON, G. M., *The Prophet Harris*. London: Longmans, Green & Co. Ltd., 1971.

HORTON, ROBIN, "African Conversion," *Africa* 41, No. 2 (1971).

JANZEN, JOHN M. and WYATT MACGAFFEY, eds., *An Anthology of Kongo Religion*. Lawrence, Kansas: University of Kansas, 1974.

LUTHERAN THEOLOGICAL COLLEGE, Mapumulo, *Our Approach to the Independent Church Movement in South Africa*. Mapumulo, Natal: Missiological Institute, Lutheran Theological College, 1965.

MACGAFFEY, WYATT, "*The Beloved City*: Commentary on a Kimbanguist Text," *Journal of Religion in Africa* 2, fasc. 2 (1969).

MITCHELL, R. C., and H. W. TURNER, *Bibliography of Modern African Religious Movements*. Evanston, Ill.: Northwestern University Press, 1966.

PEEL, J. D. Y., *Aladura: A Religious Movement Among the Yoruba*. London: Oxford University Press, 1969.

RANGER, T. O., *The African Churches of Tanzania*. Nairobi: East African Publishing House, 1969.

SUNDKLER, B. G. M., *Bantu Prophets in South Africa* (2nd ed.). London: Oxford University Press, 1961.

TURNER, H., *African Independent Church*, 2 vols. Oxford: The Clarendon Press, 1967.

———, "Bibliography of Modern African Independent Movements, Supplements 1 and 2," *Journal of Religion in Africa*, Vol. 1, No. 3, Vol. 3, No. 3 (1968, 1970).

———, "A Typology for Modern African Independent Religious Movements," *Journal of Religion In Africa* 1, fasc. 1 (1967).

WEBSTER, JOHN R., *The African Churches Among the Yoruba*. London: Oxford University Press, 1965.

WELBOURN, F. B., *East African Rebels*. London: SCM Press, 1961.

WELBOURN, F. B., and B. A. OGOT, *A Place to Feel at Home*. London: Oxford University Press, 1966.

Religion in African Literature

ACHEBE, CHINUA, *Arrow of God*. New York: Doubleday & Company, Inc., 1969.

GABRE-MEDIN, TSEGAYE, *Oda-Oak Oracle*. London: Oxford University Press, 1965.

IJIMERE, OBOTUNDE, *Imprisonment of Obatala and Other Plays*. London: William Heinemann Ltd., 1966.

LADIPO, DURO, "Moremi," in *Three Nigerian Plays*, ed. Ulli Beier. London: Longmans, Green & Co. Ltd., 1967.

———, *Oba Ko So, The King Did Not Hang*. Ibadan: Ibadan University Press, 1972.

———, "Oba Waja, The King is Dead," *Présence Africaine*, No. 62 (1967).

LAYE, CAMARA, *The Radiance of the King*. London: Fontana Books, 1965.

NGUGI, JAMES, *The River Between*. London: William Heinemann Ltd., 1965.

SOYINKA, WOLE A., *A Dance of the Forests*. London: Oxford University Press, 1963.

TUTUOLA, AMOS, *My Life in the Bush of Ghosts*. London: Faber and Faber Ltd., 1954.

Religion and Art

African Arts (Quarterly Journal). Los Angeles: African Studies Center, University of California.

BASCOM, WILLIAM, *African Art in Cultural Perspective*. New York: W. W. Norton & Company, Inc., 1973.

BIEBUYCK, DANIEL, *Lega Culture: Art, Initiation and Moral Philosophy Among a Central African People*. Berkeley: University of California Press, 1973.

CARROLL, KEVIN, *Yoruba Religious Carving*. Geoffrey Chapman Ltd., 1967.

D'AZEVEDO, WARREN L., ed., *The Traditional Artist in African Societies*. Bloomington: Indiana University Press, 1973.

JOPLING, CAROL F., ed., *Art and Aesthetics in Primitive Societies*. New York: E. P. Dutton & Co., Inc., 1971.

LAUDE, JEAN, *African Art of the Dogon, The Myths of the Cliffdwellers*. New York: E. P. Dutton & Co., Inc., 1973.

PAULINE, DENISE, *African Sculpture*. New York: The Viking Press, Inc., 1962.

THOMPSON, ROBERT FARRIS, *Black Gods and Kings*. Los Angeles: University of California Press, 1971.

WILLETT, FRANK, *African Art: An Introduction*. London: Thames and Hudson, 1971.

General Reference Book

BOHANNAN, PAUL, and PHILIP CURTIN, *Africa and Africans* (2nd ed.). New York: Natural History Press, 1971.

Bibliographical Sources

African Bibliography Series. London: International African Institute, 1958–60.

Bibliographie Ethnographique de l'Afrique Sud-Saharienne. Tervuren, Belgium, 1925–.

Ethnographic Survey of Africa (approximately fifty volumes). London: International African Institute, 1950–.

MEDIA RESOURCES

Listed below are some of the best films on African religious phenomena currently available in the U.S. and Canada. All films include English narration and commentary. Rental orders should be placed well in advance to insure booking. Prices vary from $15.00 to $35.00 and are subject to change.

"A GREAT TREE HAS FALLEN": Eight day funeral ceremonies for the late Ashanti king, Sir Osei A. Prempeh II. Shows rites and symbols of the traditional Ashanti kingship. 23 min., color. Indiana University.

ANCIENT AFRICANS: A survey of ancient African civilizations, presented through art, trade, architecture, and religion. Traces the history of African king-doms and the introduction of Islam. 27 min., color. EMC no. 8538, Indiana University CSC-2159.

BENIN KINGSHIP RITUALS: Annual renewal ceremonies of the ancient kingship of Benin, now the capital of the mid-western state of Nigeria. 30 min., color. Indiana University.

DUMINEA, A FESTIVAL FOR WATER SPIRITS: Communal rituals for the hero spirits and water spirits of the village of Soku, in the eastern Niger Delta. 20 min., color. Indiana University.

DURO LADIPO: Introduces the Yoruba playwright Duro Ladipo of Oshogbo, Nigeria. Shows scenes from his play *Oba Ko So* (*The King Did Not Hang*), based upon the legends of the king-god Shango, as performed before the Alafin of Oyo, the traditional ruler of the Yoruba. 30 min., b/w. EMC no. 7495, Indiana University, RS-700.

GARCONS ET FILLES (BOYS AND GIRLS): Scenes from initiation ceremonies for boys and girls among the Gbaya of the Central African Republic. 28 min., b/w. Harvard University.

GELEDE: Dance, music, and ceremonies of the Gelede masquerade society of the Yoruba of western Nigeria. Shows various mask types and the styles of performance associated with them. 20 min., color. Indiana University.

HAUSA VILLAGE: Daily life of a Hausa village in northern Nigeria. Includes preparations for an Islamic wedding ceremony. 22 min., b/w. Indiana University, GS-306.

HIMBA WEDDING: Marriage ceremony of the Himba of Angola and Namibia (southwest Africa). Includes scenes of divination and mock bride capture. 28 min., color. National Audiovisual Center, no. 393340.

IFA: YORUBA DIVINATION AND SACRIFICE: The Yoruba divination system as it applies to healing. 18 min., b/w. R. M. Bucke Memorial Society, Montreal, Indiana University.

LES MAITRE FOUS: Possession cult among the Songhay and Djerma peoples of Accra, Ghana. 35 min., color. University of Michigan, University of Wis-consin (La Crosse).

THE NUER: Cultural life of the Nuer cattle herders of southwestern Ethiopia. Shows spirit possession, animal sacrifice, and the *gar* initiation ceremony. Superbly photographed and narrated. 74 min., color. Indiana University GSC-1292, EMC no. 4-8106.

N/UM TCHAI: Ceremonial possession dance of the !Kung Bushmen of Namibia and Botswana. The dance is a general curing ceremony. 19 min., b/w. Documentary Educational Resources.

WERE-NI! (HE IS A MAD MAN): Ritual healing techniques among the Yoruba of western Nigeria. Shows scenes of Ifa divination, animal sacrifice, possession and masquerade cults. 30 min., color. R. M. Bucke Memorial Society, Montreal, Indiana University.

Film Distributors

African Studies Program
Indiana University
Woodburn Hall
Bloomington, Indiana 47401

Extension Media Center
University of California
Berkeley, California 94720

R. M. Bucke Memorial Society
4453 Maisonneuve Blvd.
Montreal, Canada

University of Wisconsin (La Crosse)
Audio Visual Center
Florence Wing Communication Center
1705 State Street
La Crosse, Wisconsin 54601

Documentary Educational Resources
24 Dane Street
Somerville, Mass. 02143

The Film Study Center
Harvard University
19 Prescott Street
Cambridge, Mass. 02138

University of Michigan
Audio-Visual Center
416 Fourth Street
Ann Arbor, Michigan 48103

Index

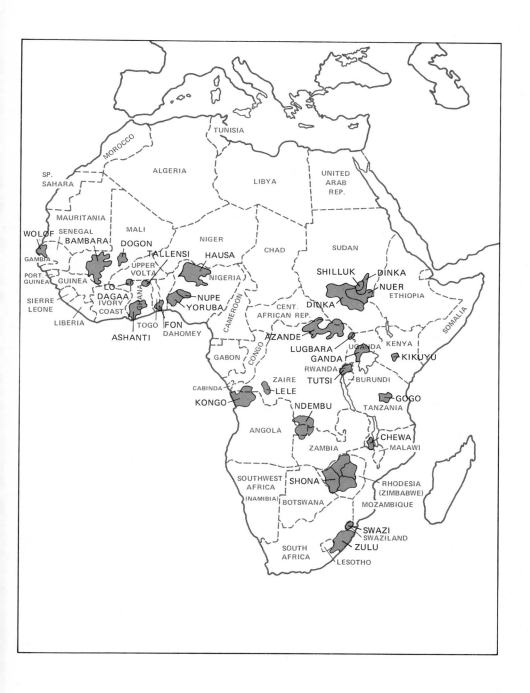